Germany
and the
League of Nations

Christoph M. Kimmich

The University of Chicago Press
Chicago and London

Germany
and the
League of Nations

The University of Chicago Press, Chicago 60637
The University of Chicago Press, Ltd., London

CHRISTOPH M. KIMMICH taught at Columbia University
and is now associate professor of history at Brooklyn
College, CUNY. He is the author of *The Free
City: Danzig and German Foreign Policy, 1919–1934* and
coeditor of *Akten zur deutschen auswärtigen Politik, 1918–1945.*

Library of Congress Cataloging in Publication Data

Kimmich, Christoph M
  Germany and the League of Nations.

  Bibliography: p.
  1. League of Nations—Germany.   I. Title.
JX1975.5.G3K54   341.22'43   75-36400
ISBN 0-226-43534-2

Contents

Preface

The Germans enjoy the distinction of being the first nation represented in the United Nations by two governments. The two Germanies were admitted to membership in September 1973, twenty-four years after the two states had been established, as a consequence of an accommodation West Germany had reached with her eastern neighbors. West Germany had been active in United Nations affairs since the early fifties, and formal admission merely ratified what already amounted to membership in all but name; for East Germany, admission signified coveted international recognition of her equal and sovereign status.

For years West Germany had vigorously opposed East Germany's admission, even at the price of her own, for fear that United Nations' acknowledgment of the division of Germany would cost her her strategy for reunification. In fact, West Germany had acted as if the foremost reason for her presence in the United Nations was to bar the admission of East Germany. Whenever she thought this interest threatened, she exerted pressure in the technical agencies, made special contributions to the budget, and instructed her permanent observer to lobby behind the scenes. On the other hand, she did little to support those activities which specifically advanced the goals of the United Nations—the promotion of international cooperation and compromise. The West German public itself seemed not unsympathetic to the new world organization; thus it is the more significant that the entire German political establishment and the press virtually ignored the United Nations and held neither its functions nor its promise in high esteem.

This undistinguished record bears striking resemblance to Germany's relationship with the League of Nations. From 1926 to 1933 Germany was an active member of the League, and the

League figured prominently in Germany's revisionist foreign policy. The Germans considered membership an opportunity to reestablish their position as a great power, rebuild international confidence in their motives and intentions, and cultivate close contact with representatives of the leading member-states. Stresemann put membership in the service of his efforts to free Germany of the punitive provisions of the peace treaty and to restore her economic prosperity, territorial integrity, and military strength. Brüning, Papen, and Schleicher, committed to a different revisionist strategy, tried to use the League's disarmament conference to reduce and then eliminate restrictions on Germany's armed forces. Hitler thought the League a hostile alliance, inimical to his ambitions, and he withdrew from it within a year of coming to power. All German statesmen from Stresemann to Hitler regarded the League as a means for advancing German interests, and all endorsed it to the extent that it in fact advanced these interests. None prized it for the advantages and protection it could offer a defeated and disarmed country; none recognized it as a new approach to old problems of international disorder and insecurity.

German policy toward the League, the premises of this policy no less than its implementation, was always an issue in domestic politics. Few Germans were convinced that the League's ideals of open diplomacy, collective security, and equality of nations had much practical value. Most believed that German membership ought to yield tangible results (whether, as in 1918–19, an easy peace, or, as after 1926, an early revision of the peace terms), and they never conceded that Germany might have to give more than assurances of good will in return. These public assumptions put the government under an obligation to justify its policy with one success after another—or face attack. Conversely, when this policy was successful, these same assumptions could be exploited, and no government failed to publicize its achievements for its own purposes. German policy toward the League, then, was as much a response to public pressures as it was an instrument for manipulating public opinion.

The League was a challenge to established traditions of foreign policy. The Germans' assumptions about the League, their formulation of policy, and the style of their diplomacy all show that they never truly understood this novel system of conducting international affairs. German diplomats were always ill at ease in Geneva, always on the defensive when they reported back to Berlin. Though they were not the only traditionalists in the corridors of the new diplomacy, they differed from the others in significant ways. They were committed not only to traditional diplomacy but also to traditional objectives. The revisionism to which they had committed themselves could not be realized within the framework of the League and the new diplomacy. Thus the diplomatic commitments which kept the Germans from supporting the League also made them accessory to undermining the vitality of the League and hastening its decline. The fortunes of this traditionalist power in the League explains in no small measure the ill fortunes of the League in the traditionalist world of the interwar years.

This book attempts to reconstruct and interpret Germany's relationship with the League—her policy at Geneva, the interplay of policy and politics, and the attitudes and opinions that inspired both policy and politics.

I have received much help along the way. At the Library of the Foreign Office in London, Ronald Wheatley guided me expertly through the vast store of filmed German documents. The archivists of the Politisches Archiv in Bonn and the Bundesarchiv in Koblenz advised me helpfully and provided me with abundant material. At the Library of the European Office of the United Nations in Geneva, Norman Field and his staff admitted me to the archives of the League of Nations, which were then in the midst of being reorganized. Grants from the Council for Research in the Social Sciences, Columbia University, enabled me to visit these archives and to film much of their holdings. The Dunning Fund of the Department of History, also of Columbia, defrayed the expenses of copying the manuscript.

John Fox, Bernd Klinkhardt, Michael-Olaf Maxelon, and Paul Wehn lent me their dissertations on various aspects of German diplomacy between the wars. Christine Fraser very kindly sent me a copy of her thesis on Germany's relations with the League in 1933. Emery Kelen, who observed life in Geneva at first hand, permitted me to reproduce some of his drawings.

Felix Gilbert shared his knowledge and recollections of Weimar diplomacy with me in several conversations. He, Hans Mommsen, and David Felix read and criticized the manuscript with much care. Rudolph Binion went through it painstakingly, challenging every dubious point and every infelicitous phrase. His moral support sustained me throughout. After seeing an early version, Fritz Stern urged me to rethink my approach and to enlarge my focus. His advice prompted me to cast the book into its present form.

My wife, Flora, was part of this undertaking from start to finish. Taking time away from her own work, she joined me in the archives, in assessing the evidence, in forging the arguments. She read various drafts, and each was the better for it. The book bears the marks of her collaboration on every page.

Celebrating Germany's entry into the League are (clockwise from lower left): Guani (Uruguay), Vandervelde (Belgium), Albert Thomas (International Labor Organization), Drummond (League of Nations), Stresemann, Chamberlain, Briand, Scialoja (Italy), Ninčić (Yugoslavia), Beneš (Czechoslovakia), Ishii (Japan), Undén (Sweden). From a menucard for a press luncheon, 1926. By permission of Emery Kelen.

1   "The Only Way to Peace," 1918–19

A society or league of nations had been advocated long before it became reality at the end of the First World War. Since the seventeenth century, political theorists, legal philosophers, and pacifist intellectuals had proposed it as a means of curbing the rivalry and strife among sovereign states. They had envisaged a supranational authority, based on common principles of law and honor, empowered to limit national armaments and arbitrate international disputes. In the nineteenth century, supranational authority was implicit in the concert of Europe, which provided a framework for great-power conferences. Yet in practice this authority never extended beyond some purely technical agencies designed to regulate communication and transportation. European governments conducted their foreign affairs according to national interest, free of outside compulsion or encumbrance, and they saw no reason to question the principle of the powerful and untrammeled nation-state. Their diplomacy dealt in alliances, balances of power, and concerts—and the threat or use of military force if other means failed.[1]

Public opinion had been largely indifferent to the notion of international authority. The World War, however, cast doubt upon the adequacy and efficacy of traditional diplomatic methods. They had not prevented (and may even have conduced to) a conflict that soon locked its participants in military stalemate and exacted a harrowing toll in lives and property. In all the belligerent countries, many came to conclude that such a catastrophe could be averted in the future only by revising the aims and the structure of international diplomacy so that the public would have a voice in foreign affairs and international, not national, interests would prevail. After 1915, such ideas were propagated by the League of Nations Society in Great Britain and by the League to Enforce Peace in the United States.[2]

Woodrow Wilson's interest in these ideas made them politically potent. They formed part of the famous Fourteen Points, his program of liberal war aims, which he proclaimed in January 1918. These aims, reflecting Wilson's interpretation of the causes of war, directed that economic barriers be removed after the war, national armaments reduced, and territorial disputes decided according to the wishes of the populations involved. At the core of the program was a "general association of nations," which was to guarantee "political independence and territorial integrity to great and small states alike." This association, Wilson explained in subsequent statements, would not be an executive organ with compulsory powers but a "tribunal of opinion," where differences would be settled with equal justice for all. It would be incompatible with special alliances, trade restrictions, and "private plots and conspiracies."[3] What Wilson had in mind was not a utopia in which all nations would live happily ever after, but a defined system of international relations which presupposed a totally new conception of diplomacy. This new diplomacy was to gather the sovereign nations into a civilized society, to subject their foreign affairs to the directives of a broad constitution, and to settle their disputes in a rational spirit safeguarded by a comprehensive peacekeeping organization.

Wilson's message was meant quite deliberately to counter the call for world peace through world revolution, which the Bolsheviks had raised after they seized power in 1917.[4] For Wilson, world peace would come through rule of law, a notion that was revolutionary in its own way. It presupposed a postwar settlement that would forgo the punitive features commonly associated with such settlements. It presupposed a world of liberal democratic states, for the new conception of international affairs required that, as in national affairs, policy be conducted openly and with the consent of the members. It presupposed also that the United States would abandon her traditional isolation and play an important role in the future affairs of Europe, for her power would be required to give life to the system she introduced.

The fourteen points, and especially the idea of an association of nations, found a mixed response in Allied Europe. They made for effective propaganda, evoking visions of a better world and of a fitting end to the slaughter and devastation, and became a catchword for people weary of war. The reaction of the Allied statesmen was more reserved. These men had war aims of their own, some of which conflicted with Wilson's program, and they were not sympathetic to schemes that seemed to favor the enemy. Above all they wanted to repulse Germany's drive for dominance on the continent, which threatened their sovereignty and their survival. And they had specific ideas of how to settle the future of disputed border areas, of colonies, and of the German fleet. Moreover, they were not convinced of the new diplomacy. They had doubts about the effectiveness of the future world community: the British found it a poor substitute for naval supremacy, and Clemenceau, the French premier, spoke of it with a touch of ridicule. Finally, the conservative war cabinets were wary of the effect Wilson's program might have on domestic politics. Their critics on the left acclaimed Wilson. These critics believed that his liberal internationalism reinforced their plans for political reform, for a just and equitable order at home, and they were eager to enlist his popularity and prestige in their purposes.[5]

Allied statesmen could not reject Wilson's program out of hand: Wilson's rhetoric affected their people, and they could not dispense with popular support (especially from the laboring classes) in the final phase of the war. More important, the Allies could not win the war without American assistance, and they might have to depend on it even after the war was over. After America had entered the war in 1917, both the British and the French governments had appointed committees to explore the idea of an association of nations and to draft practical proposals. It was not until November 1918, however, when Germany's defeat was certain and the Americans threatened to negotiate a separate peace, that Britain, France, and Italy accepted the fourteen points (with certain express reservations) as Allied war aims.[6]

At Wilson's behest, the association of nations appeared as the first item on the agenda when the peace conference opened at Paris in January 1919. A commission to draft a constitution for the association was set up under Wilson's chairmanship. In the course of discussion, Wilson gave in to British and French pressure and abandoned the idea of immediate German membership, to which he had held throughout 1918—for all practical purposes denying democratic Germany what he had been willing to give to imperial Germany. On the terms of the association, however, he made few compromises. He rejected an attempt by the British, who wanted to avoid further continental entanglements, to dilute the association's firm guarantees of territorial integrity. He was not persuaded when the French, twice victims of German aggression, proposed that the association be equipped with its own armed forces and general staff, so that it might prevent a revival of German militarism and respond to aggression promptly and effectively. And he resisted the Allies' effort to separate the peace treaty with Germany from the statutes of the association.[7]

The commission released its draft of the statutes for a league of nations on 14 February. The draft envisioned a rather loose association of sovereign states, combined into a "body of delegates" whose "executive council" would consist of the major Allied powers. It proposed to settle international conflicts by requiring a moratorium before a dispute could lead to war. During this moratorium solutions would be attempted by a legal decision from a world court or by mediation of the delegates or the council. It was assumed that world opinion would also exert pressure toward peace. If the transgressor resisted these efforts toward peaceful settlement, the members were duty-bound to apply economic and financial sanctions and to exclude him from normal international intercourse. Such a system, of course, did not abolish war completely. In allowing for war, the document was attuned in large measure to political realities.

Between 14 February and 28 April, when the peace conference in plenary session unanimously approved the final version, the draft was emended to satisfy objections of states not previously consulted and, particularly, of the Senate in Washington, which believed that the draft injured American interests. The final version now expressly denied the League the right to interfere in domestic affairs and to affect "international engagements . . . for securing the maintenance of peace" (such as the Monroe Doctrine). It also clarified the procedures the League was to follow in case of conflict. Most of the changes, however, were matters of form. The final version named the original members; it spelled out the terms of admission; it provided for withdrawal on two-years' notice. The "executive council" became simply the Council, composed of the great powers as permanent members and of a few non-permanent members, scheduled to meet as occasion required. The "body of delegates" became the Assembly, composed of representatives of all member states, to meet at fixed intervals. The council and assembly were to be assisted by a permanent Secretariat, staffed by an international civil service under a secretary-general. The seat of the League was to be at Geneva.[8]

At the conclusion of the war, the Germans were probably the most outspoken supporters of the idea of a league of nations; when Wilson proclaimed his fourteen points in January 1918, however, the Germans had shown little enthusiasm. Victory appeared within reach. An armistice had been concluded on the eastern front, and peace negotiations with the new Soviet government were under way. German troops were soon to be ferried to the west for the final campaign. Wilson's peace program therefore seemed untimely, and the settlement it offered also looked trifling. If the Germans accepted the fourteen points as a basis for peace, they would benefit to the extent to which the British and French were restrained in their territorial and economic aspirations. However, the Germans would have to renounce war aims they had cherished and elaborated since the first year of the war. In their more extreme forms, these aims included the annexation of lands east and west, the subjection of neighboring states, and the creation of a vast colonial empire in Africa. Even the more moderate versions of the war aims intended to enlarge Germany's boundaries and expand her power and influence.[9]

The German press, from *Vorwärts* on the left to *Tägliche Rundschau* on the right, responded to Wilson's message with comments ranging from the skeptical to the condemnatory. The *Kölnische Volkszeitung* was not unrepresentative in castigating the president's proposals as "shameless hypocrisy"; the *Norddeutsche Allgemeine Zeitung,* a conservative sheet considered close to the government, denounced the fourteen points as a front for "imperialist conquest in the guise of peace, freedom, and international happiness."[10] If the fourteen points were not hypocritical, as most argued, then, *Vorwärts* suggested, they were fantastic: Germany had not reached such a pass that she could be forced to give up Alsace-Lorraine, Posen, and Danzig.[11]

The major parties of the Reichstag were divided over Wilson's proposals. The conservatives were hostile. In spirit and content, the proposals were a threat to their traditional way of life and their privileges. They inaugurated a fierce campaign against the proposals, especially against the "association of nations," and carried on this campaign till Germany's collapse in the fall. The liberals and socialists, constituting the majority, were not unsympathetic to Wilson's message, for it seemed to echo their own concerns of the previous summer, when they had tried to commit Germany to a compromise peace without annexations and indemnities.[12] Chancellor Hertling was not unresponsive to pressures from the restive Left, but he could not afford to offend his conservative and military backers. He therefore endorsed Wilson's general principles but hedged his comment with reservations and qualifications. If Wilson should prove to have spoken in a just and impartial spirit, he said, the imperial government would be prepared, after all other pending questions had been disposed of, to give thought to the foundation on which an "association of nations" might be erected. But clearly, he added, Wilson's proposals were no basis for a true peace. They were cast in the language of the victor, hardly appropriate to Germany's unprecedentedly promising military situation.[13] Passing from words to deeds, Germany responded to Wilson's program by concluding the peace treaty of Brest-Litovsk in March, which breathed a spirit most unlike that animating the fourteen points, and by almost simultaneously launching a massive offensive in the west.

With the change in military fortunes came a change in attitude. The high command had expected that the offensive would force the enemy to sue for peace and would revive the martial spirit at home. But by August 1918 the German army was in retreat and domestic morale was sagging. The liberal press began to voice cautious approval of Wilson's program and especially of the proposed association of nations. Letters concerning the association poured into the offices of the *Frankfurter Zeitung,* many of them expressing extravagant hopes for amity and understanding, for a new era in the history of mankind.[14] The conservative press reacted angrily. For the *Deutsche Tageszeitung* the association remained a scheme for "Anglo-Saxon world hegemony." "Admission," it warned, "could be secured only by relinquishing those powers and those means by which the Reich came into being"—the monarchy and the army. The conservative papers worried about the psychological impact which peace speculations might have on the public and on the war effort, and they tried, unsuccessfully, to throttle the debate.[15]

The German Foreign Ministry was preparing for contingencies. Since the early spring, it had sought contact with Wilson through various intermediaries, who were authorized to discuss the fourteen points as a possible basis for peace. The ministry hoped to induce Wilson to negotiate a peace that would take account of both Germany's and the Allies' war aims. By the end of August, it was prepared to make extensive concessions to meet the fourteen points. Its legal department drafted a model constitution for an association of nations. The draft stressed "permanent peace" as the body's main purpose and pacific settlement of international conflicts, limitation of armaments, and development of international law as its main functions. Members were to enjoy equal dignity, to respect one another's territory, and to refrain from interfering in each other's internal affairs.[16] The draft made no distinction between the privileges of a victorious and of a defeated power; under the circumstances, therefore, it was favorable to Germany.

The issue became urgent at the end of September when news reached the Foreign Ministry that the war effort was at the point of collapse. Enemy offensives were pushing the German armies back in the west and were routing German allies in southeastern Europe; Austria-Hungary appealed to Wilson for a peace conference. Paul von Hintze, foreign secretary since July 1918, summarized his ministry's thinking for the high command on 29 September: inasmuch as the war could not be won, Germany would have to resort to a political settlement. Woodrow Wilson offered a peace program far more favorable than anything the European Allies held in store. Wilson's principles could be made to serve Germany: by subscribing to the "association of nations" the Germans would gain American protection against the retribution of the Allies. Most important, this was the only concrete program available; by accepting it, Germany would obligate Wilson to negotiate on these terms. Hintze proposed that the regime that had prosecuted the war be replaced by a government based on a coalition with the majority of the Reichstag.

Such constitutional reform would appeal to Wilson's democratic sentiments and lend credibility to Germany's peaceful intentions. At the proper moment, this government would ask Wilson to begin proceedings for restoring the peace and, if the military were agreeable, ask him to invite the powers to conclude an armistice. The high command accepted this plan, which resembled some of its own recent conclusions, insisting only that the proper moment had already arrived.[17]

Max von Baden, a liberal aristocrat, who was to form a new government on 3 October, was reluctant to accept the program and horrified by the precipitate request for an armistice. He proposed instead to interpret the fourteen points publicly in Germany's favor and call upon all the enemy powers to open negotiations. This would avoid the impression that Germany was capitulating and lessen the impact on an unsuspecting German public.[18] Hintze, however, remained adamant, citing the precarious military situation, and he found support among the representatives of the moderate Left who were about to become part of the new government. They urged that the government adopt Wilson's program and especially an association of nations, which, they were agreed, was "the only way to peace."[19]

Under such pressure, Prince Max gave in. The first act of his new government, even before coming before the public, was to accept Wilson's program without reservation and to request an armistice from Washington. On 5 October he spoke to the Reichstag at length about the internal changes his government was about to inaugurate, which would make Germany a parliamentary monarchy by the end of the month and put an end to Bismarck's pseudo-constitutionalism. He also committed his government to the fourteen points and to an association of nations "on the basis of equality for the strong and the weak alike."[20] This was the first official endorsement of Wilson's ideas. With premature optimism, the *Norddeutsche Allgemeine Zeitung* wrote the following day that the Allies were rapidly being deprived of weapons for Germany's political and economic defeat, since democracy and an association of nations were gaining wide acceptance.

The government's open concern gave the topic public legitimacy, and the newspapers took up the debate. Not a few which had cast doubt on Wilson's program eight months earlier now found themselves in complete accord with it.[21] Wilson's ideals, primarily his notion of an association of nations, filled the pages of the press. The government itself took a hand in the publicity. On 6 October, the cabinet decided to urge the press to emphasize the association and to say little about the less attractive points in Wilson's proposals, such as those dealing with Alsace-Lorraine and Poland. Two days later the Foreign Ministry convened a meeting of parliamentarians and constitutional lawyers to discuss ways of carrying "the idea of an association of nations" to the masses "by means of comprehensive and penetrating propaganda." The ministry proposed to consolidate its effort by establishing contact with societies and groups already engaged in popularizing a Wilsonian peace.[22] It was the first sign that the government was perhaps less convinced of the principle of an association of nations than persuaded of the political usefulness of such an idea.

The propaganda fell on open ears. The request for an armistice had revealed with staggering suddenness that the military situation, far from being as favorable as the high command had claimed publicly, was disastrous. To request an armistice was to admit defeat—and this was the final blow to public confidence. As morale collapsed, interest in the shape of the postwar world grew. At this point began the public discussion of the fourteen points. Public lectures on Wilson and on the association of nations, which proliferated at the end of the month, were filled to capacity. They ended unfailingly with unanimous resolutions in favor of an association.[23] Most Germans seemed in accord with Prince Max, who presented the association as a cure for present ills and as a source of consolation and strength in a difficult time.[24]

On 11 November the Germans signed an unexpectedly harsh armistice which deprived them of any possibility of resuming hostilities. The war was over. The government which accepted the armistice was no longer the government which had sued for it. The November revolution had deposed the old regime and swept the democratic Left into power. On 10 November a new government had been formed in Berlin, the Council of People's Commissars, in which (at least ostensibly) moderate and radical Socialists shared power equally. Though the council was not bound to the politics of the past, it introduced few changes.

Dominated by the moderate Socialists, it conceived of itself as provisional. After a constituent assembly had been elected, a regular government could be chosen, which would establish parliamentary democracy and institute social and economic reforms. Until that time, the People's Commissars wished to evade far-reaching political decisions that might tie the hands of a future government. They were, however, prepared to deal with immediate concerns—the consequences of defeat and revolution. They were willing to carry out the onerous terms of the armistice, to secure supplies before famine swept the country, to begin to demobilize the huge army, and in general to restore a peacetime economy. At the same time they tried to temper the widespread uncertainty engendered by the revolution, which continued to stir up unrest. They addressed themselves to restoring order and authority, preparing for proper elections, and negotiating an early peace.[25]

In this ranking of priorities the People's Commissars clashed with their nominal superior, the Workers' and Soldiers' Council of Berlin. This body, like most of the workers' and soldiers' councils in Germany, looked to the Soviet experience of 1917 for guidance. Thus it determined that, instead of waiting for a duly elected government, it would use the momentum of the revolution to institute a socialist democracy. It wished to purge German society of all vestiges of militarism and authoritarianism, to dissolve the army and replace it with a people's militia, and to socialize the economy forthwith. In this program the more moderate People's Commissars saw not only a challenge to their priorities, but also an alarming threat of bolshevism and civil war.[26]

Inexperienced, burdened with immense tasks, under political attack from a movement they feared, the men of the new government sought help from the civil service and the officer corps. Since neither the personnel nor the attitudes of these institutions had changed greatly, the appeal was in effect a compromise with the old order. Any qualms the Socialists might have entertained about such an arrangement were swept aside by the needs of the hour and by the conviction that the arrangement would be temporary, since Germany was about to become a democracy. They were confident, moreover, that the men of the old order would become the junior partners of the People's Commissars. The old order, for its part, was not reluctant to compromise with the

Socialists. The events of November had thrown it into panic, and the example of Russia caused it to fear for its social position and for its material possessions. Panic or no, the old order was quick to exploit the weakness and uncertainty of the new regime and to assume positions of authority and influence. Thus policy remained in the hands of men who were by tradition averse to fundamental domestic change and suspicious of international cooperation. Not only did the new regime exercise restraint in its desire to reform the country, but by associating itself with the old order, it also positively promoted continuity and obstructed innovation.

Foreign policy was the prerogative of the Foreign Ministry, which was entrusted to Wilhelm Solf, an appointee of Max von Baden. Solf was sympathetic to constitutional reform but hostile to revolution and to rule by workers' and soldiers' councils. Correspondingly, he believed that it was more to Germany's advantage to deal with the Western powers than with the new Soviet state.[27] In October, he had conducted the pre-armistice negotiations with Washington, and received assurances that the Allies would make peace on Wilsonian terms. He now held fast to the tactic of dealing solely with the United States. The malevolent armistice (especially Foch's intransigence) and the reports sent to Solf by his ambassadors in neutral countries confirmed him in the wisdom of this tactic.[28]

Solf explained his policy to a conference of representatives of the German state governments some two weeks after the armistice. Unlike the European enemies, he said, the American president had no claims to make on Germany, and he was committed to his fourteen points. As the president of a strong economic power, Wilson would be able to influence his allies "decisively."

> Germany can recover from the deep wounds of the war only if she pursues thoroughly pacifist policies. Therefore it is patent that Germany must support all wishes for the creation of an association of nations, for disarmament, for the establishment of tribunals of arbitration, for freedom of the seas, etc., openly and honestly. Only in this way can we hope to restrain the imperialism of our other enemies and to some extent to offset our current weakness.

Solf pointed out that developments within Germany might jeopardize any chance of success. He described the civil disorders as "an insurmountable obstacle to peace." The American public was hostile to the German revolution, he told the conference, and as opposed to a Socialist republic as it had been to imperial autocracy. Wilson could not help the Germans if Germany were in revolution. Solf called for order and for the early election of a constituent assembly to show Wilson that democracy was alive in the new Germany. The alternatives—revolution at home and vengeance abroad—would mean "the destruction of the Reich and the annihilation of the German nation."[29] Several members of the conference observed, not inaccurately, that what they had heard was not the voice of the "new" spirit and the "new" diplomacy, but the voice of bygone days. Others suggested that the best indication of Germany's having reformed would not be Solf's foreign policy, but his resignation.[30]

Indeed, Solf had only formulated explicitly the rationale behind much of Germany's official Wilsonianism as it was practiced by the exponents of realpolitik. As the diplomats saw it, Wilson's proposals for peace offered various benefits. First, they could be used to disguise Germany's political helplessness. By defining the fourteen points in terms favorable to Germany, the government could pretend still to be master of its fate. It insisted that the fourteen points did not require the surrender of German territory or sovereignty, and it evolved a rather nebulous concept of a conciliatory peace which evaded the implications of Wilson's program. The government then claimed that Germany's interpretation was what Wilson had meant, and that this represented the "legally binding maximum" that Germany was obliged to accept.[31] Second, Wilson's program offered a means of influencing the deliberations of Germany's enemies. Outspoken Wilsonianism qualified the Germans as Wilson's partners. As such, they became his collaborators in arriving at an impartial peace settlement. They might also be able to drive a wedge between Wilson and his European allies, who were rumored to be opposed to the fourteen points. Some members of the government inferred from various signs of American good will that the Allies were at odds and presumed that such differences could be exploited at the peace negotiations.[32] Third, whatever the peace terms, Germany's admission to an association of nations would improve her situation immeasurably. Membership would restore her dignity and prestige. As Walter Simons, the director of the legal department of the Foreign Ministry, remarked to a journalist, only as "an equal among equals" would Germany enter such an association of nations.[33] Membership would also assure "Germany to the Germans," for national self-determination—the heart of the new world order—would apply to all. Germany's unity and territory would remain inviolate.[34] And a treaty based on the principles inherent in the association would guarantee a just and impartial peace. Any other settlement would contradict the spirit of the new organization.[35]

Official Wilsonianism also had domestic ramifications. The provisional government was still unable to assert its authority; in fact it had trouble even protecting itself. In December it had been besieged by rioters and held at bay by mutinous sailors, and in January it was obliged to call in military irregulars to suppress an attempted coup engineered by radical Socialists and Communists. Though the radicals were not nearly as organized—and the workers not nearly as radical—as members of the government believed, the revolutionary rhetoric was unnerving. Moderate Socialists and bourgeois liberals joined the traditionalists to declare that Wilsonianism presupposed constitutional order and domestic stability—without which there would be famine, foreign occupation, and a harsh peace.[36] Only a constitutional, democratically elected government could avail itself of Wilson's principles.[37] Here again the idea of an association of nations was useful. The association would be the cornerstone of a new international order, and this new order might be used to assure the people that the sacrifices of the war had not been in vain. At such a prospect revolution and bolshevism might become less attractive; the lack of food and employment—the daily misery—might become less pressing. The people might support the government's commitment to Wilsonianism and reinforce the government's authority to settle internal affairs. Wilsonianism, then, was used both in the campaign for a liberal peace and in the struggle for power within Germany.

Its double function is evident in the German government's policy until May 1919, when the Allies transmitted their draft for a peace treaty. After Solf resigned in December 1918, the policy passed on to his successor Ulrich von Brockdorff-Rantzau, another diplomat of the old school, and every government, whether controlled by the Socialists alone or by a

Socialist-liberal coalition, believed that Wilsonianism coincided with its interest.[38] The Germans arranged their tactics accordingly. Members of the government, and scholars and publicists close to it, took every opportunity to address Wilson directly. Official notes were sent to the American peace delegation, and Germans spoke with Americans during negotiations for an extension of the armistice. Contact was arranged also through the various official and unofficial American missions which visited Germany and reported their findings to the president: the missions of Ellis Loring Dresel of the State Department in December and January and again in April, of Captain Walter R. Gherardi in February and March, and of Colonel Arthur Conger in March and April.[39] In an attempt to influence the peacemakers in Paris indirectly, the moderate Socialists and liberal scholars who represented Germany at international conferences (the Socialists in Berne in February and in Amsterdam in April, the pacifists and league enthusiasts at Berne in March) appealed to the like-minded in Allied countries. The theme was always the same: a new spirit prevailed in Germany, and a democratic Germany sincerely wanted to contribute to the new postwar order; true and lasting peace would come only if the privileges of national self-determination, of a just and impartial settlement, and of an association of nations were extended equally to all.[40]

The government also tried to take a leaf out of Wilson's book and use the public as an instrument of diplomacy. It was convinced that if Wilsonianism became a creed of the masses, Germany would gain a hearing abroad. As Brockdorff-Rantzau told a press conference, the echo of German public opinion would impress the Allies, even if the arguments of the German peace delegation were ignored.[41] In public speeches and interviews with the press, members of the government exhorted the public to voice its desire for an association of nations and emphasized the link between an association and a just peace. The government's tactic had two prongs. While it induced the public to appeal to Wilson and to Wilsonians the world over, it also comforted the public by arguing that Germany had contractual certainty of a Wilson peace. Had not the Germans laid down their arms for the promise of a new world order? Had not German democracy been advance payment on a liberal peace? Had not Wilson assured the Germans in October 1918 that the Allies were pledged to his principles and to membership in the association of nations? Time and time again, government and press stressed that Germany would sign no peace but a Wilson peace.[42]

The German government conveyed its propaganda through various ministries and agencies. Its chief propagandist was Matthias Erzberger, who had caught the mood of the times the previous October and published *Der Völkerbund: Der Weg zum Weltfrieden,* which carried its message in the title.[43] The most penetrating instrument of propaganda, roughly equivalent to the League of Nations Union in England, was the Deutsche Liga für Völkerbund, which the government had commissioned Ernst Jäckh to organize in December 1918. Jäckh, a consultant to the Foreign Ministry and a man on familiar terms with both the old and the new regimes, had been an enthusiast of an association of nations for some time and was therefore eminently suited to his task. The Liga, funded by the government with 100,000 marks at its outset and with 450,000 marks annually in 1919 and 1920, enjoyed illustrious sponsorship. The government was represented by Ebert, Erzberger, Solf, and Preuss (the minister of the interior), and all the parties (except the Nationalists and the Communists) joined in, as did trade union leaders and notables of academic, commercial, and industrial life. Small in active membership (about 1000) because it wanted to be a well-knit working organization, the Liga encouraged corporate membership, especially of trade unions, and soon achieved a roll of ten million supporters.[44]

Thus sponsored and subsidized, the Liga set out to propagate the idea of an association of nations among all classes at home and to profess Germany's faith in Wilson's peace proposals before the world. Lecturers traveled throughout the country. The Liga dispensed pamphlets and handbills and furnished information on all aspects of the association of nations to press agencies. It commissioned scholarly monographs and spelled out the functions and purposes of the future organization in detail. A journal, *Neue Brücken,* appeared regularly; bibliographies were assembled; offprints distributed; and a press service set up. Indeed, the Liga claimed that in 1919 most of what had been said and written in Germany about an association of nations could be traced to its initiative. The Liga received generous coverage in all newspapers except those on the extreme Right.[45]

Virtually all political parties concurred in the Wilsonianism propagated by the government and the press. Among the Socialists, international cooperation had been an article of faith and a living experience since the previous century. Before the war, the idea had been prominent in the Socialist International, in which the German Socialist party had played an important role, and it was part and parcel of the solidarity of the proletariat. The Socialists prided themselves on their long history of advocating international arbitration, which, along with international disarmament, had been the subject of resolutions at various international congresses. Philipp Scheidemann, a leader of the moderate Socialists (SPD), declared in November 1918 that his party was prepared "to serve the cause of an association of nations and a ... just and impartial peace with all the strength of devoted enthusiasm." In these months his colleagues quoted Wilson freely and at the least provocation.[46] The Independent Socialists (USPD), otherwise hostile to the moderate Socialists, from which they had split off in 1917, gave Wilsonianism uncritical support. The Independents were eager to pursue a foreign policy of genuine internationalism, and they began by publishing the documents of Germany's prewar diplomacy to demonstrate her involvement in the outbreak of the war and thus to clear the slate for a new start. In a fervent article in *Die Freiheit*, the party organ, they equated Wilson's aims with those of the international proletariat and glorified the American president as the champion of an association of free and equal nations.[47]

Next in fervor was the Center party, which endorsed international cooperation, not least because the conception was in keeping with the party's ecumenical religious orientation. On the premise that rule of law must replace rule by force in international affairs, the party committed itself to an association of nations with mutual disarmament, protection of minorities, economic equality, and obligatory arbitration.[48] The Democratic party (DDP) and the People's party (DVP), which rallied the followers of the defunct Progressive and National Liberal parties in November 1918, also included a commitment to the idea of an association of nations in their platforms. Though they were not without misgivings about the venture (the Democrats were afraid the organization might foster Anglo-American hegemony), they agreed that an association of nations was integral to the postwar world. With the parties of the left they shared a vision of membership on equal terms, or arbitrative tribunals, and of a universal reduction of armaments.[49]

Amid all this acclaim, voices of opposition from the extremes on the right and the left of the political spectrum were muffled. It was opposition tendered as much against the principle of an association of nations as against the new democratic government which espoused it; the two were inextricably linked. For the Communists (KPD), persuaded of their own view of history, Wilson's program constituted bourgeois reconstruction, not revolution. Their propaganda disparaged the association of nations as "a league of murderers, of profiteers, and of suppressors of the proletariat," and no more than a joint venture of capitalists and imperialists in new format. Like the Nationalists (DNVP), they dubbed the association a "holy alliance," dedicated to oppression.[50] For the Nationalists, who comprised the whole range of conservatives from the old empire, the association was anathema by definition. The party extolled not international cooperation, but national sovereignty and loyalty to the state and nation. No state should be subject to international control.[51]

The public, it would seem, hardly needed to be encouraged to support the association. Contemporaries speak of widespread and fervent enthusiasm (*Völkerbundtaumel*). It was an open secret that a favorable peace and a new association were interconnected. Exhausted by war and troubled by revolution, the German citizen, normally not especially interested in or informed on foreign affairs, was taken with the notion that a world should be born in which there would be neither victors nor vanquished, neither annexations nor indemnities.[52] Most active in discussion was the small band of German pacifists, the Deutsche Friedensgesellschaft and the Bund' Neues Vaterland, which had been muzzled during the war and now ventured to speak again. They, with the Independent Socialists, were perhaps the most genuinely committed to an association of nations. The pacifists organized public lectures and demonstrations to propagate the "new age of world peace." Time and again they appealed to Wilson not to permit the new association of nations to become an instrument for enslaving Germany, not to pervert the noble idea of international cooperation.[53]

The motives for the public enthusiasm were probably a mixture of idealism and opportunism. High in the government, however, Wilsonianism was endorsed out of opportunism and propagated not without cynicism.[54] The government tipped its hand by resorting to threats at the same time that it churned up a great show of acclaim for Wilsonianism and the association of nations. It warned that a harsh peace would entail awful consequences: Germany would lapse again into chaos and anarchy, bolshevism would flourish and spread to the West. In support of its claims, the government cited the uprisings that occurred in January 1919 and again in March. Clearly the government's most urgent desire was an easy peace. If the Allies would not be wooed, the Germans were nothing loath to try blackmail.[55]

This strategy, predicated primarily on the hope for American intercession, was not as effective as the Germans had anticipated. The draft statutes of the League of Nations, released on 14 February 1919, were a disagreeable surprise. The German government was quick to denounce the draft as a betrayal of the Germans' idealistic faith in a new order and a reaffirmation of the traditional system of international relations. The association as envisaged by the Allies would be a concert not of equals but of victors, designed to cast the political status quo into juridical permanence. As in times past, the victor was privileged to take spoils, and the cherished hope for an easy peace would come to nought.[56]

The country's reaction to the Allies' draft was massive consternation. Huge demonstrations in the major cities reaffirmed German confidence in the fourteen points. A rally in Berlin sponsored by the Liga für Völkerbund on 16 March became so crowded that it had to be divided and held in two places. Resolutions accepted by acclamation appealed to the conscience of all those concerned with the future of mankind to recognize that Germany's isolation would be the death of the association of nations.[57] A veiled threat to the Allies emerged in a debate engaging several newspapers as to whether an alliance with the Soviet Union was preferable to membership in the association of nations. In an attempt to halt the speculation, the semi-official *Deutsche Allgemeine Zeitung* reiterated the German view that salvation lay, not in alliances or armaments, but in the association.[58] Prime Minister Scheidemann, who headed a coalition government made up of Socialists, Democrats, and Centrists elected by the constituent assembly on 13 February to supersede the Council of People's Commissars, reaffirmed the established position. Germany wanted not a soviet republic but an association in which nations could develop freely as equals.[59]

By mid-March, news from Paris seemed to confirm what the Allied draft statutes had implied—that the peacemakers were departing from the spirit of the fourteen points. Rumor had it that Germany would not be allowed to negotiate the peace; her representatives would be given a finished treaty, to accept or reject. She might be adjudged guilty of the war, would be obliged to pay immense damages, would lose not only Alsace-Lorraine but possibly also West Prussia and Upper Silesia, and would be forced to accept the occupation of the left bank of the Rhine. These prospects persuaded the government to cling even more firmly to its strategy. In public, it continued to express unwavering confidence in Germany's case; in confidential directives to its peace delegation, it defined the limits of negotiation and concession and the projected association of nations by a narrow interpretation of the fourteen points.[60] Originally, the government had intended to charge its peace delegation simply with a broad commitment to "the creation of a permanent association of nations on the basis of equality for all nations, great or small, with the introduction of obligatory arbitration for all international disputes."[61] Now the cabinet decided that a German draft of a constitution should be brought in against the Allied scheme and that this draft should be used in a sweeping press campaign.[62]

The drafting was entrusted to Walter Schücking, a well-known pacifist and professor of international law at Marburg, who was assisted by two members of the legal department of the Foreign Ministry, Walter Simons and Friedrich Gaus. The most prominent notions in the draft were Schücking's own, which he had expressed most recently in *Der Weltfriedensbund* (1917) and *Internationale Rechtsgarantien* (1918). These ideas had also been introduced into the proposed scheme of the Deutsche Gesellschaft für Völkerrecht, an association of Germany's foremost jurists, on which Schücking had worked and on which the drafters now drew.[63] Schücking saw the practical problem as one of securing Germany's admission to an association of nations whose statutes would safeguard Germany's vital interests.[64] The

German draft was elaborate and meticulous—a monument to perfectionism, but also to inflexibility. Its basic orientation was not diplomatic but juridical; international relations were placed on a strict legal basis. The thrust of the draft was that the association of nations should maintain permanent peace by obligatory arbitration of all international disputes, legal as well as political, an idea long espoused by pacifists. This arbitration was consigned to two bodies, one for legal, the other for political disputes—the Permanent International Tribunal and the International Mediation Office. The decisions of these bodies were to be adhered to "in good faith" and, if necessary, enforced by the severance of diplomatic or economic relations or, as a last resort, by military measures. The Mediation Office, moreover, might take the initiative and "offer its services" to quarreling states.[65]

The obligatory scheme of the German proposal was reminiscent of a plan introduced at the peace conference at The Hague in 1907, which imperial Germany had rejected. As such, Schücking's draft was a conscious effort to distance the new Germany from the old. Less consciously, the reversion to the Hague plan (which Schücking had suggested in *Internationale Rechtsgarantien*) showed a desire for historical continuity and, conversely, an inability to innovate.[66] There was one more reason for the rigor of the German plan. By proposing an uncompromising obligation with no qualifications or loopholes, the Germans could outdo the Allies' draft. Simons believed that it was in Germany's interest "to counter the purely political and bureaucratic draft of the Allies with a democratic German draft which provided for positive cooperation." And Schücking thought that a "more progressive" German draft would be an effective weapon in a propaganda campaign against the Allied proposal.[67] The "progressiveness" of the German plan, an appeal to the Left in other countries, was evident also in a proposed international parliament to which national parliaments would send one representative for each million citizens, and evident as well in the new organization's responsibility to secure for workers of the member states "an existence in accordance with human dignity." Schücking was grandiloquent in introducing the draft to the cabinet on 22 April: here was a "manifesto of liberty, equality, and fraternity among nations."[68]

The Allied peace terms, presented to the Germans on 7 May, struck them as more severe than anything they could have imagined. The government and the press protested against these "unacceptable demands"; the public reacted with mass meetings and petitions and a week of national mourning. In an acrimonious session of the constituent assembly on 12 May, where speakers vied with each other in denouncing the peace treaty as a violation of Wilson's principles and a betrayal of the Germans' good faith, one lonely voice, that of Ludwig Quidde, a member of the Democratic party and a pacifist, regretted that Germany had been excluded from the League.[69] Tellingly, after weeks of contrived enthusiasm for and concern about the new association, neither the government nor the populace expressed particular outrage at the exclusion. To be sure, the first of many notes to be sent to the Allies conveyed the German draft for an association. The transmission of the note was a routine response, a propaganda ploy that Schücking had proposed to the cabinet some three weeks earlier. The note was intended to impress Wilson and the Left in Britain and France which, predictably, would condemn the peace terms.[70] Other than that, the German draft served no purpose—the Germans never pressed it further, and they accepted the Allied proposal as a basis of negotiation.

The government reverted to the matter of the League once more in its counterproposals to the treaty on 29 May. The remarks contained little that was new. The Germans objected to having been excluded despite promises that the League "would unite the belligerents, conquerors as well as conquered, in a permanent system of common rights." They warned that without Germany there could be "no true union of peoples," that within the new League the old political system—"the present hostile coalition"—would continue. Thus it would not be Germany's fault if the nations of the world were disappointed in the expectation of peace and "if conditions were created which would of necessity lead to new wars." On the condition that they be admitted to the League "as a power with equal privileges as soon as the peace document agreed upon has been signed," the Germans were prepared to negotiate a peace settlement. A guarantee of equality and reciprocity in economic affairs, spelled out in great detail, would have to be part of the covenant of the League; Germany's disarmament would have to be the beginning of general disarmament. Both requests, of course, curtailed other conditions of the treaty.[71]

In their reply of 16 June the Allies rejected all the German proposals for the League. The great propaganda campaign of the winter months had failed, for the Allies observed pointedly that they were not convinced that the German revolution represented "a permanent change." Surely Germany could not expect "the free nations of the world to sit down immediately in equal association with those by whom they had been so grievously wronged." Therefore the Allies could not accede to the request for immediate admission. The possibility of admission might be opened once the German government had given "clear proofs of its stability as well as of its intention to observe its international obligations," particularly those connected with the peace treaty. The acts of the German government would determine the length of the quarantine.[72] There the matter rested. The Germans wrote no rejoinder, and the government accepted and ratified the peace treaty at the end of June.

Exclusion from the League was the first of many rebuffs to be rationalized and assimilated. The political parties reacted with disappointment or malicious satisfaction, according to their previous attitudes. On 25 May, four days before the Germans submitted their counterproposals in Versailles, the *Deutsche Allgemeine Zeitung* carried a lead article which described the League as an alliance hostile to Germany, set on obstructing her development, destroying her property, and barring her from the world's markets. Membership, in effect, was not worth wishing for. The pacifists alone still clung to the idea of the League—"despite everything"—as the country's only hope.[73]

2 Germany Outcast, 1919–23

The peace treaty imposed upon the League certain specific responsibilities. The League was to assess the results of a plebiscite in Eupen-Malmédy, a small corner on Germany's western border, in order to determine whether that region should fall under Belgian or German sovereignty (article 34). It was to delimit the boundaries of the Saar territory and to administer the area for fifteen years, when its fate would be decided by plebiscite (articles 48, 49). It was to guarantee the status and constitution of the Free City of Danzig, a German city at the mouth of the Vistula, which provided Poland with access to the sea. A League high commissioner (and, on appeal, the council itself) was to mediate and adjudicate disputes between Danzigers and Poles (articles 102, 103). The decision on whether Germany and Austria should be permitted to merge rested with the council (article 80), as did the supervision of German disarmament once Allied control organs had been dismantled (article 213). The League was charged with overseeing the mandated administration of Germany's former colonies and with protecting the educational, cultural, and religious rights of the German minorities in the new states in eastern Europe.[1] When Germany became a member, she could represent her interests as these responsibilities were carried out. She could also gain a voice in international affairs, making up for what she lacked in military power by political counsel and influence. In the process she might help reduce the legacy of wartime antagonisms and restore normal relations among the European powers. Logic as well as prudence seemed to argue for Germany's early accession to the League.[2]

As the first meeting of the assembly in November 1920 drew near, there was wide speculation about whether Germany would apply. The governments of states that had been neutral during the war—the Scandinavian states, for example—were eager for Germany's admission. Socialist congresses, pacifist conferences, and League of Nations associations expressed their interest. The press in Germany and abroad canvassed the possibility and desirability of Germany's entry. In the League secretariat, still located in temporary quarters in London, officials initiated "discreet preparations" by sounding out influential council members and reviewing relevant legal provisions.[3]

Foreign Minister Walter Simons, who had been responsible in part for the German proposal for an association of nations in 1919, quashed the speculation. In an address to the Reichstag, he warned against dismissing the League outright but deemed an application for admission premature. If an invitation were proffered, Germany could not turn it down flatly, he thought, but she would have to insist on certain conditions. Coming closer to what must have inspired his reserve, Simons noted that "we do not want to join as long as our opponents do not wish to accept us as equals."[4]

Simons spoke for a government whose political balance had shifted from the supporters of the League to its detractors. The coalition of 1919, stigmatized by the peace treaty and weakened by an undistinguished career in office, had lost support as German democracy came under attack from those who aimed either at revolution or at restoration. The Left had assailed it for compromising its principles and promises, forsaking democratic socialism, and capitulating to the old order. The Right, quick to identify moderates with radicals, had condemned it for its principles and promises, and accused it of fostering disorder and lawlessness. The Kapp putsch in March 1920 had been a harbinger: to the extreme Right the time had seemed ripe for a takeover. In the Reichstag elections in June, the various resentments had become politically effective, and the coalition which had commanded three quarters of the constituent assembly now could not even count on a simple majority. The Independents, trading on the bitterness the Kapp putsch had inspired in the working class, sapped the support of the moderate Socialists; the Democrats suffered a serious setback; and even the proverbially stable Center party lost ground as its federalist Bavarian wing went off on its own. The People's party and the Nationalists together nearly doubled their strength. The new political constellation exposed the opportunism and hypocrisy of much of the democratic commitment of 1918–19, when simple survival and hope for an easy peace had determined political philosophy.

Germany's accession to the League, advocated warmly in the election campaign of 1919, was of little consequence in the campaign òf 1920. None of the party platforms touched on the subject. The Right saw little reason to revise the opinion it had formed the year before. It saw the League as "a syndicate of victors bent on exploiting the peace treaty." The League was not designed to provide for the "impartial settlement of international disputes"; it offered no protection against "military, political, and economic oppression." Merely to appeal to it, commented the pan-German *Deutsche Zeitung*, was to demonstrate a "perverse kind of courage."[5] The coalition parties quarreled little with such opinions. After the treaty had been signed in June 1919, these parties had expressed regret at Germany's exclusion from the League and had deplored the absence of idealism in the covenant. Unlike the Right, however, they had withheld final judgment in the hope that the League would eventually redress the imbalance between victors and vanquished. They hoped that Germany would be invited to join and that she could revise the peace treaty and reform the covenant from within the League.[6] This wishful thinking—apparent for the last time in January 1920,[7] when the League was founded officially—came to nothing, much to the satisfaction of the Right. The coalition government addressed various appeals to the League in the spring of 1920. All misfired. In April the government had tried to warn the council that French occupation of several German cities was dangerous. At the same time it accused the Belgian government of unscrupulous practices in the plebiscite in Eupen-Malmédy and protested to the League. Repeatedly the coalition expressed its indignant concern at the League's newly established administration of the Saar territory. These appeals, if they were considered at all, were dismissed by the council. The government interpreted such neglect as outright hostility. The coalition parties gave up their hopes, subscribed to Simons's skepticism, and dropped the League from their program.[8] Not until late in 1922 did the desirability of German membership in the League reappear in their platforms, and no member of the coalition parties raised the issue in the cabinet before 1923.

The *volte-face* of 1919–20 casts light on German attitudes toward the League, which seem in retrospect to have shaped Germany's relations with the League throughout the Weimar years. On the one hand, Germans of all political opinions adopted a utilitarian approach, measuring their interest in the League by the tangible advantages the League could offer. They saw such advantages less in the benefits Germany might reap in participating in League decisions than in possible mitigation of the peace settlement. On the other hand, Germans chiefly of conservative persuasion displayed a deep disdain for the League. Their disdain suggested that they saw no value or purpose in a new international order. In fact, neither in public statements nor in private conversations can we find evidence that the Germans, as representatives of a great power, wanted to take part in any responsibility for overcoming national rivalries and making a new order effective.

These attitudes, latent the year before, emerged into prominence in the summer of 1920. The June election, some nineteen months after the revolution had deposed the imperial regime, passed the affairs of the country into the hands of the moderate, conservative bourgeoisie. The new government, a coalition of People's party, Centrists, and Democrats put together by Konstantin Fehrenbach, the last president of the imperial Reichstag, abandoned projects for nationalizing or socializing the economy and for purging the reactionaries in the civil service and the army. The spirit of reform and conciliation that had animated the Socialist governments disappeared. Henceforth Weimar governments were to include or depend on parties which were uncomfortable with democratic forms of government and critical of the republic.

The League figured prominently in the German press only on the occasion of its annual assembly, the most spectacular, but politically the least significant, of its operations. Programs of instruction in schools and universities gave little attention to the League. Those history textbooks which treated the League without rancor focused on its technical and charitable functions.[9] The middle class, having lost its incentive of 1919, showed little interest in the League. What interest remained was confined to a politically unorganized minority. The pacifists, mainly intellectuals of democratic persuasion, had believed themselves on the verge of realizing a dream. They now bewailed the League and Germany's exclusion. At the same time, however, they were loath to surrender what little had been achieved toward realizing that dream. The League offered practical advantages, they argued; it was the only peaceful way of revising the peace treaty. To ignore it was folly. But even the pacifists felt obliged to qualify their championship of the League: reforms along the lines of the German draft of 1919 would have to precede German membership. Theirs was a voice in the wilderness. Reigning attitudes found expression in the fortunes of the Liga für Völkerbund. Its meetings were broken up by nationalist rowdies, its subsidies reduced, and its membership, a barometer of German sentiment, declined steadily. It shrank to a lobby of limited effect.[10]

Indicative of the level of general unpopularity was the hostile, even scurrilous, attention—to the point of downright misrepresentation—of satirical weeklies, political periodicals, and daily newspapers. Correspondents who went to Geneva called the League "a farce," "the bad conscience of the Entente," a front for the great powers. To apply for membership would be self-abasing; to join, self-destructive. The press devised a standard barrier to membership: reconciliation and revision of the peace treaty would have to open the way.[11] In the Reichstag, little was said in defense of the League. Deputies might compare it unfavorably with an "ideal" or "true" League; more often they would denigrate it as a "caricature," an "unholy alliance of victors," or as the "steward of injustice." And whenever League decisions seemed contrary to German interests, the plenum rang with charges of vindictiveness and malevolence (reported at length in the press). Symptomatic of the parliamentary attitude was the response which a statement before the Reichstag in February 1921 elicited. The foreign minister's remark that as a sanction the Allies might block Germany's admission to the League was greeted with "resounding laughter."[12]

The public's sporadic displays of hostility have been variously explained as disappointment at Germany's exclusion from the League or as reaction to the way the League treated Germany in issues connected with the peace treaty.[13] These experiences may have contributed to prevailing public sentiment. The source of the sentiment, however, lay deeper. The League was a product of the Treaty of Versailles. The populace resented the peace settlement with a deep and pervasive passion. The resentment was not confined to the conservative bourgeoisie; it reached into the ranks of the working class. It flared up when Allied troops moved in to occupy the demilitarized Rhineland; it burst forth whenever conflict erupted along the line of demarcation between Germany and Poland. It emerged when the Allies demanded that the Germans pay reparations, reduce their armaments, and deliver up their "war criminals." The Germans behaved as if, having gone the length of signing the treaty, they should be excused from executing it.

The Nationalists in particular stoked this resentment—chiefly to advance their own interests. Having recovered their nerve, they suggested that denouncing the treaty was merely a matter of courage. They heaped abuse on the German politicians who were "weak-kneed" in facing up to "the enemy." And they exploited the treaty—the consequence of a war they had themselves endorsed—to discredit the young republic. They charged the coalition parties with having placed naive faith in Wilson's hypocritical promises and having spinelessly signed the armistice and the peace, thus signing away German honor and surrendering German power. Even more moderate contemporaries blamed the treaty for political unrest and virulent nationalism, for want and inflation, shortages and unemployment. Now the coalition parties had to pay for the illusions of 1918–19, when they had propagated democracy and internationalism as a guarantee for a mild peace. They were unable to correct the distortion of their motives and intentions, unable to explain the limitations imposed upon them by circumstances. Resentful themselves of having to abandon their hopes of international conciliation and embarrassed by the popularity of the Nationalist agitation, they were obliged to join in denouncing the treaty.[14]

The settlement alone, however, could not have engendered such resentment. In attacking Versailles, the Germans vented deeper passions. For behind the frustration over Versailles lay an unwillingness to accept the collapse of the extravagant expectations which Germany's prewar stature had seemed to warrant. Imperial Germany had seemed destined to rank among the world powers, and few except the radical Left doubted the propriety or legitimacy of Germany's prewar policy. Most clung to the explanation the imperial government had manufactured to justify the war. They believed the war to have been a defensive struggle against encirclement by jealous powers who begrudged Germany her natural ascendancy, and they conveniently forgot the great aims elaborated during the war. The fixation upon Germany's prewar status shows how little war and revolution had changed public values. The massive upheavals of the years 1914–19 had left the vast majority of the Germans remarkably unreconstructed.

Bound to tradition and able to find no merit in the postwar world, the Germans could not even assess the new situation soberly. They failed to understand that the peace settlement, for all its harshness, had made Germany more secure nationally and had provided opportunities for reorientation and new departures. They mourned the sunken fleet and clamored for the restoration of the colonies which had both caused friction with England. Before the war Germany had been drawn into conflicts in the Balkans, where the Habsburg Empire had clashed with Russia. Now the empire had disappeared and with it the involvement in noisome Balkan squabbles. The reconstitution of Poland, which the Germans detested, offered them a formidable ally in Soviet Russia; the retrocession of Alsace-Lorraine opened the possibility of reducing inherited tensions with France. But the generations which had lived through Germany's rise to power continued to see the world and Germany's advantage in terms of her position in 1914. Even a mild peace would not have reconciled them to Germany's situation after 1918. To such a mind a new European order and a new spirit of international conduct were inconceivable; new politics or even a willingness to experiment with a new form of politics was out of the question.[15]

The political articulation of the public's prevalent attitude was the government's commitment to the revision of the treaty. This commitment had been expressed most forcefully by a Socialist, Foreign Minister Hermann Müller, as early as July 1919: the government would leave "no doubt" about its intentions to revise.[16] No government of the republic ever surrendered this commitment. It was the basis of foreign policy throughout the Weimar era. Germany would have to regain her freedom of action, or at least some measure of self-determination in her dealings with other powers. The main target, therefore, was the conditions of the treaty which limited Germany's sovereignty.

The government would have to extract the country from the immense material burdens of reparations, for these seemed to impede economic recovery. It would have to curtail the occupation of the Rhineland and rid itself of the lien on exports and customs revenue. And it would have to put an end to Germany's unilateral disarmament—either by bringing about general disarmament or by rearming. Once these "shackles" were cast off—and the use of the term implied that the Germans believed they lacked freedom of movement, not power—Germany could begin to make good the losses that hurt the most, the territorial amputations. In the east, Poland would have to return the formerly Prussian provinces; in the southeast, Austria should merge with the Reich; not a few even dreamed of recovering Alsace. The retrocession of territory would virtually return Germany to her status of 1914, while Anschluss would make her stronger than she had been at the outbreak of the war. Implicit in these political ambitions was a yearning for the glitter and prestige of the Wilhelmine era, for restoration.

In the Foreign Ministry, where these aims were cast into policies, prewar traditions were still very much alive. The compromise reached with the moderate Socialists during the revolution had preserved the ministry from radical change. It was saved from further interference by the return of middle-class influence on the government. To be sure, the ministry had been reformed in 1919–20, but the reform had been limited to organization. There had been some change in personnel (a number of imperial diplomats had resigned) but no change in personnel policy. The few non-professionals whom the left-wing parties had forced upon the ministry made no mark. Some had found the atmosphere not to their liking and had left; some had been sent abroad to serve in legations and embassies. Those who attained influential positions soon adapted themselves to the reigning outlook and the traditional procedures. By mid-1920 the professionals felt secure once again, and within the next three or four years the ministry returned to old hands.[17]

For the moment, revisionist policy could do no more than seek a modification of the terms. Success depended largely on tactics. The German diplomats soon found that France, convinced that her national security depended upon exacting execution of the treaty, would be intransigent. She would brook no delay or change in the Germans' obligation to reduce their armed forces and trim their armaments, and she wanted to establish a large reparations sum and a schedule of payments. The British, though committed to the same aims, were on the whole more pragmatic and more given to negotiation and adjustment. These differences, which burdened relations between London and Paris in these years, offered the Germans an opportunity for initiatives. But the German diplomats seemed to ignore the limits that the effects of the war had imposed on their activity and to entertain illusions about their room to maneuver. Accustomed to negotiating from strength, they had no experience with the tactics suited to a weak power. Their efforts to exploit differences in the Allied camp were too crude to succeed. Attempts at duplicity or evasion or at outright defiance resulted in ultimatums and sanctions. These fostered unrest at home without advancing revision in the least. To escape the impasse, some of the diplomats looked to Washington, some to Moscow, but none to Geneva.[18]

The League seemed to offer no advantages to a policy of revision or restoration. In fact it could be argued that Germany had a choice of either joining the League and renouncing revision, or abstaining from the League and pursuing her cherished aim. Since the covenant was part of the treaty, membership would only draw Germany deeper into the settlement. Hans von Seeckt, who represented views held not merely by the military but also by hardline diplomats and members of the right-wing parties, put this possibility succinctly:

> Entry would entangle Germany in the system of the Western powers, would rob her of freedom of action for possible future developments, and would relegate her to the position of an Anglo-French protectorate. If Germany cannot free herself of the worst fetters of Versailles ... she is doomed to decline.[19]

The diplomats were unmoved when Johann von Bernstorff (and other lobbyists for German membership) argued that as a member of the League, Germany could influence the implementation of the peace terms.[20] They were convinced that Germany's presence at Geneva could not have prevented French sanctions or the division of Upper Silesia.

The professionals wondered whether membership in the League would not damage Germany's relations with the United

States and with the Soviet Union, the great outsiders to the
League. It was a commonplace in the Foreign Ministry that the
United States, having rejected the Versailles Treaty because of
its connection with the covenant, wanted Germany to stay out of
the League. The Germans did not wish to affront the Americans, for they hoped for American intervention in the dispute
over reparations. The resumption of trade between the two
countries late in 1919 gave rise to the belief that the Americans
would want to protect German prosperity and stability from
debilitating reparations payments. And since both Britain and
France were in debt to the United States, Washington had the
means to apply the necessary pressure.[21] The Soviet Union, the
Germans knew, was deeply hostile to the League, believing it to
be a capitalist alliance directed against her. Membership could
not be reconciled with rapprochement with the Soviet Union,
which was advocated by Ago von Maltzan in the Foreign Ministry and favored by the military leadership and by heavy industry. Rapprochement with the Soviet Union might, at the very
least, provide a counterweight to the power of the West, and, at
best, might open possibilities of treaty revision, especially along
the eastern frontiers.[22] The German government was therefore
particularly attentive to what the ambassadors in Washington
and Moscow reported, and both Wiedfeldt and Brockdorff-
Rantzau counseled against seeking admission.[23]

The conclusions of these broad political considerations were
confirmed in a detailed analysis of the League. This analysis did
not originate in the Foreign Ministry, which never went beyond
general statements of its policy until after the French and Belgians occupied the Ruhr in 1923. The analysis lies in the dispatches of the German minister in Switzerland, which the ministry forwarded to the major diplomatic missions and to the
president and the chancellor throughout these early years.

Germany's minister in Switzerland was Adolf Müller. A man
of strong views, outspoken and acidulous, Müller had come late
to the diplomatic service. Before his appointment in January
1919 he had edited a Socialist newspaper in Munich. The professional diplomats respected his judgment, however, and they
sought his counsel even on matters which did not involve the
League. From Berne, Müller kept close watch on developments
in Geneva, and his contacts with members and officials of the

League and with the Swiss government made him a valuable and informed observer. Müller did not confine himself to routine reports. He took occasion to write whenever he felt that his government might succumb to the advice of "false friends" (such as the Liga für Völkerbund) and take rash steps toward admission. His anxieties often led him to choose sharp language and exaggerated arguments, but he had no reason to think that his plainspoken warnings would offend the officials in Berlin. The reports were unequivocal. By his own admission, Müller adhered to the idea of a "true" League with justice and equality for all. He condemned the Geneva institution as "anti-Christ" and a "travesty." Indeed, until well into 1923, Müller opposed joining the League at any time and under any circumstances. In his dispatches he elevated Germany's abstinence to a virtue and a principle. Absence invited attention, he argued, and it allowed Germany to protest the injustice of her position to the world at large.[24]

While his reports naturally reflected the shifting emphases dictated by passing events, they pursued one basic argument. The League was an alliance of the great powers, and those powers (particularly France) exploited the alliance for their own purposes. From this assumption followed a number of conclusions. According to the covenant an applicant for admission had to "give effective guarantees of its sincere intention to observe its international obligations." France would interpret this stipulation as legitimate grounds to demand a renewed acknowledgment of the peace treaty and a pledge that Germany would execute the treaty in all its particulars. She would insist that Germany disarm morally as well as materially, and she would demand assurances that Germany would not rearm. Even if Germany could escape restrictive and "humiliating" conditions, membership would damage her situation seriously. The French and their allies controlled the assembly, including those members who bore Germany no ill will and earnestly desired international conciliation. The French were determined to maintain their control, even at the cost of discrediting the assembly, and no member wished to court conflict with France. Real power lay with the council, but the council's political decisions emanated not from an impartial body, but from the chancelleries of the council members. French control extended also to the secretariat. Highly placed French staff members—Jean Monnet, an assistant secretary-general, Paul Mantoux, director of the political section, and Pierre Comert, director of the information section—dominated Secretary-General Eric Drummond, a stiff and unimaginative administrator.[25]

The absence of the United States and of the Soviet Union enhanced French influence. Müller warned against such an "incomplete" League. The United States had inspired and initiated the formation of the League, and its absence, Müller argued, reduced Europe's confidence in the League's stature and effectiveness. As Wilson's performance at the peace conference had demonstrated, America was the only power of sufficient prestige to mediate between France and crippled Germany. No one at Geneva, therefore, could urge the League to revise the unbearable peace. Without the United States and the Soviet Union, the League was a one-sided political constellation. Without the backing of these two powers Germany could not hope to influence decisions within the League. Membership would deprive her of her right to choose her own political alignments.[26]

The League's own competence, as defined by the covenant and endorsed by the French, could not advance Germany's interests. Issues which Germany found most burdensome, such as reparations, lay outside the League's province, and France would exclude them from discussion at Geneva. At Versailles, Clemenceau had claimed that the League was competent to revise the settlement of 1919. Pure deception, said Müller. Article 10, which guaranteed the "territorial integrity" and "political independence" of member states, made the League the guardian of the territorial status quo. Article 19, which allowed obsolete treaties to be revised, did not apply to the Versailles settlement. The French prime minister Viviani had argued in the first assembly in 1920 that the League could not alter the covenant, since altering the covenant was tantamount to revising the peace treaty, for which the League had no authority. In consequence, the League could hardly promote revision—indeed, in matters such as the administration of the Saar and the guarantee of Danzig's integrity and independence, the League blocked the way directly.[27]

For issues on which the League was competent, such as Anschluss, the Saar, and surveillance of Germany's disarmament, majority decisions carried. Germany could do no more than protest, and protest outside the League, Müller was fond of saying, carried greater moral conviction. Worse, Germany's presence would sanction whatever the majority decided. Germany could hardly count on the smaller states in the assembly. To be sure, they might clamor for her admission and make speeches in her behalf before the assembly, but at best, Müller concluded drily, their clamor for Germany sprang from the hope that Germany's entry would strengthen their ranks. Within the League they would pursue their own interests and, being small, refrain from challenging the great powers.[28]

For all its paranoid overtones, Müller's explanation of the League was not without foundation in fact. The League was an association of states, not a superstate, and depended for its authority on its strongest members. In the absence of the United States and the Soviet Union and because of the halfhearted interest of Italy and Japan, this responsibility devolved upon Britain and France. Yet in interpreting the League as an "Allied instrument,"[29] Müller failed to observe the lack of agreement between these two powers and its potential advantages for Germany. At the peace conference, the two states had advanced rival proposals for the covenant, and neither was entirely satisfied with the League as created at Versailles. This dissatisfaction influenced both their attitudes and their policies toward the League.

If France had her way, the League would be a coercive coalition, for if it was to be effective in preserving peace and maintaining security, it had to be powerful. This view was shared by the Left, which favored the League and collective security, and the Right, no convert to a new world order. The conservative postwar governments, prompted by the memory of two German invasions, continued to search for the security France had failed to find in the treaty and had lost again when the Anglo-American guarantee fell through. They thought they could obtain security by "putting teeth into the League," or, failing that, by enlisting members of the League in the protection of France. They sought security also in old-fashioned alliance politics, in armaments, and in thwarting Germany's attempts to recover. The French pursued this policy, which the Germans interpreted as an attempt at hegemony, with a single-mindedness that bordered on obsession.[30]

In the first year after the peace conference, the French were not eager for the Germans to join the League. As long as Germany remained outside, France could proceed against her at will and without fear of the sanctions by which the League protected its members. Thus France could punish Germany for violations of the treaty—as in 1920 and 1921—and the League could not intervene. She could also exclude the League from disputes such as those over reparations, and instead consign them to summit conferences of the powers, where the League could not act as moderator. As long as Germany remained an inconsequential outsider, France could influence League policy without reference to the welfare of the Germans. She could make the League an instrument of her foreign policy by having it assume surveillance of Germany's disarmament and raise troops for the prompt enforcement of military sanctions. Once France had realized her plans, she would welcome Germany into the League, for then membership would endorse the French security system. There was, then, a certain ambiguity about France's position: she wanted to keep Germany out of the League, but not indefinitely.[31]

In Britain and Germany advocates of German membership argued that a well-timed application could neutralize French opposition. France could not afford to be charged with obstructing the pacification of postwar Europe, as she was sure to be if she alone rejected Germany's application. In fact, application in the teeth of French opposition might strengthen Germany's moral position. The Foreign Ministry demurred. It argued that application was more a risk than an advantage. The French had threatened to quit Geneva if Germany were admitted.[32] The risk, however, was more apparent than real. If France should resign, she would offend the British—who, for reasons of their own, espoused the League as a supplement to traditional diplomacy—and France's security system depended on British support.

For the British government the League was not the instrument for enforcing the Versailles Treaty, but rather useful machinery for revising its unworkable parts. Differences could be resolved and grievances redressed before they became explosive. The British, therefore, stressed the League's conciliatory and mediatory functions and resisted schemes for extending its punitive powers. They believed that, as a standing conference

for dealing with common problems, the League provided a setting in which the discontented states, such as Germany, could be
restored to some prominence and induced to cooperate in the
maintenance of a stable international order.[33]

Neither the French nor the British prevailed. This conflict
impaired the League's effectiveness in political issues. It ren-
dered the League incapable of concerted action that might involve major powers. It cast doubt on the League's impartiality
and the efficacy of its sanctions. On matters affecting the Allies
or their followers, the council was often evasive (as when it failed
to respond to Lithuanian requests to eject the Poles from Vilna,
the old Lithuanian capital, which they had seized by force in October 1920). Or, rather than risk an embarrassing deadlock, the
council would refer troublesome issues to ordinary diplomatic
negotiations or conferences. As a result, the League was left to
deal with secondary problems.

Yet the failure of the League and the new diplomacy was by
no means a foregone conclusion. The gray record of these early
years of the League might disenchant those who had put great
hopes in the new order in 1918–19. World confidence—the
mainstay of the League—might be slow in coming. Purists might
charge the League with timidity and bewail its lack of moral
authority. But there were signs that the League might yet find its
own way, and the supporters of the League, if disappointed,
were not resigned. The assembly, led by illustrious representatives of smaller states (such as Beneš of Czechoslovakia, Branting
of Sweden, or Motta of Switzerland), assumed an identity of its
own, criticizing the work of the League in its debates and prodding the council about its responsibilities. The secretariat, whose
duties often went beyond the purely administrative to the politically sensitive, had become known for its loyalty and efficiency.
And in various countries, peace groups and League of Nations
societies pressed their governments to align national policy with
covenant principles and urged reforms to make the League live
up to its aspirations.[34]

No German government rejected the League coldly. Whether
under the chancellorship of the hapless Fehrenbach or of the
combative Josef Wirth, the government appears to have assumed tacitly that eventually Germany would join the League,
probably as one consequence of a general settlement. The

Foreign Ministry followed developments within the League, especially those related to Germany's possible admission. Foreign initiatives—articles in the press, diplomatic allusions, or resolutions of League of Nations societies—were canvassed, assessed, and circulated in the ministry and among various missions. The envoys in the major capitals were enjoined to report regularly on the sentiment toward the League and on Germany's prospects. The ministry registered the various hints that Germany should apply, but it recognized that these hints offered no guarantee that Germany would be admitted. The hints usually came from officials in the League secretariat or from smaller countries, often former neutrals, which were eager to bind up the wounds of the war or simply to offset Allied preponderance at Geneva. They carried little political import and amounted to no more than pious wishes.[35]

German political leaders took care not to display outright hostility toward Geneva. They did not want to create the impression that "the German government was averse or indifferent to the idea of the League."[36] The tone of almost all public declarations on the subject (the most conspicuous exception being the reaction against the division of Upper Silesia) was bland and vaguely cordial.[37] The government endorsed the notion of international cooperation repeatedly, and it even cultivated direct contact with Geneva. Germany had joined the International Labor Office in November 1919. German experts were active in several technical commissions of the League—those on health, transit, communications, opium traffic, and intellectual cooperation—and they participated in some of the general conferences under League auspices (at Brussels in 1920, Barcelona in 1921, Warsaw in 1922). A ready exchange of technical and statistical material between Berlin and Geneva began in 1920. Though certain diplomats objected to the continuing activity of the Liga für Völkerbund, the Foreign Ministry subsidized it with 50,000–75,000 marks a year (as opposed to 450,000 marks in 1919 and 1920).[38]

Officially the government maintained a neutral reserve. "We do not want to nurse our resentments," wrote Simons in a diplomatic dispatch, "but to let the League approach us."[39] In defining this policy for its diplomatic missions in the summer of 1921, the Foreign Ministry declared that Germany would await an official invitation. The tactic implied that upon receiving such an invitation, the German government would press for certain conditions and privileges. The ministry instructed its diplomats to explain Germany's reserve by saying that Germany could not possibly enter while member states still applied sanctions against her. The explanation indicates just what conditions the Germans intended to seek.[40]

The first direct challenge to the German position came in British soundings on possible admission in the summer of 1922. The previous year, under threat of ultimatum, the German government had accepted Allied reparation terms and embarked on a tactic of limited compliance with the treaty in hopes of persuading the Allies to modify their conditions. Germany's payments had accelerated the inflation of her currency and further undermined European solvency; her limited compliance had left France's search for security unfulfilled. Interest in Europe's political and economic stability as a prerequisite for good trade led the British to advance a program for international reconstruction and to foster the reconciliation of the great powers, including the pariahs, Germany and the Soviet Union. To this end, Lloyd George, the British prime minister, proposed a European economic conference at Genoa in April 1922.[41]

The professionals in the German Foreign Ministry were not pleased at the prospect. They had been working toward resumption of formal relations with the Soviet Union. Arrangements had already been set in motion to secure Soviet facilities to circumvent the military proscriptions of Versailles, and a provisional trade agreement had been signed. Walther Rathenau, first as minister of reconstruction and then as foreign minister, thought that the tactic of compliance should not be compromised by close contact with the Soviet Union. The Allies seemed to him the more immediate threat and, correspondingly, their good will of more immediate advantage. He had cultivated contact with the British, and the subsequent relaxation of tension seemed now to lead to some form of conciliation with the West. The professionals were afraid that such conciliation might lead to membership in the League; rumors from Geneva confirmed their suspicions.[42] Membership in the League would imprison Germany in the system created at Versailles. That, they thought, would block their revisionist plans forever. The

Rapallo treaty, pressed by Maltzan, was in part a deliberate attempt to undercut the Genoa conference and sabotage whatever accommodation might have been achieved. The maneuver was a triumph for the traditionalists—such as Maltzan and Seeckt—who harbored prewar dreams.[43]

It was at this point that Lloyd George, quick to recover from the shock and still on a course of conciliation, inquired about Germany's willingness to join the League. If Germany could be brought into the League, German revisionism, blatant at Rapallo, might be curbed. Conversely, once Germany had been harnessed to the obligations of the covenant, the French might feel less inclined to press security aims which the British considered both unrealistic and unacceptable. Lloyd George's initiative met with rebuff, but the British were undeterred. Early in May the British ambassador in Berlin, Lord D'Abernon, called at the German Foreign Ministry to ascertain Germany's position on the League. A shrewd and adroit diplomat, D'Abernon enjoyed some influence with the German government (not least because the Germans believed him to be influential with his own). His inquiry was therefore taken seriously. State Secretary Haniel, in charge during the foreign minister's absence, directed Gerhard Köpke of the legal department to draw up a memorandum on Germany's policy and wired Rathenau at Genoa for instructions. Köpke's memorandum opposed entry, citing the familiar arguments. Rathenau too was hostile. He believed that membership would aggravate Germany's difficulties. "I deem it impossible that the League could bring us any closer to a satisfactory solution of even a single one of the questions which burden us," he wrote. He wished therefore to evade any serious discussion of possible admission.[44]

Acting on Rathenau's instructions, Haniel received D'Abernon at the ministry. Stressing that what he had to say was strictly his own opinion, he told D'Abernon that a League based on equality and designed to promote world peace was a noble ideal to which he subscribed. At the moment, however, the institution at Geneva hardly embodied this ideal. The German public did not believe the League to be impartial, and the reluctance of the United States and of the Soviet Union to join only enhanced the mistrust. Moreover, the German government entertained certain reservations. It was concerned about the process of admission as outlined in the covenant. Even if Germany were to be admitted with certain immunities, a seat on the council was not assured. Even if a seat could be procured, Germany could hardly influence decisions, for the council was virtually identical with the Conference of Ambassadors, which supervised the treaty. The situation could be improved only if the council were expanded to alter the predominance of Allied powers or if the assembly were given greater authority.[45]

The British persisted. Lloyd George told D'Abernon privately that he wanted to bring Germany into the League and treat her as an equal and announced publicly that his government would welcome a German application. He was seconded by Lord Robert Cecil, a conservative member of parliament, long an enthusiast of German membership.[46] Drummond campaigned for German membership in London, and secretariat officials espoused it in Geneva. In Germany, the cry was taken up by pacifists, Socialist deputies in the Reichstag, and democratic newspapers.[47] To hinder what might become an uncontrollable campaign, the Foreign Ministry drafted an article over the name of prewar minister Bernhard Dernburg, a well-known Democrat, for publication at the end of June. The article claimed that the treatment Germany had received at Geneva was responsible for her reluctance, and that the League had offered little justice and equality. It called for the democratization of the League and for a council seat for Germany to insure such reform.[48]

On 12 July D'Abernon approached the chancellor on German membership. Wirth put certain questions to him. How did Britain think Germany's entry might affect "the great political questions on which Germany's fate depends"—reparations, military control, French sanctions? Would Britain promise not to interfere in German affairs once Germany had joined?[49] Ten days later the ambassador broached the subject with Maltzan. Maltzan, who believed that Germany's salvation lay in alliance with Russia, cited the Foreign Ministry's favorite gambit: public opinion was an insurmountable obstacle.[50] On 25 July Wirth addressed to D'Abernon a résumé of Germany's position. The résumé had been drafted in the Foreign Ministry and reflected the ministry's thinking. There were certain conditions Germany must set: Germany would have to be admitted without "a renewed acknowledgment of the Versailles Treaty," and a permanent seat on the council would have to be hers on admission. The conditions, D'Abernon did not doubt, were tantamount to a rejection of the British soundings.[51]

These stirrings in the summer of 1922 brought out the latent interest on the Left. After Rapallo, Germany's international position had deteriorated (quite contrary to expectations in the Foreign Ministry). When she stopped paying reparations in August, citing her rapid inflation, and requested a moratorium on payments through 1924, the French under Poincaré took reprisals. The League, as the *Vossische Zeitung* put it, might be a way out of these difficulties.[52] At the party congress in September the Socialists resolved to ask the government to disregard even the warranted criticism directed at the League and to seek admission as soon as "a position compatible with the importance of Germany's culture and economy" had been assured. The Socialist minister of justice, Gustav Radbruch, appealed to the chancellor privately to include the topic on the agenda of the cabinet. The Democrats discussed the matter at length at their party congress in October, and "Germany's early entry" was the theme of the German pacifist congress that same month. Surprisingly, Otto Hoetzsch, a moderate conservative, declared at the party congress of the Nationalists at Görlitz in October that German representation in the League—to be sure with full equality and a seat on the council—would be politically useful, since Germany's interests in Danzig, the Saar, and Upper Silesia were proper concerns of the League. He suggested that negotiations with the great powers begin.[53]

The Foreign Ministry was obliged to respond to these pressures. In February 1923 League affairs within the ministry were transferred from the competence of the legal department to a separate section—Referat Völkerbund—directly responsible to the state secretary.[54] To head this section, the ministry appointed Bernhard Wilhelm von Bülow, a nephew of the prewar chancellor. Bülow came with excellent qualifications: a critical turn of mind, a great knowledge of international affairs, a good grasp of the legal dimension of diplomacy, and experience and expertise. He had entered the diplomatic service in 1911, had attended the conferences of Brest-Litovsk and Versailles, and had resigned shortly after the peace treaty had been signed. In his temporary retirement he had devoted himself to a careful study of the League, and he had published the results in a number of articles and in a substantial, rather critical book, which appeared in autumn of 1923.[55]

The Foreign Ministry had already consulted Bülow several times in 1922, and his views on policy toward the League, advanced very persuasively, colored the ministry's thinking thenceforth. Bülow's analysis was less Francophobe than Müller's. It was a mistake, Bülow argued, to regard the League as anything but a political body—"the extension of the Paris peace conference." The League council, which set the tone, consisted of the victorious powers and assured their predominance. The Allies defined the tasks of the League. Its competence extended to maintenance of the status quo of 1919, but it had no power to interpret or revise the treaty. From this premise it followed that the German government should assess Germany's relationship with the League by political standards. If Germany were to think in terms of joining, she should also think in terms of making the League serve her political purposes. It followed further that the state of Germany's relations with the Western powers was the sole determinant of her chances of admission. Only when the Allies abandoned their hostility would entry be possible. Admission would be the consequence of improved relations, and not their cause (as the pacifists argued).[56]

Bülow was skeptical of the value of membership and, like Müller, he warned against the siren songs of the neutrals and the Left. In a memorandum he submitted to the ministry in September 1922, he summarized his objections. He dismissed the motives behind various entreaties as insincere. The major powers wished to bring Germany into the League (though not into the council) in order to subject her to the discipline of the organization (*Vereinsdisziplin*), to oversee her external affairs, and to bring her into a European bloc that could be directed against Russia or even against the United States. The neutral and small powers wanted to bring the League closer to universality and to lessen the powers of the Allied victors. The secretariat wanted to infuse new blood into the League, which was having difficulties. The continued absence of various major powers impeded its functioning, and the Allies' control over the execution of the peace treaty deprived the League of all worthwhile tasks. These impediments had already caused certain members, especially

non-Europeans, to tire of the League. Entry therefore would
benefit no one but the League, and it would curtail Germany's
freedom of action and hamper her revisionist policy. She would
be limited to aggressive opposition or docile acquiescence;
neither was desirable.[57]

As head of the new section, Bülow set out to acquaint himself
at first hand with the state of Germany's relations with the
League. In April 1923 he visited Geneva. Members of the secretariat, he found, believed Germany's admission unthinkable
until Franco-German relations returned to normal. Bülow
found other suspicions confirmed; the officials were unshake-
ably committed to the peace settlement, which they regarded as
the basis of all their activity. As a result of his visit, the ministry
decided that Germany should continue to confine her relations
with Geneva to nonpolitical matters.[58]

In the summer, however, interest in Germany's entry quick-
ened. In January the French and Belgians, exasperated by Germany's evasiveness over reparations, had occupied the Ruhr.
They intended to take over the management of Ruhr industries
as "productive guarantees" for reparations. This callous disregard for the League spirit, the insistence that might makes right,
angered all friends of the League. Neutral statesmen had urged
that the League intervene to settle the crisis and to solve the
reparations problem. In May, British Liberals were in touch with
Friedrich Sthamer, the German ambassador in London, and
with the Foreign Ministry. Their message: Germany should join
the League to protect her political interests.[59]

The Foreign Ministry believed that neither the intervention of
the League nor German admission to the League would facilitate a solution. In fact, the diplomats feared that an intervention
might draw Britain closer to France and retard a solution. They
were heartened to discover that at last the British had refused to
act with France in enforcing the peace terms. Reports from
Sthamer that the British government hoped for a German initiative suggested that mediation would come from London. But a
German proposal, submitted in May, failed to elicit such mediation. Little different from earlier proposals, hedged with conditions, it disappointed the British and was promptly rejected by
the French and Belgians. Nonetheless, the German government,
supported by the major newspapers, held fast to its policy.[60]

This inflexibility had its counterpart in domestic policy. The government encouraged and subsidized passive resistance in the occupied Ruhr. In retaliation, the French increased their forces, separated the Ruhr from Germany proper, and took sharp reprisals for German sabotage. Neither side would relent. Time, however, was with the occupier. How long could the German government afford a policy which, though it attracted support like nothing since 1914, drove the country to ruin? Most spectacular, the currency, already badly inflated, became altogether worthless. In January the mark stood at ten thousand to the dollar; six months later it had increased elevenfold. Millions saw their savings vanish and their standard of living decline. The financial crisis encouraged menaces to the republican regime, to the country's unity, and to national security. While young Nazis paraded in Bavaria, Communists gathered to await the day the government would become bankrupt. Separatists agitated in the Rhineland, and after the Lithuanians had seized Memel, rumors circulated that the Poles were about to occupy Danzig and East Prussia.[61]

By June, the crisis was acute and attitudes toward the League underwent a change. On the thirteenth, Sthamer reported that Cecil, now Lord Privy Seal in the cabinet, had drawn up a scheme which would strengthen the League's peacekeeping functions by making military sanctions mandatory and automatic. Since Cecil's plan was likely to affect his government's foreign policy, Sthamer thought it conceivable that Germany might be confronted shortly with a decision about entering the League. He suggested that Germany try to influence the project and proposed that Count Harry Kessler, a former diplomat turned cosmopolitan patron of the arts, who happened to be in London and knew Cecil personally, establish contact. The German government responded promptly. In a second proposal to the creditor states only the week before, it had offered to accept a new international settlement of reparations. Therefore it wanted to court favor with the British. It approved Kessler's proposed conversation. Should Cecil allude to Germany's joining the League, Kessler was to summarize Germany's standing position on the subject without, however, presenting it as anything but his own private opinion. The conversation took place on 19 June, and Kessler immediately relayed Cecil's enthusiasm for Germany's entry, adding his own fervent endorsement. He reported that Cecil had told him that British fears of a German war of revenge would be allayed (and Germany's prestige consequently enhanced) if the German government requested admission. A council seat, he said, was virtually assured, and there would be no humiliating conditions.[62]

The report caused rumination in the Foreign Ministry. If Cecil could indeed influence British policy, Germany could not remain indifferent, for she could not afford to offend Britain. Sthamer was asked his opinion. He responded with a warning. To be sure, Cecil's entry into the government raised certain hopes, but the government as a whole, Sthamer thought, did not share Cecil's views. Cecil merely spoke for himself. Britain could not be expected to oppose France on the issue of Germany's admission, and the French would doubtless resist.[63] Bülow, also consulted, reported directly to the chancellor and cautioned against a German initiative. In the legal department, Gaus refrained from urging a particular course but opined that entry might be used as a bargaining point in breaking the stalemate in the Ruhr. And Maltzan, the architect of Rapallo, who had succeeded Haniel as state secretary the previous December, seemed to think that Germany would have to swallow this "bitter pill" and join.[64]

Foreign Minister von Rosenberg, a professional diplomat, was undecided. "Conditions at home and abroad might possibly make our entry a necessary part of the settlement of the European question," he noted. It was important, therefore, to shape developments so that entry would come "at the proper moment and under the most favorable circumstances." He instructed the ambassador in London to obtain more information on the British view from Curzon, the foreign secretary. As the ostensible reason for his interest, the ambassador could mention the recent American proposal that Germany and America become members of the Permanent Court at The Hague, and he could justify his interest by saying that the German government did not want to neglect this opportunity to affirm its continuing commitment to the idea of international justice. He added for Sthamer's information that Sthamer might permit Germany's interest in the Hague court and in possible participation in Cecil's assistance pact to be construed as evidence of Germany's willingness to draw closer to the League.[65] Sthamer balked at these instructions, and the Foreign Ministry acquiesced in his reluctance when no further encouragement arrived from Britain.[66] At the same time, the ministry ignored the agitation of German Socialists and inquiries of members of the League secretariat.[67] Bülow repeated his warnings against broaching the subject, and Müller supported him, arguing now not absolutely against joining the League, but against "premature, unprepared, and unconditional" entry.[68]

The deteriorating situation in Germany led the government to grasp at straws. On 29 July Rosenberg instructed Sthamer to inform Curzon that the unabated crisis in the Ruhr was creating desperate conditions in Germany, where the government faced threats from radicals on both Left and Right, and the populace was about to lose "faith both in the state and in itself." Sthamer was to say that the government was determined not to lose political and economic control. He was to ask confidentially whether Germany could expect support, if only moral support, from Britain, and he was to inquire if there were not some measures by which the Germans might relieve the situation without offending the British. Such measures might include taking the Ruhr case to the Hague court or requesting that Germany be admitted to the League.[69] Never had Germany gone so far toward admission.

Curzon threw cold water on the idea. Germany would be prudent, he told Sthamer, not to seek admission in the face of existing difficulties. She would be wiser to await events. Moreover, Germany should attach no conditions to her admission, nor should she expect a seat on the council. Bülow concurred with Curzon's estimate of the situation; he thought that further diplomatic collaboration with the Western powers was necessary before the distance between Berlin and Geneva could be bridged.[70]

Bülow was right. On 6 August Berlin learned from its envoy in Vienna that the French were raising objections to Germany's possible admission. If negotiation should begin, the French told the Austrian government, France would demand a pledge that Germany would observe all her obligations—a euphemism, the Foreign Ministry concluded, for the stipulations of the peace treaty. This was the first of many such reports to reach Berlin.[71]

Müller reported in September that the French delegation to the assembly had explicit instructions to vote against Germany's admission and was authorized to threaten France's withdrawal if Germany were admitted. That same month the assembly studiously evaded the subject. Even Cecil commented that a German application would founder upon the conditions of the covenant, inasmuch as Germany had obviously not satisfied her obligations under the treaty.[72] The Germans were obliged to settle the reparations issue and the Ruhr tangle outside the League.

3   To Locarno, 1923–25

The occupation of the Ruhr, by which Poincaré tried to extract reparations and to strengthen his country's security, injured France gravely. Germany's passive resistance made the occupation costly, and the unstable franc plummeted. At first the French public had supported the occupation, but support gave way as measures taken to ensure order in the Ruhr—arrests, expulsions, even executions—inflamed international opinion against Poincaré's venture. The premier, however, was intent on having a showdown. He would not let domestic difficulties or international isolation deter him from forcing Germany to capitulate.[1]

Capitulation was bound to come. Among the few Germans to recognize and acknowledge this was Gustav Stresemann, who had become both chancellor and foreign minister at the height of the crisis in 1923. Until the revolution Stresemann had been a leader of the National Liberals, loyal supporters of the Hohenzollern dynasty and enthusiastic adherents of German war aims. In 1918 he had rallied the more conservative members of his party to the People's party, which had concluded an uneasy peace with the republic. Stresemann himself never lost a nostalgic attachment to the monarchy. He commanded enough ambition and enough realism, however, to become a *Vernunftrepublikaner* after 1919. In the Reichstag he had made a name for himself as the spokesman of the moderate Right (with occasional lapses into more radical right-wing rhetoric) and as a tactician of remarkable skill and determination. He demonstrated these qualities by putting together a coalition comprising both Socialists and his own party in 1923.[2]

Stresemann had watched the escalation of the Ruhr crisis with alarm. He regarded the occupation as a prelude to the permanent annexation of the Rhineland and as part of a deliberate policy to consolidate France's continental hegemony at Germany's expense. He believed that the crisis, which brought financial chaos, political radicalization, and stirrings of separatism in Bavaria and the Rhineland, was driving Germany to the verge of disintegration. He was convinced that, unless Germany succeeded in averting catastrophe, she would have to abandon her hope of recovering her position among the European powers. Passive resistance, far from settling the crisis, was about to bankrupt the state—economically, morally, and politically. Active resistance or some kind of Anglo-German alliance against the French, advocated by some traditionalists, was out of the question. If Germany were to be safe, let alone prominent, her government would have to find a new approach.[3]

Germany, Stresemann argued, would have to acknowledge the defeat of 1918 and its consequences. She had lost the capacity to impose her will by military and political pressure. She could expel the French from the Ruhr and secure an acceptable reparations settlement only with the aid of Britain and the United States. Like his predecessor Cuno, Stresemann assumed that the two powers were inclined to help because both were distressed at the international repercussions of Germany's monetary collapse, both were interested in Germany's trade and market, and Britain, if not the United States, did not want France to become the dominant power on the continent. Unlike Cuno, however, Stresemann realized that Germany could count on such help only if she became conciliatory. She would have to seek accommodation with the great powers in a system which balanced European interests. Accommodation would require concessions—or "sacrifices"—for Stresemann understood that the Western powers, too, had claims they wished to satisfy. It was therefore logical that he should replace a policy of bluster and defiance with a policy of compromise.[4]

The government's first step was to terminate the Ruhr crisis—that is, to capitulate. Stresemann reiterated Cuno's offer to accept the recommendations of an "impartial international body" on the sum total of the reparations debts and the form of its payment. He declared that Germany was prepared to guarantee the western frontier as fixed at Versailles.[5] Then, at the end of September, he rallied the Reichstag parties (except the Nationalists) to his decision to abandon passive resistance. He could now tackle the inflation, which meanwhile had reached grotesque proportions. By November he had introduced a new currency, balanced the budget, and restored financial stability. Once Germany was on a surer economic footing, the possibility of making proper payment of reparations, of reviving the economy, and attracting foreign credit seemed less remote. At the same time, the government regained control of the domestic situation. It put down a mutiny of army irregulars at Küstrin, who had conspired to seize the government as the first act in a general "war of liberation." It deposed the coalition governments in Saxony and Thuringia, where Communists had joined Socialists preparatory, Berlin suspected, to revolution. It prevented the constitutional conflict with the Bavarian government, which had challenged Berlin's authority, from flaring into open insurrection or worse. The woeful failure of the Hitler putsch was a signal event: it marked the end of the civil strife that had plagued Germany since the war. When Stresemann's government fell at the end of November, the foundations had been laid for foreign and domestic confidence in the republic and for a foreign policy of accommodation.

Stresemann's decisions ended the international impasse. The British government, which had suggested in April 1923 that German willingness to pay reparations was a precondition for any settlement, now distanced itself from France's tactics against Germany. The United States, troubled all along by Germany's economic chaos and waiting for Germany to take the first diplomatic steps, now pressed for a solution. The French, buffeted by inflation and in fear of isolation, were obliged to make concessions. A commission of financial experts, headed by Charles Dawes, an American banker, convened in December 1923 to unravel the reparations issue. Its report, released the following April, established a sliding scale of annuities, to be tied to specific revenues and secured by railway bonds and industrial debentures. The report also provided for a major loan to preserve the stability of the German currency while the scheduled payments got under way. Approved by all the powers—albeit reluctantly by France—the Dawes plan promised to make reparations bearable and restore international economic cooperation. The final settlement was reserved for negotiations scheduled for July and August in London.[6]

The change in the international atmosphere revived the issue of Germany's entry into the League.[7] Again the impulse came from Britain, where the country's first Labour government had taken office in January 1924. Ramsay MacDonald, the new prime minister, was known to believe in the League. His government, the London embassy reported, thought the League a proper "clearing house" for the disputes which troubled relations among Europe's great powers.[8] MacDonald had repeatedly stressed his government's conviction that both Germany and Russia ought to join the League. Word reached German diplomats that in the September assembly Britain would urge Germany's admission. Richard Haldane, lord chancellor in the new cabinet, spoke to Ambassador Sthamer about Germany's attitude toward the League in what the ambassador termed "unmistakable if cautious soundings."[9]

Rumors of British interest led German Socialists to raise the subject in debate in the Reichstag. Stresemann, no longer chancellor but still foreign minister, defined the government's position on 28 February. His remarks were general. He explained (with overtones that would hardly be missed in London) that the German government had no need to reach a decision on whether to join the League, for it had received no invitation. There could be on doubt about Germany's commitment to international solidarity, he went on; though the institution at Geneva embodied this ideal only imperfectly, Germany was in principle not opposed to membership. Germany's conditions—a permanent seat on the council and no humiliating procedure preliminary to admission—were well known. Should she join, she would strive to make the League universal, at least in Europe.[10] The euphemism was transparent, and in a confidential session of the Reichstag's Foreign Affairs Committee, Stresemann was explicit: "Our relationship with Russia will always be of the greatest significance for us, economically and politically. Any League action which involved us against Russia would encumber us more than any other state."[11]

While Stresemann was defining Germany's position before the Reichstag, Bülow was in London exploring the intentions of the new government. After conversations with numerous politicians and publicists (among them Lord Parmoor, Labour's representative to the League), he concluded that the British had no firm policy on Germany's admission. The British in general and the Labour government in particular undoubtedly were well disposed toward the League, and many favored Germany's admission. But there was no clear indication whether Germany would have a seat on the council, whether she should apply or await an invitation, whether she would have to acknowledge the peace treaty once again, whether the British government could override French objections to her admission. Bülow recommended that Germany leave the initiative to Britain. Time favored Germany, and the less the Germans commented on their attitude, at least until summer, the better.[12] Müller, in Berne, was also pessimistic. At the meeting of the League council in March, he reported, no one had seemed interested in promoting Germany's admission. The British had brought forward no new policy, and the French had agitated busily against Germany's conditions behind the scenes. Indeed, if decisions taken on matters affecting Germany (Danzig, Saar) were any indication, interest in Germany's membership had waned.[13] Implicit in both these reports was the opinion that, as long as Poincaré held power in France, Germany had little prospect for admission on her terms.

In May the French repudiated Poincaré and *la politique de la Ruhr,* and installed a left-oriented government reputed to be friendly toward Germany. Premier Édouard Herriot told the Chamber of Deputies that as part of his official policy he favored bringing Germany into the League "when she had put her house in order."[14] After MacDonald and Herriot announced their intention to attend the meeting of the assembly in September, the British press resumed discussion of Germany's admission. Officials at the London embassy were besieged with questions. In Berlin, Lord D'Abernon queried Stresemann on Germany's attitude, and Drummond, passing through, emphasized the advantages of membership.[15]

The Foreign Ministry, as on earlier occasions, discounted these gestures and insinuations. They were motivated by purely selfish reasons, Bülow told Stresemann. The powers wanted to subject Germany to control by the League; the secretariat wanted to provide the League with "new impetus to overcome its internal difficulties." All would seek to secure Germany's admission as cheaply as possible: they would accord her no privileges and no permanent seat. Entry into the League, Bülow concluded, was not yet ripe for discussion.[16] This conclusion was confirmed by warnings from the diplomatic missions: Berne reported opposition from the smaller council powers, Paris advised that French conditions were unchanged, and Washington predicted American displeasure.[17]

Domestic politics also seemed to augur for restraint. Unlike the latest parliamentary elections in Britain and France, which had brought left-wing parties to power, the Reichstag elections in May (the first since 1920) had given significant gains to the Nationalists. Their success at the polls put them in a position to destroy Stresemann's conciliatory foreign policy, for which they expressed a great loathing. While their attempt to join the cabinet had foundered on their unreasonable demands, they could still block the legislation required to put the Dawes plan into effect. If the government was to avert this threat to its policy, it could not afford to upset the Nationalists by opening negotiations—or even discussion—about Germany's accession to the League. State Secretary Maltzan, well aware of these implications, informed Germany's missions that the government intended to take no initiative toward admission in September.[18] And before setting off for London for the reparations talks, the German delegation decided that if the issue of Germany's membership should come up, they would handle it "as cautiously as possible."[19]

At the London conference all the former belligerents accepted the Dawes plan, and the French pledged to evacuate the Ruhr within the year. The topic of Germany's entry into the League arose only in a casual exchange between Carl von Schubert, the head of the western department, and Miles Lampson of the Foreign Office.[20] The omission astonished the Foreign Ministry. When MacDonald raised the question before the assembly in Geneva on 4 September, the ministry was altogether at a loss.[21] In words greeted by strong applause, MacDonald declared that the League "cannot afford" to allow Germany "to remain outside."

> There is not a single question regarding armaments, regarding the conditions of peace, regarding security, regarding the safety and the guarantee of the existence of the small nations—not a single one—that we can discuss amongst our-

selves with a menacing vacant chair in our midst. . . . The London conference created a new relationship between Germany and the other European states, and that relationship should now be sealed and sanctified by Germany's appearance on the floor of this Assembly.

Taken by surprise, Herriot could only respond weakly. The articles of the covenant, "which presuppose the fulfillment of engagements regulating disarmament," set forth procedures for admission. There could be "neither exception nor privilege"; "respect for treaties and pledges must be the common law." To the press, Herriot described Germany's entry as "premature."[22]

MacDonald's speech, cordial and inviting, lacked concrete content; Herriot's speech listed precisely those obstacles which lay between Germany and the League. Both speeches aroused excited discussion at Geneva and in Germany. The Reichstag had been recessed after ratifying the Dawes plan, and the German reaction appeared mostly in the press. The socialist and democratic papers—*Vorwärts, Vossische Zeitung, Frankfurter Zeitung*—welcomed MacDonald's initiative, interpreting it as a direct and urgent invitation. The Socialists, who had interpellated the government in June, expected an immediate affirmative reply. Paul Löbe, a Socialist and president of the Reichstag before the May election, who had advocated entry in January 1922, wrote an open letter to Stresemann, demanding that Germany apply for membership forthwith.[23] When Lord Parmoor told journalists in Geneva that Germany's admission had been mentioned at London, the Socialists accused Stresemann of duplicity in having denied that it had been discussed.[24] Not to be outdone, the nationalist papers *Deutsche Tageszeitung* and *Kreuzzeitung* denounced the Left and urged the government to be prudent in Geneva. They polemicized against joining, citing all the old arguments and even some new ones. When the Left praised MacDonald, the Right quoted Herriot.

The government was obliged to respond, but its response was slow. Not only was it reluctant to act impulsively, especially in matters connected with the League, but it was also hampered by a lack of clear information on which to act. Count Kessler, who had been asked to serve as a semi-official liaison with MacDonald, reported directly from Geneva. Apparently he construed his mission very broadly and interviewed various delegates, the unimportant as well as the important. His dispatches shifted from skepticism to enthusiasm. He concluded that the moment for entry had arrived. Insensitive to explicit cautioning from Berlin—where Maltzan advised that Germany join only "as proof and result of general détente and trust" and warned against action which would be "rued"—Kessler suggested that he be accredited to the secretariat so that he might represent Germany's position.[25] On 10 September Müller arrived in Geneva from Berne to secure clearer information. He reported that no matter what Kessler might say, a permanent seat was by no means assured. The French insisted on a waiting period for Germany and wanted guarantees of complete and lasting disarmament permanently and effectively controlled. Müller recommended that Germany secure diplomatic assurance of a seat before the cabinet discussed entry.[26]

Stresemann tried to calm the furor. At a press conference he deplored the newspaper campaign: Germany's entry was not a matter of partisan concern but a question of the country's best interest. Appearances notwithstanding, the League had made no official offer, and the government surely could not be expected to leap at a rhetorical invitation. At a cabinet meeting on 15 September, for which the ministers had interrupted their vacations, Stresemann summarized the situation. It was clear that Germany's conditions would not be met; application, therefore, was senseless. To escape the reproach that the government had ignored an invitation, he had asked Lord D'Abernon to obtain a formal statement of the prospects of a permanent seat.[27]

The Foreign Ministry too tried to check the momentum of the debate. In two extensive memorandums prepared for the cabinet, Bülow argued against precipitate action. The French would undoubtedly make difficulties. Unless the government were assured of its various conditions—and Bülow listed nine of these—membership was worthless. If Germany managed to force her way into the League, the repercussions would damage the institution and reduce its usefulness. Müller, whom Stresemann solicited for advice, agreed. A permanent seat, which required the unconditional assurance of every member of the council, was an indispensable prerequisite. A display of reluctance would only strengthen Germany's hand. When the public had been prepared and negotiations had ensured the conditions, she should apply. Only then would she be admitted without obstacle; only then could she participate without disappointment.[28]

The cabinet met for three hours on 23 September. It neither questioned nor debated whether Germany should join the League; rather, it discussed tactics. Stresemann held forth at great length about Germany's past associations with the League, about the drawbacks and advantages of membership, about the conditions Germany should set and the prospect of their being accepted. He reported on D'Abernon's information; MacDonald in London was more sober-minded than MacDonald in Geneva. The British government, D'Abernon had said, could not guarantee Germany's conditions, nor could it advise her on an issue of such magnitude. MacDonald, however, had suggested that the Germans canvass the other powers. The cabinet concurred with Stresemann: the government should announce that it was willing in principle to join the League but that the moment was not favorable for an application. It agreed too that the governments represented on the council should be sent a memorandum inquiring about their opinions of the German conditions.[29]

The memorandum, drafted in the Foreign Ministry, was approved by the cabinet on 25 September but not made public.[30] On 29 September it was transmitted to the governments represented on the council—Britain, France, Japan, Italy, all of which held permanent seats; and Belgium, Czechoslovakia, Brazil, Spain, Sweden, and Uruguay, whose tenure was limited to three years. The German government, the memorandum began, convinced that the London conference had opened the way to fruitful cooperation within the League, would seek early admission. Before it could apply, however, it needed clarification of certain decisive questions:

1. While Germany hoped for general equality for all states within the League, she expected to enjoy the privileges which the covenant accorded certain powers. She required guarantee of a permanent seat on the council and proportionate representation in the secretariat. Would the powers agree? According to the covenant, a permanent seat could be established by unanimous decision of the council. A permanent seat has always been

Germany's primary condition—"our minimal demand."[31] The early Allied drafts of the covenant had forseen a seat for Germany, and the German government believed its claim to this privilege legitimate. A seat was a matter of prestige "commensurate to Germany's status as a great power."[32] Tangible affirmation of status as a great power would end Germany's isolation and guarantee her equality. It would also assure that the government's application gained necessary domestic support; the Foreign Ministry never ceased to point out that membership without a permanent seat was "domestically untenable."[33] A permanent seat also had practical value, for it gave Germany influence over issues in which she had a direct interest. She could act on questions which the peace treaty assigned to the League and shape them in her own interest; she would participate in the great political issues of disarmament and collective security.[34]

2. Germany, disarmed and therefore at a disadvantage in military conflicts, should not be expected to accept any of the obligations arising out of article 16, which defined the League's sanction against aggression. She would have to insist on her neutrality. Did the powers agree? Article 16 was the heart of the covenant. It defined the military, economic, and financial sanctions the League might apply to preserve the peace. In effect, Germany was asking to be relieved of joint responsibility for keeping the peace; she would not contribute troops, allow troops to cross her territory, or join in blockades or boycotts. This request for absolute neutrality was the doing of the Foreign Ministry; the cabinet had considered the issue secondary—"desirable but not essential." Germany might be treated "like Switzerland," which escaped military but not economic obligations.[35] In the memorandum—and before the public—the German government argued that, without armaments, Germany could not risk reprisals or become the battleground for the League's wars. The argument was sufficiently true to be credible, but the real reason lay deeper: Germany did not want to disrupt her relations with the Soviet Union. Unlike Ambassador Brockdorff-Rantzau in Moscow, Stresemann did not consider Rapallo the best means of revising the Versailles settlement. But he knew that Germany needed Russian support. Without it she would be unable to bargain with the West. Moreover, a large segment of the public favored ties with Russia and would protest their severance.

Severance was a real possibility. The Russians thought of the League as an imperialist alliance against the Soviet Union. If Germany remained outside the League, Russia would have a useful buffer against the League's anti-Soviet designs. Fearing that the German government was now planning to change its policy, the Russians intervened: if Germany entered the League, they argued, she would "renounce the future," would accept the Versailles borders, and, by becoming a satellite of the West, would inevitably "collide with Rapallo." Whatever the government's intentions, it would be drawn into actions leading to conflict with the Soviet Union. These arguments, advanced while the German government was debating the issue, were to become standard fare in the twelve-month battle the Russians waged against Germany's pro-League—and thus pro-Western—orientation. Pressed by Brockdorff-Rantzau and Maltzan, the German government raised reservations about article 16 to escape the predicament and forestall collapse of its relations with Russia.[36]

The two remaining conditions were minor. The German government was prepared (3) to accept the League's admissions formula, which asked for guarantees that the applicant would fulfill its "international obligations." By accepting the formula, however, the government did not acknowledge the parts of the peace treaty it had protested—such as the delineation of the eastern borders or the division of Upper Silesia, and particularly the imputation of war guilt in article 231. The government also declared (4) that after joining the League it would lay claim to a colonial mandate. This condition appeased the colonial lobby in Germany because compliance would nullify the Allied charge that the Germans had been incompetent and inhuman colonial administrators.[37]

The memorandum was a commitment in principle, but also an offer with strings attached. As such, it served a double political purpose. On the one hand, it responded to domestic and international pressure to heed the call from Geneva. Thus it improved Germany's position within the community of European powers and mollified the Left, on which Chancellor Marx's minority government depended. On the other hand, the stiff conditions which the memorandum named assuaged the conservatives and the Foreign Ministry. The diplomats were fundamentally opposed to precipitate action. They were convinced that the measured tone of the memorandum would indicate to the world that a great power could not be hurried, that it was aware of its prestige and prerogatives. The memorandum entailed no great risks; it passed the initiative back to the League powers. If the League were willing to fulfill the demands, Germany would join on advantageous conditions.[38]

By the first week of December the council powers had tendered their replies. No power blankly opposed the demand for a permanent seat. The French government agreed on the condition that Germany abide by the covenant; Brazil and Spain, each ambitious for a permanent seat of her own, replied in general phrases. The council powers referred the other conditions to the League as a whole, for the council could speak only for matters which affected it directly. The council powers did specify, however, that Germany would have to enter the League without conditions.[39] On 12 December, less than a week after receiving the last reply, the German government had formulated its answer, addressed this time to the secretary-general in Geneva to be placed "before the competent departments" of the League. The tone was cordial, the message unchanged. Germany reiterated her view that the obligations of article 16 were an unreasonable burden upon a "centrally located and completely disarmed" country. Germany could not "waive her right to neutrality." She asked not for a "special privilege," but that she "be at liberty to determine how far she will take an active part in international conflicts." She would now await the League's proposal on reconciling her disarmament with her responsibility to take part in any sanctions the League might impose.[40]

The undiplomatic haste of the German reply was prompted by several considerations. The officials of the Foreign Ministry had thought first to submit the replies from the council powers to the Reichstag, possibly even to the public. They changed their minds, as Bülow explained to Brockdorff-Rantzau, because they were afraid the public might construe these replies as an open invitation to seek admission. The Reichstag might react rashly, water down the conditions which appeared to stand in the way of admission, and meddle in a delicate international issue. If the notes from the council powers remained unpublished, the government could represent its prompt response as a request for further clarification. It could then publish the two

German memorandums to gratify the public's curiosity.[41] A prompt response to Geneva was no great liability. A memorandum addressed to the League itself, the Foreign Ministry calculated, would not be answered until the assembly met the following September. The delay would remove the subject from partisan discussion, and it would postpone a decision until Germany's situation had improved.[42]

The situation which seemed so favorable after the conclusion of the Dawes agreement had deteriorated by December. The Dawes plan had settled the problem of reparations for the time being, and the Allies turned their attention to Germany's disarmament, long a matter of contention. They were suspicious of Germany's efforts to disarm and wanted the Inter-Allied Military Control Commission to resume its regular investigations, which had been suspended during the Ruhr crisis. The German government resisted, not least because the army had been rearming secretly and illegally. A compromise was reached in June: the Control Commission would conduct a general inspection, and if the findings were satisfactory, it would reduce its functions and staff. The inspection was not carried out without incident. Uncooperative army officers raised obstacles; public hostility threatened the inspectors' safety. By mid-October rumor had it that the commission was dissatisfied with what it had uncovered. The rumors were disturbing, because if Germany were found in default, the Allies might prolong their occupation of the northernmost (or Cologne) zone of the Rhineland beyond January 1925. They had occupied the entire Rhineland in order to enforce the peace treaty. According to article 429 they would be obliged to evacuate the first (Cologne) zone in five years, the second (Coblenz) zone in ten, and the third (Mainz) zone in fifteen if the Germans fulfilled the peace terms faithfully. By November the German ambassador in Paris reported his impression that the French would not evacuate.[43]

In a related move the Council of the League had responded to French pressure in September and accepted a draft report which recommended that the League assume authority over Germany's disarmament after the Control Commission had been disbanded, in accordance with article 213 of the peace treaty. The report suggested that any League member be empowered to call for investigations, that the council decide on investigations by a simple majority, and, worse, that permanent inspection stations (*éléments stables*) be erected in the demilitarized Rhineland. In December the British had concurred in this plan, and a committee was charged to submit practical details by the next session of the council in March 1925. The Germans feared that military control might not be over after all, that in the future their neighbors would seize upon any pretext to initiate investigations. They feared also that the prolonged occupation of the Rhineland and the envisioned inspection stations would once again encourage separatism.[44]

Berlin was also disturbed by the so-called Geneva Protocol, an ambitious Anglo-French attempt at European security, which the League assembly had endorsed unanimously in October. The Protocol proposed to strengthen the League's peacekeeping functions by making arbitration compulsory in all disputes that might lead to war and by tightening the sanctions of the covenant. It reconciled Britain's reluctance to undertake unlimited commitments and France's reluctance to trust the League instead of her own superior power. The result would be a reliable and seemingly watertight system for settling international differences. Such a general system of security, the Foreign Ministry was quick to see, would preserve the European status quo. If the Protocol were accepted and Germany were to join the League, she would find herself fettered. If it failed to be adopted, as seemed likely after the Conservatives returned to power in Britain in November 1924, the French might be compensated with a tripartite pact among Britain, France, and Belgium. Together the three Western powers would then maintain the status quo by enforcing the peace treaty.[45] As Stresemann was to say of the security problem, "A solution without Germany is a solution against Germany."[46]

These apparently intertwined prospects threatened to destroy the détente which had followed the Dawes agreement. The Germans, while accepting massive financial obligations, had gained political advantages. The French had lost the option of using reparations for political purposes, and they had begun to lift the occupation of the Ruhr. The United States and Britain—whose investors, demonstrating their confidence in Germany's future, had subscribed eagerly to the huge Dawes loan—had acquired an interest in Germany's welfare. This broad improvement in Germany's external position had opened opportunities for initiatives in foreign policy. Now it seemed that Germany was not to escape the French security system after all; she would remain an outcast among the European powers; she would continue to be subjected to sanctions. Such a setback would discredit the approach Stresemann had initiated in 1923, when he had made accommodation both the guiding principle of his diplomatic strategy and the emphatic commitment of Germany's foreign policy. In his public speeches in the autumn he had more than once stressed that the policy that had led to the Dawes plan was the policy that would restore Germany's sovereignty and international status. A reversal now would strengthen the hand of the opposition, and if it should lead to political turmoil, might halt the economic recovery that was beginning. If that were to happen, Stresemann told the cabinet at the end of December, he believed that he would have to resign.[47]

It was D'Abernon who proposed a way out. Long an exponent of drawing Germany into the Western orbit, he was disturbed by the possibility that Austen Chamberlain, the foreign secretary in the new Conservative government, might commit Britain to French security "in what would amount to an anti-German defensive league."[48] On 29 December he suggested to Schubert, who had just succeeded Maltzan as state secretary in the Foreign Ministry, that Germany might revive Chancellor Cuno's proposal of December 1922 (reiterated by Stresemann in September 1923) that the major powers pledge not to wage war against each other for a generation.[49] To Schubert, whose gruff and suspicious manner concealed fine political instincts, D'Abernon's suggestion seemed timely. Not only did it offer a means of relieving Germany's immediate situation, but it also coincided with Stresemann's plans for Germany's long-term advantage.

Stresemann's acceptance of the consequences of the lost war defined only his methods, not his goals. He was as committed to restoring Germany's sovereignty and to redrawing her frontiers (especially in the east) as any Weimar foreign minister. He planned to achieve this goal by making Germany part of a community of economic and political interests in Europe. Germany could not enter such a community as long as France mistrusted her. France, Stresemann understood, had sought nothing so urgently as security, both in the peace treaty and in her policy since demonstrate that she was no threat to French security, France might not insist on keeping her within the limits of the Versailles settlement and might not try to weaken her permanently. A security pact which recognized the inviolability of the French frontier would surrender what appeared irretrievably lost anyway—Alsace-Lorraine. It would help ward off a crisis over evacuation, and it offered an alternative to the Geneva Protocol or a tripartite pact. Stresemann therefore pursued D'Abernon's suggestion. The announcement on 5 January that the Allies would not evacuate the Cologne zone confirmed him in his course.[50]

In great secrecy the German government proposed a pact to Premier Herriot on 9 February. Germany offered to guarantee the status quo along the Franco-German border (including the demilitarization of the Rhineland), and she was willing to conclude treaties for peaceful resolution of legal and political disputes with states willing to reciprocate.[51] The German proposal expressly circumvented the League, the logical guarantor of such a pact. Since the events of the previous year had brought rapprochement between Germany and the League, her motives require explanation.

The Foreign Ministry deliberately preferred a regional pact to a general settlement under League auspices. It was prepared to accept the loss of Alsace-Lorraine, but not of those areas of West Prussia and Upper Silesia which had been incorporated into Poland.[52] It intended, therefore, to distinguish between the eastern and the western borders. The ministry knew that the public would endorse such a distinction. Thus the ministry evaded the auspices of the League by offering arbitration treaties which would meet France's foremost objection to the German offer—the absence of a parallel guarantee of Germany's eastern frontiers.[53] The ministry's second reason for evading the League was an old and recurrent motif in Germany's relations with Geneva: the ministry was unwilling to impair Germany's relations with the Soviet Union. The memorandum of September 1924 had already cast a pall over these relations, and the Germans' repeated reservations on article 16 had been a concession to the Russians. Brockdorff-Rantzau, a committed advocate of the Soviet case, warned in November against destroying a valuable relationship by what he deemed a worthless connection with the League. A pact with the Western powers, as was now proposed, would surely irritate the Russians—but it would not cause a break if the League were not involved.[54]

Germany's flanking maneuver proved impossible. When the German ambassador mentioned his country's proposal to Chamberlain on 30 January, Chamberlain wondered why the Germans did not solve the security problem simply by joining the League. In Paris, Herriot told Ambassador Leopold von Hoesch that the League could not be "bypassed permanently" by a "partial settlement" of the security question.[55] These were straws in the wind. By February 1925 it was evident that the British government would not accept the Geneva Protocol, and France, opposed to admitting Germany to the League in September 1924, now began to favor admission. At the end of February, long before Paris commented officially on the German proposal, word reached Berlin that the Allies would insist on the competence of the League. By March it was official: D'Abernon reported to Schubert that according to Chamberlain in Geneva, the British and the French would accept a pact only if Germany joined the League "on the same footing as the other powers." The League's response to the December memorandum, which arrived unexpectedly on 14 March, reinforced Chamberlain's point. Germany should expect no privileges on article 16—equal rights presupposed equal obligations. However, Germany, like all other members of the League, would be able to determine "to what extent she was in a position to comply with the Council's recommendations" on military sanctions.[56]

The Foreign Ministry knew that it had miscalculated. The question of Germany's entry into the League, which the Germans had believed buried until September, had suddenly become *höchst akut*.[57] The League had replied promptly to the German memorandum and, as Schubert was to concede, had met many of Germany's reservations. Gaus, head of the legal department, observed that it would now be difficult to remain aloof "without creating the general impression that we basically do not wish to join the League."[58] More important, a link had been forged: if Germany wanted to conclude a security pact, she would be compelled to enter the League without condition or privilege. Unconditional membership would nullify the advantages of a regional security pact. The Germans believed that the

the conclusion of the treaty. It followed that, if Germany could Polish government, alive to the implications of such a pact, had induced France to insist on membership, and that the British government had concurred in order to escape having to commit itself in eastern Europe. Furthermore, unconditional membership would alienate the Russians. Stresemann suspected that the Western powers might in fact be trying to estrange Germany from the Soviet Union by drawing Germany into the League. Quite against their will, the Germans might be forced to choose between East and West after all.[59]

Was the security pact worth the price? The ambassadors in London and Paris, whose opinion Stresemann requested, gave conflicting answers. Sthamer argued that Britain wanted "to inhibit Germany's political independence" and therefore would not modify her position on Germany's admission. He urged that, if Germany were forced to choose, she forgo entry even if this meant forfeiting the pact. Hoesch was more positive: "We cannot sacrifice vital needs to general political perspectives." If Germany abandoned her present course, she might see *Poincarismus* revive in France and face a crisis like that of 1923. No sacrifice would be too great if the pact were to open the way to the evacuation of the Rhineland and the final abolition of military control. Germany should risk being obliged to join the League, and she should risk a dispute with Russia.[60] Stresemann seemed to side with Hoesch. He instructed Brockdorff-Rantzau to tell the Russians that article 16 would not impair their relationship, for joining the League would not cost Germany "the possibility of neutrality toward Russia." As a member of the council, Germany could prevent any League action against the Russians and soften the League's anti-Soviet bias.[61] Obviously, Stresemann was preparing for eventualities.

Meanwhile, the Foreign Ministry "decided neither for nor against entry." It replied to the note from the council, not with an application, but with a simple acknowledgment.[62] In press conferences and diplomatic dispatches, Schubert explained that because of the "political developments" since December, when Germany had sent her inquiry to Geneva, Germany's entry could no longer be deliberated in isolation. It was now linked to the general situation and would depend on the development of this situation. In conversations with Allied diplomats, Schubert tried to keep the question of entry separate from the security negotiations. Germany, he argued, could not "be expected" to decide about joining the League until the immediate issues— evacuation, military control, permanent inspection stations— had been resolved satisfactorily. Moreover, because Germany required stronger assurances on article 16 than the council had made, the whole matter would best be left for later negotiations.[63] Already a step away from Germany's original position, however, Schubert conceded that a formula to meet Germany's reservations could no doubt be found.[64]

On 16 June the French delivered the answer to the German pact proposal and published the secret German note. Unlike the British, they had been interested in the German proposal from the beginning,[65] but neither Herriot nor Aristide Briand, who succeeded him as foreign minister in April, wanted to respond without exploring alternatives and ramifications. Stresemann's proposal clearly would improve France's security. The French, caught up in financial and economic difficulties, were no longer willing to bear "the costs of active antagonism"—high military expenditures and sanctions.[66] The British, who might have supplied an alternative, considered bilateral alliances and general accords (like the ill-fated Geneva Protocol) unsuitable instruments for European security. On the other hand, the proposal had obvious liabilities: it would limit France's freedom to enforce the peace treaty as she saw fit, and it would alienate her east European allies. To offset these liabilities, the French would have to enlarge the compass of the pact.[67] The British, once they were past their initial hesitation, actively sponsored the pact. In the proposed multilateral agreement they saw a way to satisfy France's needs and at the same time to induce Germany to abandon part of her campaign against Versailles. Unconditional membership in the League would draw her into the postwar order of which Geneva was the symbol and the guardian. The possibility that the security pact might loosen Germany's ties with Russia made it all the more acceptable.[68]

The French reply, in which the British concurred, brought forward a number of reservations. The French wanted to ensure that the pact did not infringe upon their commitments to the successor states. They realized that a pact which guaranteed the inviolability of the Rhine frontier would block the passage of troops sent to the assistance of the eastern allies. The prospect was the more real if Germany remained outside the League and free of its obligations. Therefore the French specified that Germany would have to join the League on the terms the council had outlined in March. The pact should in no way alter the peace treaty or any subsequent provisions for the occupation of the Rhineland. Finally, the guarantee of Germany's western borders should be supplemented by treaties with Poland and Czechoslovakia. These treaties, to be guaranteed by the signatories of the security pact, would subject all disputes to obligatory and binding arbitration.[69]

The publication of the exchange of memorandums informed the German public for the first time of the details of the German proposal. Back in March, disquiet had rippled through the Reichstag parties when the League's memorandum arrived in the midst of rumors about a German diplomatic initiative in Paris. Stresemann had tried to allay these misgivings. In conversations, in small gatherings, and (anonymously) in the press, he expounded the advantages of his policy. His concern was particularly with the Nationalists, whose extreme wing protested his renunciation of "Germany's inalienable claims" to Alsace-Lorraine as "the gravest sin against Germany's future."[70] The Nationalists were the second largest party in the Reichstag. Slightly more tolerant of the republic since they had come under fire from the far Right, and pressed by their industrial and agrarian backers, they had at last joined a cabinet in January 1925. Stresemann had been instrumental in bringing them into the government. As long as they were outside, he was hampered in his freedom. Any government that followed a policy of accommodation was bound to lose support, as the Reichstag elections in 1924 had shown. Stresemann knew that even if he could not commit the Nationalists to his foreign policy, their presence in the cabinet would soften their opposition in the Reichstag and allow him greater flexibility. Now he was anxious to intercept their retreat from responsibility. The pact, he argued, would frustrate Allied plans for "an aggressive and offensive alliance against Germany" and would put up strong barriers against future invasion by the French. The right to reclaim Alsace by force was a small price to pay for the guarantee that the Rhineland would remain German and that the periods of occupation might be shortened. Finally, the pact offered the possibility of "new boundaries" in the east. As a member of the League, Germany could defend "national" interests in her expropriated territories and lend support to "legitimate Russian claims." Germany would never allow herself to be drawn into an alliance against the Soviet Union.[71]

The Nationalists were not convinced. Until the French replied to the German proposals, however, they found little they could attack. They comforted themselves with the hope that the French would reject the German offer. Now the French reply indicated that the French were willing to negotiate. Moreover, by insisting on the League, they formally fused the two issues which the Foreign Ministry had wanted to keep separate. Right-wing propaganda rose to the occasion. In the press, at party meetings, in political associations and lobbies, the conservatives vented their animosities toward France, the League, and a "pact of renunciation." The pact, if it materialized, would put an end to all hope of revising the peace treaty. Joining the League meant unconditional submission to the Western powers and the acknowledgment of Germany's borders east and west. Strese- mann was a traitor and should be put in the dock.[72]

The opposition which emerged in the cabinet had more seri- ous implications for the future of Stresemann's policy. Word reached him that the Nationalist ministers, prodded by some of their colleagues in the Reichstag, were determined to wreck the security pact.[73] In the cabinet meeting of 24 June, however, he found that the opposition was not restricted to the Nationalists. Seeckt was to describe the session as "a fierce fight about the foundations of our foreign policy."[74] The Nationalists de- nounced the pact as a "trap" which would bring Germany into the League on Allied terms and destroy the possibility of revi- sion in the east. Several ministers of the Center party expressed their hope that the pact would fail. Seeckt, who served as spokesman for the opposition, claimed that the pact was alto- gether in France's favor. It would determine Germany's fron- tiers in the west irrevocably, and he for one could not condone the surrender of Alsace-Lorraine. Germany's foreign policy should be directed toward Russia, as in Bismarck's day. Joining the League—which he had opposed vigorously since the peace conference—would deprive the country of its opportunity to fight military control or to realize Anschluss. Article 16 would impose intolerable obligations. Germany should regain power, and then all that had been lost could be recaptured.[75] The cabinet meeting is indicative of the extent to which Germany's national policies consisted of nationalist slogans defended with moral fervor. Few were able to emancipate themselves from their recollections of past glory and to understand either that the national interest called for flexibility or that accommodation with France had advantages which might outweigh Germany's territorial claims.

Stresemann's response to this campaign is a measure of the importance he attached to the success of his venture. He argued that the proposals opened the door "to intervening once again actively in international affairs."[76] To those less emotionally engaged than the Nationalists, he pointed out that his policy was the only one possible under present circumstances. If the negotiations broke down, Germany could expect France to resume her harsh tactics. The Americans would refuse to extend further credits, and the economy would collapse. To the Nationalists he threatened to resign, a step which would have broken up the coalition. The Nationalists were confronted with a choice between principle and politics: they might acquiesce in Stresemann's policy, or they might break up the government. Their interest in maintaining the cabinet, which they found politically useful and personally attractive, prevailed. Pressed by Chancellor Hans Luther, they buckled under Stresemann's threat and consoled themselves with the thought that a final decision on the pact was yet to come.[77] To all, Stresemann pointed out that without the pact Germany could not regain sovereignty over her territory, could not press for the evacuation of the Rhineland ahead of schedule, and could not settle the question of military control. More important, the pact opened possibilities of revision. This argument was impressive—and in Stresemann's conversations it often tended to supersede the idea of accommodation, which was in fact as important to him. Accommodation came to be accepted as a tactic: Germany would renounce her territory always with the mental reservation that she need forgo these claims only as long as she was weak. The Germans also enjoyed a more immediate prospect of gratification:

the notion that temporary acceptance of the western frontier would soon produce opportunities to revise the eastern borders.[78]

Schubert likened the drafting of Germany's answer to the French note to the squaring of the circle. The response, which was delivered on 20 July, reflected the multitude of political and diplomatic considerations which the Foreign Ministry had to satisfy.[79] The German note agreed that the pact would not constitute a change of the peace treaty but added that it need not block peaceful alteration of existing treaties. For example, the German government expected that the atmosphere created by the pact would not fail to ameliorate conditions in the occupied Rhineland. The note expressed preference for narrowly defined arbitration treaties—in effect rejecting the comprehensive treaties of the French note. While the German government denied any necessary connection between concluding the pact and joining the League, it agreed to enter the League. In point of fact, the Germans abandoned here their attempt to keep the two issues apart. They realized that the Allies could not be moved— that there would be no security pact unless Germany joined the League. At the same time, the French note furnished ample reason why membership would be advantageous. The proposal that France guarantee the eastern arbitration treaties implied that she could decide when these treaties had been violated and initiate military action against Germany. This in effect permitted France military action outside the League's provision on aggression and sanction and gave France a strong position in case of war on Germany's eastern frontiers. By joining the League, Germany could sidetrack the French proposals. Germany's advantage was manifest, especially if she were to enter with reservations on article 16. The German note, therefore, insisted that Germany's conditions still retained their validity and that the French demand for unconditional entry was unacceptable. Some provision which took account of the special military, economic, and geographic situation of Germany would have to be found.[80] This request for a formula—anticipated in April—marked a retreat from the earlier insistence on absolute neutrality. Germany no longer demanded special privileges; she was willing to settle for an interpretation which would exempt her de facto from the article's obligation. By dropping the legal and political conditions on article 16 and moving toward an interpretive formula, Germany was opening the door to compromise.[81]

The Germans had come a long way. In September 1924, when they had dispatched their memorandum to the council powers, they had been in full control of the decision on when and whether to join the League. In March and April 1925, they had tried to separate this decision from the security negotiations. They had tried to make it conditional upon favorable settlement of the problems of evacuation and military control, had even thought of using it as a counter offer in a subsequent diplomatic exchange. Now Germany had lost control of the timing, had acceded to Allied conditions, and had tacitly abandoned preconditions and thoughts of a bargain. Diplomatic—even juridical—reasons had prevailed; the security pact seemed worth the price.[82] In this conclusion, the government found support among the Left. To placate the Right and the Russians, it retained its formal reservations about article 16.[83]

The French reply to the German note, delivered in Berlin on 24 August, ignored Germany's offer to compromise on the conditions of her membership in the League and reiterated the earlier demand for application without conditions. It neither met Germany's reservations on the arbitration treaties, nor did it confirm her hopes for ameliorating the terms of the occupation in the Rhineland.[84] Obviously the written exchange had reached its limit and negotiations would have to be arranged. On 15 September the Allies invited the Germans to meet them in Locarno early in October.

Now that an accord was close, both the Russians and the Nationalists launched a final campaign. But for all the barrage of propaganda, neither of the major opponents of Germany's rapprochement with the West believed that it would alter her course. The German government had been conferring with the Russians since the previous September. In December 1924 the Russians had proposed a neutrality pact of broad dimensions, but the Germans had evaded actual negotiation for fear that disclosure of a pact incompatible with membership in the League would wreck negotiations with the West. In no case did Stresemann want to be obliged to choose between East and West. He argued in effect that Germany's entry into the League represented no change in her relations with the Soviet Union, that in fact it was an advantage. Germany's reservations on article 16 would buffer the Russians from the West—precisely what the Russians had argued about Germany's absence from Geneva. By June 1925 Stresemann was ready to give the Russians a written assurance which de facto would meet their demand for German neutrality. The Russians had not been receptive, but Stresemann had gone no further. By September the Russians appeared to accept the general situation and tried to gain what was possible. Foreign Minister Chicherin visited Berlin on 30 September, the eve of Locarno, in an attempt to make sure that Germany would stand by her reservations as well as to expand the possibilities of the written agreement the Germans had offered. When Chicherin left, Stresemann had Russian approval of entry in return for Germany's obligation to frame her reservations in such a way that a neutrality agreement with the Soviet Union would be possible.[85]

The Nationalists drew up extensive preconditions for the pact: an Allied pledge to evacuate the Cologne zone, a settlement of the disputed points of German disarmament, an express renunciation of war guilt.[86] In the cabinet, however, these "preconditions" became "topics" for the agenda of the conference. Stresemann thought that "the greater part of the demands could be satisfied." When the German delegation went to Locarno, it carried the cabinet's directives to the effect that the reservations toward the League enunciated in September 1924 still held and that the terms for the pact in the July note applied.[87] The conditions which the Germans enumerated in September had in fact largely been met. A permanent seat on the council was assured. Germany's title to colonial mandates had been recognized in principle, and it was understood that she would pursue this matter after entry. A mildly phrased note, dispatched by the German government on 29 September and received by the Allies with relative composure, had removed the issue of war guilt. Only the German contentions on article 16 remained to be settled at Locarno.[88]

The conference at Locarno, well prepared by an earlier meeting of the participants' legal experts in London, reached agreement quickly. The security pact, initialed on 16 October, provided for maintenance of the status quo on Germany's western frontier, including demilitarization of the Rhineland, guaranteed by Britain and Italy. Germany and France, and again Germany and Belgium, pledged not to resort to war and to submit disputes to arbitration. With Poland and Czechoslovakia, Germany agreed to arbitrate disputes, but this arbitration was neither obligatory nor guaranteed. An annex to the pact upheld Germany's reservations on article 16: a member of the League was "bound to cooperate loyally and effectively in support of the Covenant and in resistance to any act of aggression to an extent which is compatible with its military situation and takes its geographical position into account."[89] The pact was scheduled to be signed on 1 December in London; it was to come into effect upon Germany's accession to the League.[90]

At Locarno the Germans achieved what they had set out to do. They found their way out of their immediate difficulties: the Allies agreed to begin to evacuate the Cologne zone on 1 December (though the Germans had not fully met the objections raised by the general inspection), and they assured Stresemann that while the League held the right to investigate violations of disarmament, practical application would be settled in consultation with Germany.[91] The guarantee that the status quo in western Europe would not be altered by force opened the way to détente with France and precluded resumption of Poincaré's fierce policies of 1923. The settlement in the east was a moral victory for Germany. Since these borders were not protected by binding arbitration, they were by implication of a lower order of sanctity than the borders in the west—a good augury for one of the most cherished hopes of German revisionism.[92] Among the less tangible gains of the conference was a new aura for Germany's diplomatic presence. The other parties to the agreement recognized her as a legal contractor in good standing. Her new status restored her dignity and prestige in international affairs. Germany was to enter the League under the most favorable circumstances possible—as a permanent member of the council who enjoyed immunity from significant obligations incumbent upon other members. These terms secured Germany maximum influence at Geneva and at the same time obviated Soviet displeasure at her presence in the League.[93]

Membership in the League had been a condition the Western powers had exacted for Locarno. But membership also fitted into Stresemann's plans. As he had said at one point, membership would yield "unimagined possibilities" for his foreign policy.[94] This policy proceeded from the recognition that a disarmed Germany could achieve her goals only by economic and political means. The Dawes plan had laid the foundations. It prepared the way for economic recovery, made Germany attractive to foreign investment, and opened foreign markets to her. Trade negotiations with Britain and France had begun in 1924. German and French industrialists were discussing bilateral cartels. These economic ties supplemented a political community, at whose center lay membership in the League. Stresemann expected that this political and economic community would not only be a setting for cooperation with the Western powers, it would also offer Germany an opportunity to exploit her partners. In time Germany could both rely upon and impose upon the other powers in advancing her revisionist aims.[95]

4   Germany Joins the League, 1926

The Reichstag ratified the Locarno pact on 27 November 1925 and authorized the government to join the League. The government, however, caught in political uncertainty, decided to temporize. The Nationalists had left the cabinet in protest against Locarno and had made common cause with other intransigents in attacking Stresemann's policy as a grand betrayal of Germany's interests. They derided Stresemann's much-touted expectations of the benefits Germany would derive from the "spirit of Locarno," and they belittled the alleviations in the occupation regime in the Rhineland, which the Allies conceded early in November. The rump cabinet had resigned shortly after Luther and Stresemann had signed the pact in London. Not until late January did Luther manage to form a government (with several of his former ministers but without the Nationalists) capable of taking important decisions.[1]

Stresemann had worried that the Nationalists' defection would influence Paul von Hindenburg, the aged field marshal of World War I, who had been elected president of the republic in April.[2] Hindenburg had been passive during the months of preliminary negotiation and had voiced cautious approval upon the delegation's return from Locarno. And though he had wavered once or twice, he had responded to his ministers' urging and accepted the pact.[3] He had not, however, become reconciled to Germany's joining the League—"like most military men he is sceptical about the efficacy of any alternative to war," Stresemann told D'Abernon.[4] Hindenburg was encouraged in his misgivings by his friends and unofficial advisers, mostly former military officers and conservative noblemen.[5] No sooner had the Germans signed the pact in London, than he intervened directly. In a letter to the chancellor he expressed the conservatives' long-standing reservations. The German government, he urged, should not enter the League until the conditions stipulated before and at Locarno had been met. It should elicit firm assurances that membership did not imply that Germany recognized her boundaries, and insist that Germany's interpretation of article 16 was binding. It should seek guarantees that the League would improve the protection of German minorities abroad and provide Germany with colonial mandates. It should also require the Western powers to attend to matters in the Rhineland and to settle the disputes over Germany's disarmament. The Nationalists cast these same reservations into a resolution for the Reichstag, which the government was bound to consult once more before filing its application.[6] Both the letter and the resolution were attempts to sabotage the Locarno pact, which came into force only upon Germany's entering the League.

In the Foreign Ministry, Bülow objected to attaching further conditions to Germany's membership. Germany's entry into the League was not a matter simply of relations with France or Britain, was not a subsidiary aspect of Locarno. To reduce Germany's offer to join from the untrammeled decision of an equal power to a mere bargain would debase her membership. Moreover, even discussing these reservations would introduce a damaging delay into the proceedings for admission. Germany could not be admitted at a special session of the assembly called for that purpose; her admission would appear on the agenda of a regular September meeting. Germany would forfeit the prestige which special treatment imparted, and by forfeiting this asset she would compromise her opposition to the petty practices of usual procedure within the League. At worst, Bülow thought, such a delay could bring about the collapse of the Locarno strategy, for "great initiatives in foreign policy cannot be disrupted at will." Then Germany would face a blank future: "continuing accommodation with the Western powers" would be replaced "by tensions of unpredictable outcome." The Nationalists should realize, Bülow remarked, that "we decided to enter the League not as a concession to other powers, but to gain a new point of departure for the promotion of German interests."[7]

The Western powers provided the circumstances that helped to defeat the conservatives' opposition to German membership in the League. At the end of January, they reaffirmed their pledge of the previous November to reduce the occupation forces to the lowest possible level, and with a "grand gesture" that made a "deep impression in Germany," they withdrew their last troops from the Cologne zone. On 3 February the Foreign Affairs Committee of the Reichstag dismissed the Nationalists' resolution and confirmed the government's authority to petition for membership. The prime ministers of the German states, convened for consultation before the government made its decision, overcame the intransigence of the Bavarians and endorsed the government's plan. On 8 February, after a final meeting of the cabinet, the government dispatched its application to Geneva.[8] Four days later, the League council called an extraordinary session of the assembly for 8 March.

Victory over internal opposition was not enough. Within days of Germany's application, an international crisis erupted and threatened to undo the entire arrangement. Several members of the League attempted to use Germany's admission to the council to gain permanent seats for themselves. Brazil and Spain, both non-permanent members of the council since 1920, and Poland, seeking a seat for the first time, were the most prominent contenders.[9] None of these countries could lay claim to being a great power and thus to eligibility for permanent status on the council. Their untimely clamor for special privilege was in part the League's own doing. The size of the council, its division into permanent and non-permanent members, and its geographic representation had caused dispute since 1920, for the covenant had left these matters unresolved. In 1922 the number of non-permanent seats had been increased from four to six, but the quarreling continued. Some members claimed that their geographic regions were unrepresented; others resented being defined as small powers, eligible solely for non-permanent status; still others, determined to democratize the League, objected on principle to the distinction between great and small powers. This tangle of problems grew into an open fray in the spring of 1926.[10]

Britain and France were responsible for the timing. In May 1925 the French had committed themselves to helping Poland acquire a permanent seat the moment Germany was admitted to the League. The Poles, eager to claim status as a great power, knew that a seat would offset Germany's influence in disputes over the treatment of minorities. The French wanted Polish membership for the sake of a favorable political balance and to compensate Poland for discrimination against her in the Locarno pact. At the end of January 1926, Chamberlain had promised Briand to support Poland's aspirations. In return he expected France not to sabotage the Spanish candidacy, which the British cabinet had endorsed the previous November.[11]

The German Foreign Ministry had a fairly clear notion of these developments even before the cabinet decided to apply for membership. Stresemann, however, was unwilling to assume the risks of delayed application and did not mention the subject at the meeting on 8 February, at which the ministers discussed Germany's permanent seat in some detail. The ministry was troubled especially by Chamberlain's approval of the Poles' hopes, for British backing made the seat a virtual certainty.[12] Dirksen of the eastern department analyzed the implications. Germany, he argued, would be deeply humiliated if the Poles received a permanent seat at the same time as the Germans. Worse, a permanent seat for the Poles, especially with British support, would be an almost insurmountable barrier to revision of the eastern boundaries. It would also compromise Germany's Locarno policy irreparably: her entry into the League would be eclipsed, her efforts to loosen the Franco-Polish alliance checked, her hopes for territorial revision relegated to the distant future.[13] At a meeting of the cabinet on 11 February, the chancellor called a seat for Poland "intolerable": it would put Germany into a totally new situation. The government would have to forestall such an award.[14]

In the next weeks the Foreign Ministry campaigned vigorously. Its protests, which did not mention specific states, implied that the Allies were guilty of trickery. Neither at Locarno nor at London had they intimated that Germany would have to share with other states her reception into the League council as a permanent member.[15] The Germans protested at Paris and Brussels, but directed their complaints chiefly at Britain, where the press was attacking the government. Schubert and D'Abernon conferred frequently, and Sthamer presented the German case to Chamberlain. The Germans stressed their concern for the principle that permanent seats were the prerogative of great powers and submitted that seats for lesser powers would di-

minish the importance of the council.[16] The protests made little
impression. The indifference in Paris was "catastrophic," and
Chamberlain's evasiveness showed that Germany could expect
little sympathy from him.[17] The Germans, however, were not
prepared to make concessions. On 19 February the Foreign Affairs Committee resolved that Germany would enter the League
only on the condition that she alone be given a permanent seat
upon admission. On 24 February the cabinet agreed unanimously that unless Germany were assured a permanent seat on
the council as then constituted, the government would withdraw
its application.[18]

The Germans could afford to be intransigent, for they were
not alone in their opposition. The Swedish government, a non-
permanent member of the council, objected fiercely to enlarging
the council beyond permanent German membership. Foreign
Minister Östen Undén assured the Germans that Sweden would
resist the admission to permanent status of any but the great
powers—Germany, the United States, and the Soviet Union.
The Swedes were not motivated by concern for Germany in
particular, though they welcomed her admission to the League
as an opportunity to reduce tension in the Baltic. Rather they
were interested in keeping the League free from a preponderance of any one group of states (such as the "French bloc"), for
as representatives of a small neutral country they saw in the
League a guarantee of international stability and peace. In their
contact with the Swedish government, the Germans were careful
to confine their arguments entirely to the issue of principle
(rather than expediency or prejudice), in order not to offend
Undén's "purely ideological orientation."[19]

Sweden's firm opposition, communicated to the governments
in Paris and London, was a serious obstacle, since the covenant
required unanimity for any change in the constitution of the
council. By the end of February, therefore, Britain and France
turned toward possible compromise. First D'Abernon in Berlin
and then Philippe Berthelot, the secretary-general at the Quai
d'Orsay, intimated that Germany would be admitted in March as
planned and that she might return the favor by subsequently
dropping her opposition to changes in the council.[20] The professional diplomats (especially Hoesch and Bülow) opposed any
such bargain. Legally and technically, they argued, Germany's

position was invulnerable; the Western powers would give in rather than risk losing the Locarno pact if Germany refused to join the League.[21] Stresemann, however, after securing Undén's approval, kept open the possibility of compromise by defining Germany's position as unalterably opposed to enlarging the council in March but not unamenable to change in the future. He agreed to Chamberlain's proposal that the Locarno statesmen meet at Geneva before the formal session of the assembly to "reach a working agreement."[22]

The Locarno statesmen met at Geneva on 7 March in an inauspicious atmosphere. The international publicity of the previous weeks had narrowed the opportunity for compromise.[23] The diplomatic bickering had exposed the fragility of the détente and had drawn attention to persistent differences. For some ten days these differences were the center of debate. Briand was committed to Poland's candidacy, Chamberlain to Spain's—both in their embarrassment accused the Germans of bad faith, of proposing ever new conditions. Both wanted at least some assurance from Germany that their respective protégés would eventually be admitted to a permanent seat. At the same time Spain and Brazil had put the League in jeopardy. Spain threatened to resign, after warning Germany that their relations would undergo grievous change if her own claims were not satisfied. Brazil, contrary to her assurance of disinterest in 1924, informed Germany that she would support her candidacy only if the Germans did not block Brazil's aspirations.[24]

The meeting, at which Luther and Stresemann faced Chamberlain, Briand, Vandervelde, the Belgian foreign minister, and Scialoja, the Italian representative to the League, brought the differences in the open. The Allies rejected the imputation of disloyalty, and made a case for each candidate. They argued that since the Locarno powers had not agreed to preserve the council in its existing form, the Germans had no cause to oppose the other candidates. By the same token, the Germans replied, the Allies had no cause to alter the composition of the council at the very moment when Germany was to enter. The Germans acknowledged Allied difficulties but made plain that the German government, accountable to a public still mistrustful of the League, would insist on admission to an otherwise unaltered council. Stresemann offered to declare upon admission that the

Germans were in principle amenable to changes and were prepared to join a commission to examine the whole question of council reform. The meeting adjourned amicably but "no nearer an agreement at the end than at the beginning."[25]

Luther thought that the Western powers appreciated that Germany could enter the League only when the dispute over the council seats had been settled to her satisfaction. Secure in this faith and convinced of the justice of their case, the German delegation in Geneva maintained its position steadfastly. It realized, of course, that surrender or compromise would not be tolerated at home. The Reichstag would not accept a settlement which gave permanent seats simultaneously to Germany and to Poland. Hindenburg had again reminded the chancellor of the political difficulties which such a settlement would occasion, and Luther prudently kept the president abreast of the negotiations.[26]

On 11 March the admissions committee of the assembly delivered its unanimous recommendation that Germany be admitted to the League. All that remained was the settlement of the council question. The British and the French put forward a succession of compromises. On 9 March, Chamberlain had offered to commit himself to voting "against everything except a permanent seat for Spain and a temporary seat for Poland." Such a solution would eliminate the Polish claim to permanent status and defeat the ambitions of other states. Stresemann turned this down as irreconcilable with the German position.[27] On 11 March the French proposed that Germany accept Poland as a non-permanent member after her own admission to the council. The proposal mentioned neither Spain nor Brazil. This too the Germans rejected. Still another compromise, tendered by Chamberlain and endorsed by Briand (who claimed that he would have to resign if it were turned down), met the same fate: the Germans declared that they could not tolerate a new non-permanent seat created ostensibly to maintain a balance between permanent and non-permanent seats. Such a settlement, they said, differed little from previous suggestions, since Poland ultimately would be elected to the seat. Luther told Chamberlain that Germany would not abandon her determination to oppose any changes until her own admission was a fact.[28]

The situation was now critical. The Western powers agreed

that German intransigence made further private talks "painful"
and that the issue should be referred to the council. Chamberlain, depressed, thought that Germany's refusal to make concessions would be "a misfortune for the League, a disaster for
Germany, and a grave peril to the policy of reconciliation."[29] The
Germans too were in a quandary. To be sure, they had preserved their position unaltered, but they knew that if they failed
to be admitted to the League, the Locarno policy would be terminated, their relations with the Allies would deteriorate, and
they would not realize their hopes for the final elimination of
military control and for changes in the occupation regime of the
Rhineland, which had been under discussion since Locarno. The
assembly, idle for nearly a week, was becoming impatient. The
sustained deadlock was turning public opinion against the Germans. The press began to blame them for the crisis. Afraid that
support at home might collapse, the German delegation furnished the newspapers with elaborate explanations and justifications of its position. The Swedish delegation complained of
extraordinary pressure from the British, and the Germans
thought they saw indications that the Swedes' resolve was
crumbling.[30]

On 14 March Undén proposed a way out. Troubled by
Briand's insistence that he was prepared to risk rupture rather
than return to Paris without at least the prospect of a seat for
Poland, the Swedish foreign minister suggested to Luther that
Sweden resign her seat in favor of Poland. He believed that
unless the crisis were resolved shortly, the League would suffer
catastrophic damage and Europe might lapse into political anarchy.[31] The German delegation debated the proposal: it could
protest changes in the composition of the council by council
vote, but it could not protest changes by resignation. Not pleased
with the prospect of Sweden's resignation, the Germans came up
with the alternative that Czechoslovakia be asked to vacate her
seat. In this way the council would retain its political balance:
one French ally would replace another. Schubert was delegated
to apprise the British of this development. Lampson, to whom
he spoke, spontaneously suggested that perhaps several states
could resign and open their seats to new elections.[32] At dinner
that evening Luther proposed to the Swedes that both they and
the Czechs leave the council, to be replaced by Poland and a

neutral power, possibly the Netherlands. The Germans would find such an arrangement easier to defend at home. The Swedes agreed, and Stresemann won Briand to the idea. In the council meeting on 15 March both Undén and Beneš, the latter with little enthusiasm, agreed to the plan. Germany would enter without further additions to the council, and the assembly would elect two states (one being Poland) to the vacant seats. The end of the crisis seemed in sight.[33]

It was not to be. Mello-Franco, the Brazilian delegate to the council, declared that his government was determined to veto Germany's admission to the council unless Brazil were given a permanent seat. No pressure could budge the Brazilians. Distraught at this last-minute sabotage, Chamberlain and Briand took the problem to the German delegation. They said they did not favor admitting Germany to the League at the risk of her being excluded from the council. Luther and Stresemann accepted a suggestion to postpone Germany's admission until the assembly met in September. Meanwhile a committee would be appointed to study and settle the differences over council membership, and Germany would be invited to sit on this committee. On 16 March the Locarno powers published a joint communiqué regretting the fiasco. Reaffirming Locarno, they expressed the conviction that Germany's entry would be accomplished in September.[34]

It would have been no surprise had the sorry outcome at Geneva inflamed the opposition in Germany. In fact only the political extremes expressed pleasure at the episode, and only the far Right assaulted the government for this humiliation.[35] The press reproved the government for its tactics: German diplomacy had not prepared the way properly, and Germany had nearly succumbed to a base Allied scheme to inflate the council and hedge Germany in with Allied minions; the delegation deserved censure for failing to leave Geneva the moment it became apparent that admission could not be accomplished. The press's chief reproach, however, was directed at the League itself: that a non-European, second-rate power should paralyze the politics of Europe's great powers was grotesque. Something was seriously wrong with an organization which permitted such a fiasco. The final communiqué also helped calm the atmosphere: it joined strong pro-German sentiment to the implicit acknowledgement that the European powers would now treat Germany as if she had entered the League.[36] On 18 March the German cabinet—one in the belief that if there was no cause for rejoicing, there was none for despair—unanimously approved the delegation's tactics at Geneva. On 23 March the Reichstag voted for the government's policy and rejected a proposal by the Nationalists, supported by the radicals on the Right and Left, to have the government withdraw its application.[37]

To his diplomatic missions, as to the Reichstag, Stresemann assessed the episode positively. The League had suffered, to be sure—its reputation had declined, its moral authority had been challenged. It was unfortunate, moreover, that admission to the League, a milestone in Germany's foreign policy, had not been achieved. Still, Germany had emerged unscathed and strengthened. The delegation had thwarted the Allies' scheme to pack the council, and the final communiqué obligated the Allies to treat Germany as if the Locarno pact had come into force. The negotiations at Geneva, Stresemann told the Reichstag, had shown that Germany was a power of equal standing. The government would not withdraw its application. Since the League had recognized Germany's position, the Germans could now adjust their policy to further developments. Moreover, as Stresemann wrote to the missions, it made little sense to scuttle the Locarno policy, for the policy was fruitful and no alternative of equal promise was available. That a policy encountered obstacles, he declared in public, was no proof that the policy was wrong. In fact Stresemann saw certain advantages in the debacle. He instructed his diplomats to point to the "great injustice" done at Geneva and to Germany's exemplary patience under trying circumstances. To redress the situation and resuscitate a badly battered "spirit of Locarno," the leading powers would now have to offer concessions in the negotiations on the Rhineland occupation forces and the abolition of military control.[38]

The League's invitation to join the committee which was to study reform of the council arrived in Berlin on 20 March. The officials of the League section in the Foreign Ministry, who were displeased about this turn of events, recommended that Germany should decline. They argued that she would compromise the principles which she had defended so successfully if she now agreed to negotiate. She would alienate the small states, whose support might prove useful after Germany had entered the League. Moreover, the very composition of the committee, comprising both members of and candidates for the council (including Germany and Poland), would predetermine the conclusions the committee would reach. The pending applications would all be approved; a minority report by Germany and one or two like-minded states would have little impact. Bülow suggested that if the government were astute, it would refrain from taking a stand on what was purely the business of the League and rely on the assembly, which he assumed would reject the committee's report.[39]

The Foreign Ministry's decision, approved by the cabinet on 31 March, did not heed Bülow's recommendations. Stresemann seems to have had a keener appreciation of Germany's political advantage, for he claimed himself to have suggested to the council powers that Germany sit on the committee. He explained that Germany's participation assured that the committee's ultimate proposal would carry a German stamp. Germany's absence might be construed to her disadvantage, and too much was at stake to court the displeasure of the Allies.[40] Finally, Germany's participation would preclude the reproach that the German government was about to change its policy, for in February Stresemann had agreed to a neutrality pact with the Soviet Union. The pact was to be concluded after Germany had joined the League so as not to hinder that transaction, but the fiasco at Geneva forced Germany's hand. The Russians, aided by the right-wing parties in the Reichstag, pressed the Foreign Ministry to act promptly, and Stresemann saw that by doing so he might distract attention from the recent debacle. He agreed to sign the pact at the end of April—and to join the League committee to offset the impact of this treaty.[41]

On 12 April Stresemann accepted the League's invitation, with the proviso that Germany's presence on the committee would in no way prejudice her freedom to decide whether to join the League. At the end of the month Hoesch was appointed to represent Germany, and Bülow and Gaus were to serve as his aides. The cabinet agreed to give Hoesch wide discretion in his task. The cabinet would accept any settlement which assured Germany a permanent seat and excluded Poland from this privilege. Clearly the delegation was not to be uncompromising; Germany, as Bülow noted, wanted a settlement so that the Locarno pact could finally come into force.[42]

The committee sat in Geneva from 10 to 17 May. The sentiment which emerged in the initial discussions generally opposed an increase in the number of permanent seats on the council beyond Germany. When Spain officially claimed a permanent seat, the committee decided to postpone debate and turn to less delicate matters. Lord Robert Cecil, representing Britain, offered a proposal which would expand the number of non-permanent seats from six to nine. One third of these were to be filled every year for a three-year term. By a majority of two-thirds the assembly could declare three of the incumbents eligible for re-election—in effect making them semi-permanent members of the council. The increase broadened the opportunity for League members to sit on the council, but the smaller states and Hoesch (who was reserved in public sessions but active behind the scenes) opposed the semi-permanent seats as blatantly political. They suggested a compromise: re-eligibility should be determined not upon election or during tenure, but upon the expiration of a term, in recognition of valuable service or of pressing necessity. The committee adopted the proposal with this change.[43]

The Germans were pleased with the outcome. In the Foreign Affairs Committee, to which the German delegates reported on 19 May, even the Nationalists approved the result.[44] The dispute over permanent seats, conspicuously ignored by the League committee, had solved itself. Poland, it appeared, had given up her aspirations, and the leading powers, Gaus wrote to Schubert, had made it clear to the other candidates that they had no hope. By June, when the League committee's report was to receive a second reading, some accommodation was to be reached with Spain and Brazil. The latter had been informed that her threatened veto would not be tolerated. Gaus concluded that the crisis of the March session was over and, "as far as humanly possible," entry assured. Of course the issue had not been resolved without hard feelings, especially among those who had sided with the Poles. The committee had adopted recommendations which ignored French interests. That this might cause difficulties was apparent in the tension between Germany and France during these weeks, especially over the concessions that Germany expected and demanded for the Rhineland.[45]

Unexpectedly the committee's recommendations ran into trouble. On 8 June the League council postponed the second reading, arguing that more time was needed for negotiations with Spain and Brazil. Two days later, amid general surprise, Brazil tendered her resignation from the League. At the end of July the Spanish representative, who had been cool toward the council during its June session, requested the second reading of the report. At the same time the Poles asked the leading members of the council to change the committee's recommendations. The Poles requested that the tenure of non-permanent members be extended to five years and that eligibility for re-election be voted at the beginning, not at the end, of the mandate. They requested further that all new members be elected together, so that Poland and Germany might enter the council simultaneously. These were major alterations—an attempt, as Chamberlain remarked, "to renew, in a different form it is true but still with little disguise, the claim to a permanent seat on the Council."[46]

The French, themselves dissatisfied with the recommendations, were willing to entertain these requests—not least because Briand thought that a positive response to Poland might mollify Spain and Brazil. In fact the French government offered Spain the very privileges Poland demanded if the Spanish government would accept a non-permanent seat. To the Germans it appeared that a situation analogous to that in March was developing: the French were making promises and the British, while asserting their determination to secure Germany a permanent seat on the council, would not declare themselves on other issues. Both Chamberlain and Briand seemed inclined to revise the report of the committee.[47]

When word of these changes reached Berlin early in August, the Germans protested. Once again they directed their fire primarily at the British: a revision of the committee's recommendations would put Germany into a "grave position." The Germans would oppose such changes categorically, and "chaos" would result. In Paris, Hoesch told Berthelot that any such arrangement could only end in calamity, expecially for France. To rally support, Stresemann instructed his missions in Berne,

Brussels, Rome, and Stockholm to present Germany's objections. Any revision, they were to say, was bound to lead to complications, and the German government would therefore countenance no fundamental changes.[48]

The French were unhappy at the Germans' vehemence; the British were overwhelmed. On instructions from Chamberlain, D'Abernon warned Stresemann "solemnly" against raising new conditions. If Germany's admission miscarried this time, the Locarno détente would collapse. At the same time Chamberlain tried to appease the Germans: to bring Germany into the League was Britain's "first and paramount object," but surely the Germans too had an interest in keeping Spain in the League and in propitiating Poland.[49] For all their angry rhetoric, the Germans were not eager to cause difficulties. The government was too well aware of the advantages of the Locarno détente to cause its destruction. The cabinet convened on 13 August to discuss a letter from Hindenburg, in which the president reiterated his reservations about the League. "Application to the League" should be made conditional on a reduction of the occupation regime in the Rhineland and on a binding promise that Allied military control of Germany would be terminated. Stresemann argued that Germany had made no little progress in these matters and that the problems which remained certainly did not warrant withdrawing her application. The cabinet agreed.[50]

When Briand suggested that Fromageot, his legal adviser, travel to Berlin to negotiate a possible compromise with Gaus, Stresemann accepted "gratefully." The two jurists agreed on a settlement. Non-permanent members of the council could be declared eligible for re-election at the beginning of their tenure, but the assembly retained the right to replace them with other non-permanent candidates at the expiration of a term. This arrangement brought all eligible members into competition; the preliminary declaration of eligibility for a second term became purely a matter of prestige. The three powers accepted this solution and were unmoved when the Spanish government renewed its demands and threatened once again to resign.[51]

The League committee sat again from 30 August to 3 September. To everyone's amazement, the smaller powers rejected the carefully wrought compromise, arguing, true to their consistent policy, that a compromise which simply balanced the political interests of the great powers was not necessarily sound policy for the League. In the face of this opposition, the committee returned to the recommendations it had adopted in May. These were now accepted once again, with a small emendation in the procedure governing eligibility. As in the earlier report, eligibility would be voted at the end of the term of office, but an exception would be made at the elections of September 1926. At this election a vote of two-thirds of the assembly might make a state eligible for a second term with the proviso that this vote could be disavowed if another incumbent non-permanent member of the council should be declared re-eligible when his term expired in 1927 or 1928. To placate Poland, it was agreed that such a disavowal might take place only "under exceptional circumstances," but the assembly's right to elect whom it wanted was assured.[52]

From this stubborn contest for prestige and position, which had been carried on with legal subtleties and much sophistry for almost two years, Germany emerged victorious. She could expect to enter the League on the terms she had set in September 1924. It was a triumph not only for Stresemann, but also for the political parties which had backed him since he had concluded the Locarno agreement. On 4 September 1926 the council adopted the committee's recommendations: it voted to give Germany a permanent seat on the council and to increase the number of non-permanent seats from six to nine. On 8 September the assembly voted unanimously to accept Germany as a member of the League with a permanent seat on the council. The German delegation, led by Stresemann, left Berlin that evening. Two days later Germany joined the League. Stresemann pledged Germany to peaceful collaboration. He expressed the hope that justice would govern relations between nations, that general disarmament would pave the way to lasting peace, and that mutual confidence would surmount the differences between nations. In response Briand reached heights of eloquence in welcoming Germany into the League. The world would now witness "a common will to labor together for the peace of the world." Chamberlain was euphoric at this evocation of the spirit of Locarno: "Everything passed off as I would have wished."[53]

Germany's admission to the League culminated a strategy which Stresemann had inaugurated in 1923. The economic détente opened by the Dawes plan led to the political détente of the Locarno pact. In her accession to the League, Germany returned to a position of international influence; as a permanent member of the council, she achieved formal parity with the great powers. It was the first step in Stresemann's grand design. He had brought Germany into the concert of European powers, and in this setting he could begin to revise the peace settlement.

5   Stresemann and the League

At the time of Germany's negotiations for membership in the League there was speculation about whether she would appear at Geneva as the smallest of the big powers or as the biggest of the small. The Scandinavian governments especially had beseeched the Germans to rally the small states around them and act as a counterweight to the great ones. In the Foreign Ministry the question was never more than academic.[1] Germany's choice was clear in the conditions she set for membership: she would have to be assured a permanent seat on the council, to be admitted in a manner consonant with her eminence. Once negotiations had begun, the Germans' ambitions also appeared in their lively interest in the visible trappings of status—particularly in prominent representation on the League's secretariat, the most important organ of the League after the council and the assembly. At Locarno the Western statesmen had assured the Germans that they would enjoy "parity" in the secretariat, and since the Germans paid the same dues as the French (1.9 million gold francs per annum), they argued that their representation should equal that of France. When Drummond visited Berlin in February 1926 to settle the administrative details of Germany's prospective membership, Schubert asked him for the post of a deputy secretary-general (like the Frenchman Joseph Avenol), two directorships, four or five chiefs of section, and a ranking official in each of the secretariat's eleven sections. Drummond balked. These demands could not be met without creating new (and conspicuously unnecessary) positions—a prospect Drummond rejected not merely for financial reasons but also because the precedent would lead to importunate requests from other states. Drummond offered the position of an under secretary-general (to join the Italian and Japanese) and a higher post in each of six sections.[2] Ultimately, Drummond and Schubert compromised on an under secretary-general who would also be a director (of international bureaus and intellectual cooperation),[3] ranking positions in eight sections, and suitable representation on most of the standing commissions.[4]

In the League, the Germans were careful to conduct themselves in a manner befitting a great power. Only when illness kept him away in the· summer of 1928 was Stresemann not present—and then he was represented once by Schubert and at another time by the chancellor himself.[5] At every session he was accompanied by a great retinue from his ministry and by assorted experts from other ministries. A more conspicuous gesture was the presence of certain prominent parliamentarians in the German delegation to the assembly—Bernstorff (DDP), Breitscheid (SPD), Hoetzsch (DNVP), Kaas (Center), and Rheinbaben (DVP). The German delegates took their responsibilities seriously and discharged their duties conscientiously. They were urbane, peaceable, and obliging. When called upon, they came forth with proposals, solutions, or mediation. They were energetic rapporteurs on economic questions (reflecting Stresemann's concern with Germany's economic recovery), and outspoken champions of covenant principles at the annual assembly in September.[6] In the secretariat, the German officials had a hand in shaping the work of the League—preparing the sessions of the council and the assembly, drafting reports and resolutions, handling public relations, and supervising information offices in various member countries.[7] Outside the corridors of the League, Stresemann and his associates conferred with the foreign ministers or diplomatic representatives of the various member states who sought assistance, cooperation, or plain good will.[8] The Germans built up a loose following among neutrals like Holland and Sweden and former wartime allies like Hungary, whose interests they could represent. After a year of membership, a German diplomat recorded with satisfaction that the Germans had participated in all important decisions at Geneva. Their activity there, he predicted, would give them a strong and influential position—"of great significance when Germany returned to world status."[9]

Yet Germany was no ordinary great power. She bore the title and the League endowed her with the symbols representative of the title, but she had none of the attributes that defined the other great powers. She was disarmed, her economy and economic policies were still of little consequence beyond her borders, and in the absence of military and economic power, she was not a formidable political force either. Her status as a great power, Bülow once observed, existed only "on paper" and depended on the good will of the other great powers.[10] Germany differed from the other great powers in a second respect: her political orientation was unique. The other powers were the victors of the war. They had founded and then shaped the League to preserve the order they had created in 1919. Germany, foremost among the losers of the war, had now joined their organization. In the context of the League and from the point of view of its founders, she was a subversive force. She differed from the other powers on most issues before the League—a revisionist power among the defenders of the status quo.

These differences had bred misgivings among the Western powers long before Germany joined the League. In January 1926 the British Foreign Office had told the minister at the London embassy that "private, political, and diplomatic circles" suspected that Germany would be a "troublemaker" in the League. The Germans, the minister was cautioned, would do well to restrain themselves in pressing their demands.[11] In September, French right-wing newspapers, not normally among the exponents of the League, sounded the alarm: "the vultures have been let into the dove-cote."[12] These apprehensions proved excessive, for Germany's presence at Geneva changed the League less than the distance between her orientation and that of the other leading powers implied. Under Stresemann, German policy at Geneva aimed at détente. Germany's representatives were therefore at pains to observe the amenities and to cultivate good relations with the other members. They saw to it that their deviant political program never provoked open conflict in the council or assembly.[13] They took no action when German officials in the secretariat complained that they were snubbed or ignored.[14] And if it happened that some proposal ran counter to their revisionist intentions, they would skillfully employ the instruments of the League—principle, precedent, substitute motion—to undercut and defeat it.[15]

In fact, the Germans had no need to disturb League routine

with their demands, for like the other leading powers, they pursued their purposes outside the official machinery of the League. Briand, Chamberlain, and Stresemann took advantage of the regular sessions of the council—four times a year—to engage in a personal exchange of views. The "Locarnites," as Chamberlain dubbed them, would gather in each other's hotel rooms, joined by a few associates and an interpreter (and at times by representatives of Belgium and Italy). Their confidential meetings became a "standing institution" and often assumed greater importance than the public sessions of the council.[16] The Locarnites would discuss matters affecting their countries and Europe in general. Foremost in their deliberations were Germany's grievances about the peace treaty—military control, foreign occupation, and, later, reparations. Here they negotiated and compromised, seeking to reconcile Germany's desire to cast off her treaty obligations with the Western powers' doubts about Germany's willingness to abide by these without constant surveillance. They would also address themselves to the problems of the smaller states and, in a manner reminiscent of the concert of powers in the nineteenth century, coordinate their policies to bring about a settlement.[17] Finally, and often considered most significant, they would take up issues that should properly have gone before the League whenever such issues bore directly on their national interests or on relations among them. When a suspicious arms shipment was discovered at Szent-Gotthard on the Austrian-Hungarian border in January 1928, they agreed to forgo a full-scale League investigation in order to accommodate the Germans, who feared a disagreeable precedent.[18] And not infrequently, they would decide in advance on positions to be adopted or resolutions to be accepted in the sessions of the council.[19]

These meetings were popular with the participants, particularly in the beginning, and took place even when there was no urgent business to conduct or little prospect of agreement. They were not always harmonious, for the three statesmen held different views on European affairs and especially on the peace treaty. Each was enmeshed in political constraints of his own, whether in unstable political conditions at home, unresolved differences (Germany and Poland), or preoccupations elsewhere (Britain and the Near East). The success of the meetings may be attributed to the personalities of the participants. Though of different social origins and diverse political outlook, these men had a common bond. None was a professional diplomat, and all preferred the informal meeting, for they shared good memories of Locarno and of their association in March 1926. They believed that personal conferences produced results and cleared away obstacles, and that face-to-face encounter was more effective than ambassadorial démarches or diplomatic notes.

Stresemann considered this personal contact the most important advantage of membership in the League. In 1925–26 he had told his German audiences that membership would permit the Germans to press their interests and to block further discrimination against them in European affairs. It would enable them to profit from the principles to which the League was committed (such as national self-determination) and to exploit an international forum of great influence.[20] After Germany had joined the League, however, Stresemann made little use of the institution and the opportunities it offered for advancing his aims. These he pursued in private meetings with the Western statesmen.[21] Here he argued Germany's case with passion and conviction, appealing to his partners' political instincts and reminding them of their joint commitment to Locarno and their close association. He cited the expectations of the world, which saw in the ministers' collaboration the guarantee for the conciliation inaugurated at Locarno. He cited the expectations of his own public, which wanted returns for its "sacrifices," and he was not averse to some gentle blackmail. Stresemann was persistent, but he knew when to bend. He was prepared to make concessions and, being versed in the vagaries of public opinion, to put certain restraints on his public oratory.[22]

Briand responded to this approach, as he responded to parliamentary questioning at home, with his natural eloquence and optimism. He echoed Stresemann's commitment to conciliation, and, like Stresemann, he never lost sight of his national interests. Like most of his countrymen, he feared that Germany, though impotent at the moment, would seek to dominate Europe economically and financially and that, once restored, she might "destroy the political order which was the expression of her defeat." He knew that a policy of suppression, of perpetuating the discrimination of the peace treaty, was impossible to sustain.

He hoped that a policy of generosity tempered with firmness would reconcile Germany to her postwar status. Accordingly, he welcomed Germany into the League, lauding her prominence, while he persisted in trying to make the League an effective shield of French security (as, for instance, in the protracted disarmament talks).[23] In the private meetings of the statesmen, he was prepared to meet Stresemann's requests as long as they did not impinge on the security France had achieved in the stipulations of the peace treaty. He was rarely obstinate, though he could be dilatory and was given to magnifying his concessions in torrents of protestation. When Stresemann fell to bullying his partners, Briand, who hated scenes, would try to assuage him with sanguine hopes—which were subject to misinterpretation in Berlin and often got Briand into hot water in Paris.[24]

Chamberlain found this summit diplomacy more to his liking than the formal League procedures. He was uncomfortable with the public style of Geneva politics and unsympathetic to extending League authority to issues he thought better left to national governments. Meeting in private with the European foreign ministers, he could assert the authority of a respected country and assume the traditional British role of arbiter. Pragmatic and direct, talented at negotiation, he brought to bear on these discussions his determination not to let Europe fall back into old animosities and his interest in giving Germany "her rightful place once more in the councils of the European powers."[25] He was always on better terms with Briand than with Stresemann, and because he never entirely lost his distrust of Germany and remained suspicious of her ambitions, he tended to side with Briand in dealing with Stresemann's demands. Ultimately, he was to prove a disappointment to the Germans—as well as to the parliamentary opposition at home.

From 1926 to 1929, these private meetings made the League a concert of the great powers. By superseding the normal diplomatic channels as well as the League, these summit negotiations became a political fact unto themselves, the concrete manifestation of the spirit of Locarno, which Stresemann particularly was prone to invoke. For a few years, they transformed European politics and, for the first time since the war, provided a sense of order and stability.

Representatives of the smaller powers, members of the secretariat, journalists, and supporters of the League and the ideal of open diplomacy resented the "Locarno tea parties." They had expected that the council, strengthened by the accession of Germany, would rise to prominence, replacing the Allied Supreme Council and the Conference of Ambassadors, and that the League would abandon its preoccupation with the execution of the peace treaty and turn its attention to the precepts of the covenant. The League, they hoped, would renew efforts to enlarge its peacekeeping functions and to improve its technical apparatus.[26] The Locarno tea parties dashed these hopes. Some feared that the League would suffer if the power brokers of Locarno arbitrated Europe's disputes behind closed doors, without recourse to the League's machinery or contact with the League itself. Others believed that these private meetings would reduce the League to uselessness as they became habitual and began to upstage the council sessions. The press directed what seemed excessive attention to these meetings, and its reports implied that the real business at Geneva took place here and not around the council table or on the floor of the assembly.[27]

The German government could not ignore these criticisms. In defending the tea party politics before the Reichstag's Foreign Affairs Committee, Stresemann observed that his government was interested above all in settling the problems arising from the peace treaty. It would have to foster close relations with the two Western powers—especially with France, for all questions of his foreign policy (military control, evacuation, reparations, disarmament, and even the eastern borders) impinged on French national interests.[28] Bülow, in explaining Germany's alignment with the great powers to the diplomatic missions, argued in the context of the League. The very size of the council—enlarged in 1926 over Germany's warnings—had "necessarily" caused it to break up into smaller groups. Moreover, the League was not yet mature enough for questions of global importance; its competence still lay chiefly in its technical services. The League would overcome its weaknesses only if the great powers agreed on a policy of solidarity.[29]

Germany's escapade with the "optional clause" is exemplary of the profound ambiguities of her position at Geneva. The Germans arrived in Geneva in September 1927 to find that the Polish government planned to introduce in the assembly a proposal for a general non-aggression pact. The Poles wanted to outlaw war under any and all circumstances and to commit the signatories to settling international disputes peaceably. Their proposal stood in the tradition of earlier attempts to extend the League's functions in maintaining the status quo. It was likely to win broad sympathy. The Germans interpreted it as a thinly veiled attempt to do for their eastern borders what Locarno had done in the west. To approve it was impossible, to oppose it solitarily "extraordinarily embarrassing." The Polish proposal would therefore have to be thwarted.[30]

Stresemann found an ally in Chamberlain, who was "horrified" at the idea and assured Stresemann that under no circumstances would Britain assume a position divergent from Germany's. Briand, who ordinarily took the part of his Polish ally, agreed that such a pact was "unnecessary." But he intimated that he was not averse to a general resolution that bound the members of the League to the peaceful settlement of their differences.[31] The Germans also prepared for the possibility that the proposal might come before the assembly. Their subterfuge was the so-called optional clause of the statute of the Permanent Court at The Hague: adherents to the clause agreed to lay their disputes before the court for arbitration. The clause itself was of little practical significance; its obligations, said Gaus, did not exceed those Germany had assumed at Locarno. Its symbolic significance, however, was great: very few states (and none of the great powers) had espoused the clause, very much to the chagrin of the small powers. If Germany signed the clause, her delegates could count on the support of the small powers in the assembly.[32]

The concerted pressure of the great powers obliged Poland to adopt a compromise. In a parley of the powers' legal experts, the draft was reworded to limit its strictures to aggressive war and to scrap obligatory arbitration on all differences. The proposal was now to be sponsored by Poland with the explicit support of the great powers—to underscore the transformation that had taken place. When it came before the assembly, Stresemann gave it his full approval (for, as he told Berlin, "no state can declare in the assembly that it is not prepared to abjure aggressive war"). At the same time, to great applause, he announced Germany's espousal of the optional clause.[33] The Foreign Ministry congratulated itself on its tactics. The cooperation of the great powers had sidetracked an "eastern Locarno"; the personal relationship of the three statesmen had proved agreeably firm. By making a great display with the optional clause, Germany had "recovered contact with the small powers."[34] This feat of improvisation bewildered the German under secretary-general, who, after two years in the secretariat, asked Stresemann whether Germany had a League policy, and if so, what it was.[35]

Stresemann never addressed himself to the possibility that Germany, unencumbered by earlier embarrassments of the League, might have transformed the League and strengthened "the frail foundations of peaceful cooperation." The Germans ignored their chance to give new impetus to the international order represented by the League. They let the impact of their triumphant reception into the League slip away. They dismissed as fair-weather friends the small member-states which had rallied to them during the reform negotiations in 1926, when Germany had professed allegiance to covenant principles. Conventional membership served the purpose of reintegrating Germany into European affairs. At one with the great powers, the Germans preferred to pursue their vital aims, not by developing the League, but by making it a backdrop for their private conferences. And they cared little if this abuse injured the League's reputation and further reduced its vitality.[36]

German membership in the League was not merely a diplomatic issue. It also figured in domestic politics, as Stresemann well knew. For good or ill, whatever took place at Geneva would excite German interest and have domestic repercussions. A German correspondent who covered Geneva between the wars recalled that the Germans, who had virtually ignored the League from 1920 to 1926, now turned to its sessions with "lively interest," and the press reported in long columns the speeches of the prominent and the activities of the council and the assembly.[37] The topic remained controversial. In Germany the League had a past to live down, and many looked on Stresemann's policy in Geneva with suspicion. The Center party carried a brief for the German minority in Upper Silesia and watched its fortunes at Geneva. The Social Democrats were mindful of the development of the League's disarmament talks. Others, such as the

Nationalists, who still adhered to prewar standards of international diplomacy, directed their attention at Germany's conduct and overall success. And everyone who disagreed with Stresemann's foreign policy welcomed any "setback" at Geneva—even an unavoidable compromise or adjournment—as an excuse for denigrating him and his work.

Stresemann's activity at Geneva therefore had an obligatory aspect. If he wanted to preserve his political support and forestall debilitating public criticism, he would have to perform well and to comport himself as the proud representative of a great power.[38] Stresemann resented this obligation, for it encumbered the conduct of his diplomacy, and he often deplored the absence of the public solidarity necessary for the successful prosecution of his policy.[39] This policy, he believed, was the only realistic policy for Germany. It would restore the country to greatness, and, he thought, would help reunite its divided society and stabilize its regime.[40] Membership in the League was indispensable to this policy: it supplied the necessary credentials while he sought contact with the Western statesmen. His strategy at Geneva required that he be flexible, and that he be able to concede a point or compromise on an issue. It was also geared to a set of priorities that checked its pace: certain issues were to be of primary, others of secondary importance, and on the latter he was willing to hold back. He was determined to preserve autonomy in these decisions for himself and his ministry.

He bent his efforts to heading off criticism. Contemporaries record that he spent the morning in his ministry and the rest of the day gathering support and politicking in the Reichstag and the chancellery. He worked on Hindenburg, who followed Germany's progress at Geneva closely and did not hesitate to denounce the politics of compromise. He insisted that the delegation to Geneva always include Hermann Pünder, the state secretary in the chancellery, in order to forestall sudden interference from the cabinet in Berlin and to assure his fellow ministers that he would not move onto perilous ground. And the presence of parliamentarians in the delegations to the assembly, which on one level served to demonstrate Germany's commitment to the League, served on another to involve the Reichstag parties more intimately in Stresemann's policy at Geneva.[41]

Above all, Stresemann spared no effort to publicize the activities of his delegation at Geneva. He was his own best publicity agent. Like Briand, who also felt impeded by opposition at home, Stresemann used the League as a forum from which to address the German public, and he shaped his rhetoric accordingly. He never tired of calling press conferences at Geneva or granting interviews or even planting his own (usually anonymous) commentary in various German newspapers. And he reported regularly and in some detail in the confidential meetings of the Foreign Affairs Committee of the Reichstag and, in less detail, to the plenum.[42]

His reports were imbued with the satisfaction he felt about his new role at Geneva. He himself savored the dignity implicit in Germany's status at the meetings of the League. He basked in the international popularity accorded him: reporters dogged his footsteps, photographers and cartoonists recorded his every mood. He hailed the Nobel peace prize, which he received jointly with Briand in December 1926, as a token of international trust and respect. As evidence for Germany's importance he cited his participation in the great powers' efforts to settle the tensions between Albania and Yugoslavia in 1927 or the border conflicts between Lithuania and Poland in 1927–28. And he treated Chamberlain's request for Germany's good offices in the dispute between the British and the Russians in 1927 as highly significant.[43]

Stresemann's reports on Geneva, at least for the first two years of German membership, were invariably positive. He stressed less the ideal of international peace and understanding than the benefits Germany would gain from the harmonious collaboration with her former enemies. No one could deny that German interests preoccupied the League, he told the Reichstag, and that now the Germans could be advocates in their own cause. Every council session confirmed anew the wisdom of joining, and he adduced the delegation's accomplishments to prove his case.[44] Among these were the satisfactory resolution of disputes about German minorities and about the "lost territories" of Danzig and Memel. He took credit for prodding the council in March 1927 to insist that French troops be withdrawn from the Saar, where they had been garrisoned since the end of the war, and to appoint an Englishman to head the Saar's governing commission. He reported how he overcame the resistance of the council and succeeded in averting permanent League control of German disarmament. And he insisted that the Germans' experience at Geneva "justified the expectation" that the Western powers would show a "loyal spirit of accommodation" in settling such issues as the evacuation of the Rhineland and the restoration of the Saar.[45] In fact, in many of his public speeches he was nothing loath to imply that treaty revisions would follow logically (and almost automatically) from the changes wrought by Germany's accession to Locarno and the League.[46]

In the years immediately following Germany's entry into the League, Stresemann's public relations were excellent. This was the time of prosperity and relative peace. The standard of living rose as production and trade flourished and the chronic unemployment receded. In the Reichstag and the press, controversy over the direction of foreign policy rarely assumed serious dimensions. The political parties, while they retained their differences over social and economic issues, agreed that a foreign policy which acknowledged Germany's limitations and tried to work within them deserved endorsement—or at least toleration. Stresemann kept his support in the Reichstag—from the Socialists, long dedicated to a doctrine of internationalism, and from the liberal parties of the middle, which favored a policy that encouraged trade and foreign credits. All of them were satisfied as long as the League appeared to promote Germany's recovery.[47]

Even the Nationalists appeared to reconcile themselves to accommodation with the West. In the fall of 1925 they had vociferated against Locarno; in November 1926 Hoetzsch publicly acknowledged the validity of Germany's entering the League (though he disparaged the notion of international understanding and demanded that Germany pursue a "German policy" in the League).[48] When the Nationalists returned to the government in the first cabinet shuffle after Germany's entry into the League, they did so on terms set by Stresemann and Chancellor Wilhelm Marx. Those terms stressed the government's commitment to a clear line of international accommodation, to Locarno as the law of the land, and to loyal cooperation within the League. As members of the cabinet, the Nationalists held to a generally pragmatic approach and even gave occasional mild approval to Stresemann's policy.[49]

In these circumstances, Stresemann could ignore the relent-less carping of the radical Right in the press and the attacks from extremist deputies. He was also able to sidetrack or accommo-date members of the Reichstag or the cabinet who pressed him to insist on certain prompt returns and to be more rigorous in prosecuting his policy.[50]

In the long run, Stresemann's dual role—diplomat and public-ity agent—was more than he could handle. In his capacity as diplomat he urged the Germans to be patient. The League worked no miracles and offered no panacea, he told an audience in East Prussia in 1927. In the Reichstag he explained that com-promises were not tantamount to weakness and delay not tan-tamount to failure.[51] The sober advice aroused little enthusiasm, for in his capacity as publicity agent Stresemann had long since raised hopes and expectations. In Berlin he seemed on occasion to forget what he knew in Geneva—that a power seeking ac-commodation must be responsive to the political needs and feel-ings of other powers. He seemed to give in to the temptation to interpret his expectations as achievements and to describe Briand's sanguine promises as goods delivered.[52] The expecta-tions which he raised interfered in turn with his diplomacy, ob-liging him to force issues and to press for prompt results. And when he cited public expectations to justify his importunings, Briand and Chamberlain suspected that these expectations were of his own making. They, for their part, were obliged to explain that they could not accommodate him, for the excitement in the German public had alarmed their own constituents.[53]

Stresemann's difficulties with his dual role arose also for reasons beyond his personal responsibility. His League policy was never "internationalist" in the sense that it could tolerate foreign impediments to Germany's self-affirmation unless con-strained to do so. His policy was spuriously internationalist—in the sense that Germany used the League as a means of recover-ing national power, *faute de mieux* and until further notice. Ger-many's "future attitude toward the League," wrote one of Stresemann's diplomats in November 1927, would "depend es-sentially" on the resolution of the political questions closest to Germany's heart (like reparations, the evacuation of the Rhine-land, and the eastern borders).[54] But even such a circumscribed connection with the League went further than the German public was willing to go; its old adversity to the League had not moderated.

6   Rhineland and Reparations, 1926–29

In September 1926, when Germany joined the great powers as a permanent member of the League council, her subjection to Versailles was still very much in evidence. Foreign troops stood in the Rhineland and the Saar, foreign reparations agents supervised the operations of Germany's central banking system and her railways, and foreign military officers kept watch over her diminished army and limited armaments. All were in Germany to enforce the terms of the peace treaty; all in some fashion abridged Germany's national sovereignty; all served to remind the nation of the defeat of 1918. Their presence therefore was a political issue, and no German government escaped the obligation to rid the country of these restraints.[1]

The occupation of the Rhineland had been considerably modified after Locarno. The Cologne zone, garrisoned chiefly by British and Belgian troops, had been evacuated in January 1926. The remaining occupation forces (overwhelmingly French) had been reduced to 70,000 men stationed in the second (Coblenz) and third (Mainz) zones—an area of about 9,000 square miles inhabited by some 3.5 million Germans. Various administrative ordinances passed by the Inter-Allied Rhineland High Commission in Coblenz, a civilian agency of the three occupying powers, had been abrogated or revised. Local German officials now had much greater leeway in exercising their authority, and the local populace found the occupation much less onerous. (In fact, a good many Rhineland entrepreneurs found it downright profitable.[2]) The German government had acknowledged these changes rather grudgingly. Instead of citing them as evidence of diplomatic progress, it promptly pointed out that they fell short of expectations. The Germans claimed that the occupying powers had failed to keep their promise of November 1925, when they pledged to reduce their forces in the second and third zones "to a figure approaching the normal." Such a figure, the Germans contended, would be around 46,000, the size of Germany's prewar garrison in the area. The occupying powers (while themselves divided on the exact meaning of the phrase) rejected this contention, and the dispute had not been resolved when the Germans entered the League.[3]

Of greater import was Germany's interest in the full evacuation of the Rhineland before 1935, the date stipulated in the peace treaty. In unguarded moments Stresemann spoke of "getting the strangler off our neck."[4] After Locarno it was unlikely that the western powers would resort to military sanctions should the Germans appear to evade their treaty obligations. Nevertheless, as long as foreign troops remained in the Rhineland, Germany was vulnerable to incursion, or as had happened with the Cologne zone, to a prolongation of the occupation. More significant, the occupation was a focal point of resentment for the Germans, constituting, as the British consul in Mainz put it, a "great moral burden." "For many Germans," he observed in 1927, "the Occupation is the insolent crow of the vainglorious Gallic cock, and it is chiefly as such that it is hated and fought against."[5] Full evacuation had been a topic of Stresemann's conversations and speeches since the summer of 1925, when the Locarno pact was still in the making. In 1926 he more than once took occasion to aver that continued occupation was inconsistent with the spirit of Locarno, and he told the Foreign Affairs Committee that before long he would ask the Western powers to withdraw their armies. Connected with this objective was his determination to restore the Saar—then administered by the League and garrisoned by the French—before the plebiscite scheduled for 1935.[6]

The reparations issue, so productive of political quarrels at the time of the Ruhr, had lost much of its virulence. The Dawes plan provided for a workable system of payment based on Germany's capacity to pay, and the prosperity of the mid-twenties made payment relatively painless. Germany paid gradually rising annuities, which would reach their upper level (2.5 billion marks) by September 1928. The annuities were made up of certain tax revenues and of railway earnings, and were secured by railway and industrial bonds. The Reparations Commission, headed by the American Parker Gilbert as agent-general, supervised the scheme and transferred the payments to Germany's creditors. Gilbert was empowered to suspend their transfer whenever he believed the stability of Germany's currency to be in danger. Stresemann regarded the Dawes plan as no more than a short-lived expedient. Within two or three years, he asserted in 1925, the annuities would exceed Germany's financial capacities. Then, he predicted, another international conference would be convened, which would recommend some kind of final settlement.[7]

The Inter-Allied Military Control Commission, which had "controlled". Germany's disarmament since 1920, had been reduced to a skeleton force after Locarno. It was to depart as soon as the Germans had satisfied what remained of the objections raised by the general inspection of 1924. These included certain fortifications the Germans had built on their eastern frontier, the manufacture and export of war materials, and the size and organization of the police. Months of negotiations had produced no settlement; the Germans had temporized, persuaded that the developing détente would work in their favor, but the Western powers, especially the French, were not disposed to give way.[8]

Stresemann considered the evacuation of Rhineland and Saar and the revision of the Dawes plan his primary objectives. The complete abolition of the Control Commission was unfinished business, amenable, he thought, to early conclusion. He was confident that Germany's presence in the League and his own personal diplomacy at Geneva would bring these issues to satisfactory resolution.[9]

Many Germans believed that the prompt evacuation of the Rhineland would be a natural consequence of joining the League, and when Stresemann and Briand met at Thoiry in September 1926 it appeared that these expectations might be realized.[10] This private meeting had a long background. At Locarno the year before and again in March 1926 at Geneva, Stresemann and Briand had canvassed the idea of meeting à deux to discuss the issues that troubled relations between their countries. In May, as France was struggling with runaway inflation, Berthelot, the secretary-general at the Quai d'Orsay, had mentioned to Ambassador Hoesch that the French might want to secure financial aid from a seemingly prosperous Germany in exchange for reducing the period of occupation in the Rhine-land.[11] Then, in June, Briand had urged that Stresemann meet him soon for an exploratory conversation, a proposal evidently endorsed by Poincaré, who returned to power as prime minister the following month. Through unofficial channels, Stresemann conveyed his assent, and early in September he obtained the approval of the cabinet. He promised his colleagues that, if he and Briand could not negotiate an overall settlement, he would continue to press for other, more immediate returns.[12]

At Thoiry, unencumbered by publicity and basking in the euphoria of Germany's entry into the League, the two foreign ministers dispensed with detailed agenda and turned to a discussion of a "comprehensive solution." In essence this solution proposed to exchange prompt withdrawal of French troops from the Rhineland and the Saar for assistance in France's financial crisis. Germany could render such assistance by a slight change in the Dawes plan. If some of the railway bonds Germany had deposited as security with the reparations commission were put on the open market, the return might enable France to pay her debts and put her finances in order. Of the 1.5 billion marks that might conceivably be commercialized, France would receive around 700 million (or 52 percent, according to the reparations schedule in effect). Stresemann thought that Germany could offer another 300 million for the repurchase of the coal mines in the Saar. He also found Briand agreeable to a settlement of the differences over Germany's disarmament and to unhampered negotiations with the Belgians about the retrocession of Eupen-Malmédy.[13]

Stresemann was intrigued with the possibility of a general settlement of this nature. Four days later he told members of Geneva's German colony that Germany would exercise sovereignty over her soil once again and would restore the right of self-determination where it was still violated (apparently an allusion to union with Austria).[14] To the Foreign Affairs Committee he said that at Thoiry France had abandoned her commitment to the kind of security that obliged her to stay on the Rhine. Poincaré himself had conceded that Germany's presence in the League was incompatible with further French presence in the Rhineland. The moral, if not the legal, basis for occupation was gone. He cautioned that no one could say what kind of settle-

ment might result—or indeed whether there would be a settlement at all. It was not merely a question between himself and
Briand—or Germany and France—but would affect the
finances, economies, and the politics of the world. In fact,
Stresemann was not without misgivings, especially about the
technicalities of the arrangement. If Germany were to offer the
railway bonds on the open market, she would have to surrender
the transfer protection built into the Dawes plan. No private
investor would purchase bonds if the transfer of money might
be blocked any time the reparations agent believed Germany's
currency was threatened by inflation. Chancellor Marx, whose
initial reaction had been that the news of Thoiry was "too good
to be true," shared these doubts, as did his colleagues in the
cabinet. However, the ministers seemed willing to assume certain risks for the sake of a general settlement.[15]

Authorized by both the French and the German governments,
committees exploring the technical aspects of the Thoiry scheme
got busy in Paris and Berlin.[16] Within weeks, however, difficulties arose which seemed to confirm the pessimistic predictions of
the professional diplomats. The financial markets in New York
and London would cooperate in the scheme only if the French
ratified the war debt funding agreements, concluded earlier that
year, which determined sum and payment of France's war debts
to the United States and Britain. The parliament in Paris opposed ratification. Washington and London remained obstinate,
even though they favored Franco-German reconciliation. When
it emerged that ratification would have to precede commerciali-
zation, French interest in the undertaking cooled.[17] At the same
time, Poincaré's government seemed to gain control of the inflation of the franc, and France's self-confidence revived. Poincaré
had never been enthusiastic about Thoiry. In September he had
associated himself with his cabinet's lukewarm attitude toward
Briand's action. While he had done nothing to disavow his
foreign minister's policy, Hoesch suspected that he was
prepared to intervene at any moment. Poincaré believed that
during his absence from office (1924–26), France's position had
deteriorated, and he was determined to stop this decline. He
believed that rapprochement with Germany was acceptable, but
not at the price of French rights. Evacuation of French troops
from German territory, coming hard on the heels of the

Locarno agreements and Germany's entry into the League, meant the final decay of the security system of 1919. Poincaré's misgivings found an echo in the widely held suspicions of German motives—excited again by Stresemann's imprudent speech to the German colony at Geneva (which Poincaré had taken opportunity to criticize repeatedly)—and in the skepticism of the major Parisian dailies.[18]

As the Thoiry scheme lost its attractiveness, Briand came under attack, even from his associates at the Quai d'Orsay. As early as 22 October, Hoesch reported that the French thought the bargain unfavorable and believed that as the price for evacuation, Germany ought to be required to recognize the status quo on her eastern border or to renounce explicitly any and all intention of union with Austria. Berlin, of course, rejected such suggestions out of hand—but Stresemann understood that they meant the French were retreating from their willingness to make a deal. On 10 November Hoesch reported that Briand had told him that the technical obstacles had brought the Thoiry scheme to an "unavoidable standstill."[19]

The Reichstag parties, which had followed Stresemann's cue and shown cautious optimism, now began to scold. Josef Wirth, a member of the Center party and a former chancellor, demanded that the French recognize the "sacrifices" Germany had made—joining the League, conversing at Thoiry, disarming beyond prescribed limits—and respond with concessions of their own. The moderate Nationalists (like Hoetzsch and Cuno Westarp) called the Thoiry conversation a pipedream. The radical Nationalists, who knew that a success for Stresemann was a success for the republic, gleefully dubbed his policy "a policy of illusion." Stresemann reacted mildly. There was as little room for overweening optimism, he said, as for pessimism. "A comprehensive solution" involved various powers and was therefore inevitably complex and drawn-out.[20] Stresemann's words touched on a fundamental truth. The Thoiry episode had confirmed his belief that the Germans, though obliged to deal primarily with the French in resolving their postwar problems, could not ignore Britain and the United States, much less take action against them in some kind of Franco-German entente. It had demonstrated as well that as long as reparations and allied war debts remained unsettled, the Germans would be hampered in using economic means to promote political ends. Stresemann was expressing more than official optimism when he assured an audience in Hamburg that if the meeting at Thoiry had done no more than set these issues into motion, it had not been in vain.[21]

The German government accepted the Thoiry impasse and did not expect that the Rhineland would be on the agenda when the statesmen met at Geneva in December. The Germans did not want to broach the subject themselves for fear of jeopardizing the negotiations about military control. At issue here was both the future of the Inter-Allied Military Control Commission and the scope and nature of the League's powers to investigate infractions of disarmament in Germany. The Control Commission, Briand had told Stresemann at Thoiry, was to be abolished as soon as the remaining disarmament questions had been cleared up. But these questions, the subject of negotiations in Paris, had resisted resolution. Similarly, no final decision had been taken on the plan, evolved in 1924–25, by which the League would assume the functions of the Control Commission. The delay was deliberate, the result of a promise of the Western statesmen at Locarno to defer a decision until Germany was a member of the council. Now, at the end of 1926, the powers were agreed that the time had come to settle both these issues. This offered Stresemann, under pressure from the military (and from Hindenburg), the prospect of getting rid of the commission and limiting the League's competence as successor to the commission.[22]

When Stresemann and Briand met at Geneva, the evacuation of the Rhineland was discussed in greater detail than the Germans had anticipated. Briand assured Stresemann privately that the Thoiry arrangements were proceeding satisfactorily. Once the debt agreement was ratified—in January 1927, he presumed—the financial markets would open to the scheme. Briand then introduced a new aspect into the discussion: the French public was concerned less with the financial side of the bargain than with national security. At the moment the Rhineland was demilitarized and unfortified, and secured by the presence of Allied troops. What security would France have if these troops were withdrawn? She needed some sort of monitor in the Rhineland—even if only "in token form," he added deprecatingly. At a conference of the Locarnites on 6 December, Briand expanded on this delicate allusion, putting the matter squarely into the context of military control. The Control Commission would disappear shortly and the authority to investigate disarmament violations would pass to the League, but according to the peace terms this authority did not extend to the demilitarized zone. Therefore, some unobtrusive, "possibly invisible" agency would have to be erected in that area, to be charged with ascertaining and reporting infractions to the council. The French public, alarmed by recent revelations of secret German rearmament, would then become more amenable to evacuation. Chamberlain seemed to favor this proposal, remarking that the scheme had no legal foundation but might be interpreted as an extension of the Locarno pact. An impartial agency would watch not only the Germans but also the French and the Belgians. He stressed that of course Stresemann was entitled to concessions in return for his agreement—concessions he had defined to Stresemann the day before as possibly the evacuation of the second zone of the Rhineland and abbreviated occupation of the third. This, he had declared, was surely a good price for "allowing a few gentlemen to kick their heels in the Rhineland."[23]

Briand's proposal revived in another shape the idea of a permanent organ of inspection, which had so dismayed the Germans two years earlier, when it had been recommended by a League committee.[24] Now, once again, the link between French security and an occupied Rhineland—suggested in France's reluctance to evacuate the Cologne zone in 1925—became explicit. No less explicit was that Chamberlain (and Vandervelde, for that matter) acknowledged this link.

Stresemann raised two objections to Briand's proposal. The scheme would cheapen the Locarno agreements, for it would seem that these solemn pledges were not enough. The consequent loss of good faith among the powers would nullify any security France might gain. Second, the proposed agency would be a sinecure. Ultimately it would serve only the purposes of those who mocked Locarno. Schubert, too, ridiculed the scheme. He cited the demilitarization of the Rhineland, the Dawes scheme, and the international guarantees of Locarno to Chamberlain to demonstrate that France was fully secure. Stresemann showed no willingness to accept, suspecting, as he reported to Berlin, that the two statesmen had spoken of evacuation primarily in an attempt to gain "further concessions" on the issue of military control. Overt indifference to the topic was therefore politic. He was confident that opinion in France was turning against continued occupation, and that the question was best postponed till the next meeting of the council in March 1927.[25]

Stresemann was satisfied with the results of the conference. The three ministers agreed that the Control Commission would be withdrawn by 31 January 1927 and that the remaining points of contention—fortifications on the eastern frontier and the manufacture and export of war material—should be negotiated between Germany and the Conference of Ambassadors. If there was no agreement by the end of January, these matters should be referred to the council. The Control Commission was not to be replaced by a standing control agency of the League, as the French had wanted, nor would the Rhineland be treated differently from Germany proper. The council's right to inaugurate investigations under authority of article 213 was not challenged, but the council accepted the German contention that the investigations should be limited to ad hoc instances.[26] In the results of these discussions Stresemann saw a vindication of the strategy he had chosen. The way was now clear for dealing with problems "that may far surpass in significance those now settled," he told audiences at home; 1927 would be "the year of evacuation."[27]

It was to be almost two years before negotiations on the evacuation of the Rhineland began. The French public—and the French government—was not ready for such an act of reconciliation. After the settlement of military control, Briand had encountered much hostility at home. At Poincaré's prodding, the cabinet censured him for going beyond his instructions. The nationalist press accused him of capitulating to Stresemann. As Stresemann conceded privately, Briand's political difficulties were caused mainly "by our perhaps rather excessive urgency in the discussion of evacuation."[28] Now that the French no longer supervised German disarmament ("the first and advanced line of their defences against the enemy," in the words of the British ambassador in Paris), evacuation became a loaded issue. Opponents claimed that France would lay herself open to German attack, and the influential military cited the lack of fortifications on France's eastern borders and the imminent reduction in conscripts' tour of duty as proof of France's vulnerability. Evacuation would also imperil France's allies in eastern Europe, for as long as foreign troops garrisoned the Rhineland, the Germans were unlikely to try revising their eastern borders by force. But security was not the only issue. As Thoiry had shown, evacuation was also a bargaining point. Now that Poincaré had stabilized the currency, France no longer needed to make a deal. In any case, she was not prepared to bargain with a German cabinet that even then was negotiating a new coalition with the Nationalists. To regain his position, Briand distanced himself from the discussion at Thoiry, and on 19 January, before the chamber's Foreign Affairs Committee, he implicitly withdrew his support from evacuation.[29]

This placed Stresemann in difficulties of his own. Briand had given him to understand—or Stresemann had chosen to interpret Briand's remarks to the effect—that French public opinion would permit an agreement on evacuation before the year's end. Stresemann had released this information to the press, and the press had begun a campaign for early evacuation. Stresemann had also used the prospect of early evacuation to win over the Nationalists in the negotiations for a new cabinet. His colleagues in the cabinet were pressing for evacuation—or at least for concrete concessions "to compensate for the inevitable disappointment over the delay." Now Briand retracted what had seemed a solid commitment.[30]

When Stresemann met with Briand and Chamberlain during the session of the council in March 1927, he went to considerable pains to resolve the matter. As chairman of that particular session, he exercised much skill and finesse, steering delicate issues safely through the council, once or twice reversing his own position in the interest of harmony. Speaking to Briand in private, he made a strong plea for evacuation. The German public demanded it; no one could understand "why the peace between France and Germany had to be upheld by bayonets." All thought further occupation "incompatible with the spirit of Locarno." He himself would try to postpone a "formal" request for a while, but sooner or later he would have to act. Stresemann then seized upon Briand's own speeches: had not Briand cited the advantages that Locarno had brought to France? Germany could not help wondering why there had been no change.

Briand, "tired and listless," also talked of public opinion. The
concessions he had made in December had undermined his position, and there was nothing he could do about evacuation at the
moment. He had told his countrymen that article 431 of the
peace treaty, which provided for early evacuation should Germany fulfill her treaty obligations ahead of schedule, gave Germany a legal case for evacuation, but he hinted that not
everyone was convinced that the article was already applicable.
He only hoped that as the nations drew closer, changes would be
easier. Briand promised that he would make a special effort to
have the occupation army reduced substantially as compensation for the delay in evacuation.[31]

Stresemann found little support from Chamberlain. In
January, at the height of the German press campaign, Chamberlain had instructed his ambassador in Berlin to reprove
Stresemann for the Germans' "lack of conciliation." The Germans should not regard Locarno as simply an "opportunity to
exact concessions" from the Western powers. Now Chamberlain
admitted to a "bad conscience" about the strength of the army of
occupation and promised to use his influence with Briand to
have the forces reduced. He protested that his government was
unwilling to withdraw British troops unilaterally, since the
British would lose all influence in the matter of total evacuation
and all power to press the French into joint action. Now that the
Thoiry scheme had aborted, evacuation might be possible if
Germany would make a concession—"nothing but a gesture"—
toward the French,· such as the agency they had discussed in
December.[32]

At the council sessions in June and September, the three
foreign ministers collaborated on international affairs, and they
supported one another on matters before the council.[33] But
neither Briand nor Chamberlain gave Stresemann more than
general assurances of their interest in evacuation. In fact,
Briand expressly asked Stresemann not to raise the subject while
France was preparing for parliamentary elections: "no moment
could be worse for opening such a discussion."[34] All Stresemann
could achieve was a reduction of the occupation armies (to
60,000), granted on the eve of the assembly in September, and
only after he had conceded yet further disarmament inspections
by Western military experts.[35]

These various rebuffs confirmed what Hoesch had been saying since January: evacuation was not practical politics at this point.[36] The close political community Stresemann sought with the Western powers had not yet matured. Neither Locarno nor Germany's entry into the League had relieved the French of fear of their neighbor, and Germany's expectations, loudly proclaimed, had not endeared her to the French either. The British, indignant over what they deemed German rapaciousness, were inclined to let France set the tone of relations with Germany. Stresemann realized that Germany must persist—gently. At Geneva he deferred to the French and compromised on issues before the council; and he worked steadily to improve his relations with Chamberlain. While he voiced his growing frustration in the "secret conclaves" of the Locarnites, adducing the chorus of critics at home, he refrained from making a formal claim. And among his colleagues in the government he counseled against a public campaign that would embarrass the West.[37]

In speaking to German audiences, Stresemann tempered expressions of disappointment with expressions of hope. In March, after his return from Geneva, he had conceded that Germany had come no closer to settling the questions that interested her. Evacuation, however, was the "natural consequence" of the policy inaugurated at Locarno, and his conversations at Geneva had shown that the Western statesmen shared this belief. Over the summer, after the Germans had satisfied the last of the contested disarmament demands, Stresemann came to contend that Germany could request evacuation officially under article 431. She had met her treaty obligations; the Western powers should now meet theirs.[38] In December, Stresemann advised the cabinet that the "decisive step" on evacuation might come the following September. At Geneva, Briand had informed him of a "complete change" in the political climate in France. The coming elections, Briand had predicted, would bring him a favorable majority, and he would then try to settle at one stroke all remaining differences between France and Germany.[39]

Before the two statesmen met again at Geneva in March 1928, each had been obliged to take a public stand, and their positions had been clarified. During the election campaign in France, Joseph Paul-Boncour, the chairman of the Foreign Affairs

Committee in the chamber and a frequent delegate to the League, had told journalists that France required further security and that the government ought to consider the international control of the Rhineland.[40] The reaction in Germany was predictable. The political parties, also preparing for an election, seized upon this pretext to debate the government's foreign policy. Stresemann spoke to the Reichstag on 30 January and again on 1 February. He met the clamor by expressing Germany's impatience about the delay in evacuation. Germany was legally entitled to evacuation; evacuation was a logical consequence of the Locarno agreements; the delay was an "insurmountable obstacle" to Franco-German reconciliation. At the same time, Stresemann intimated that his government might be willing to oblige the French in matters of compensation and security. Germany would entertain discussions of a financial settlement (à la Thoiry) and even of some kind of surveillance after evacuation.[41] But he stressed that Germany would not purchase evacuation for a price beyond the stipulations of Versailles—clearly an allusion to the French notion of permanent inspection.[42] On 2 February Briand responded in the French Senate. He spoke in the aftermath of Poincaré's general reappraisal of the situation and, it appears, with Poincaré's approval. The Locarno pact, he remarked pointedly, was no cornucopia of favors for Germany, and it did not supersede other postwar treaties. The Western powers occupied the Rhineland to guarantee the payment of reparations. France was prepared to examine the possibility of a financial settlement. Stresemann, he urged, should come up with some proposals.[43]

Stresemann's two speeches had voiced disappointment, stressed expectations, and invited some sort of bargain. Briand's reply, as Hoesch saw it, had been an attempt to appease his domestic critics without alienating the Germans. He made clear that he had not been converted to Stresemann's views, and in this, Hoesch said, he was supported by the French public. But more important, Briand, speaking in an official capacity, had publicly suggested the possibility of negotiating the evacuation of the Rhineland. Hoesch commented that the auguries were much more favorable than after the meeting at Thoiry.[44] He admitted, however, that Briand's proposal seemed "rather obscure," and he reported with some disquiet Berthelot's observation (repeated in March to a skeptical Schubert) that the Thoiry scheme was not feasible, and that some kind of overall settlement involving reparations, interallied debts, and evacuation might offer a solution. For this, Berthelot saw no chance of progress before the spring or summer of the following year, certainly not before the inauguration of the next American president in March 1929.[45]

After the elections, when the Foreign Ministry began to plan an offensive for the fall, circumstances had changed again. The Reichstag elections in May, the first since Locarno, had strengthened Stresemann's hand. The Nationalists had lost representation, and the Socialists had gained. For the first time since 1923, the cabinet included Socialists, who shared power with members of the Democratic, Center, and People's parties. The new Socialist chancellor, Hermann Müller, dedicated his government to achieving prompt evacuation, restoring the Saar to Germany, and preparing a new reparations agreement.[46] In France the parties of the Right had come into power and Briand's influence had declined. Conversations with Poincaré and Briand convinced Hoesch that the French government could not withdraw its forces from the Rhineland at this time even if it wanted to. Hoesch urged the Foreign Ministry not to press for evacuation, especially for evacuation without compensation. France would agree to evacuation only in return for a definitive settlement of reparations. Ultimately this interest would oblige the French government to take the initiative, and it was simple self-interest for the German government to bide its time.[47]

Hoesch's counsels did not prevail. Since the previous fall, Stresemann had been insisting that Germany could expect substantial progress once the German and French elections were over. The results of the Reichstag election, which could be construed as a public endorsement of the Locarno-League policy, made such progress all the more important.[48] If the Western powers could not be moved by Stresemann's Geneva diplomacy—and their protests against Müller's policy declaration appeared to confirm this—a more formal initiative was in order.[49] This initiative was devised by Schubert, who had assumed many of Stresemann's duties because Stresemann was ill and away from Berlin. Schubert did not dispute Hoesch's view that the Dawes plan must be revised. He believed, however, that revision would be slow in coming and should not be linked to evacuation. Evacuation was urgent. If the policy of accommodation was to be taken seriously, it must show results. Schubert proposed that the German government ask the occupying powers bluntly whether they were still interested in pursuing the Locarno policy, whether they intended to work together with Germany on all questions of European politics. If so, they should be asked whether they were prepared to discuss concrete plans for evacuation, since evacuation was not to be the final result of the Locarno policy but only a necessary stage in its development. Schubert urged that the government should not wait until the assembly in September but should take diplomatic steps immediately.[50] Stresemann authorized Schubert to act. On 28 July, Schubert instructed the ambassadors in London, Paris, and Rome, and the minister in Brussels to announce that in September Stresemann intended to open discussions on the total evacuation of the Rhineland.[51] It was a first small step away from Stresemann's politics of accommodation.

On 22 August Schubert explained this tactic to the cabinet. The government could no longer acquiesce in the dilatoriness of Briand and Chamberlain without creating the impression that it accepted the existing situation without protest. It would have to secure a clear expression of intent from the occupying powers, which it could use in public. The government would argue that evacuation was indispensable to a final détente between France and Germany, that this was not a special favor to Germany but a simple matter of prudent politics. If the tactic failed and the Western statesmen refused to budge, the government might consider making a legal claim under article 431 or appealing to the arbitration tribunals established under the Locarno pact. If the revision of the Dawes plan should be mentioned in this connection, the Germans would consent to exploratory talks, but they would insist that the problem of reparations be kept separate from the issue of evacuation.[52]

At Geneva the Germans had difficulty making contact. Chancellor Müller, who led the delegation because Stresemann was too ill, found Briand prepared to listen but not prepared to accept their conversations as binding. When Müller put Germany's case for evacuation, Briand edged away, saying that the subject affected several powers and could not be negotiated by France and Germany alone. For the French government, he added, occupation was collateral for debts owed and could be lifted only if France were "offered something" in return. Müller promptly announced his willingness to discuss reparations, but in the same breath he rejected the attempt to link reparations with evacuation. To Lord Cushendun, who substituted for the ailing Chamberlain, Müller presented the same arguments, only to find the British delegate sympathetic to the French position and as eager as Briand to evade serious discussion.[53]

The meetings with Briand and Cushendun on 11 and 13 September, to which the Belgian, Italian, and Japanese representatives had been invited, became serious nonetheless. They had been preceded by a rather heated exchange between Müller and Briand in the assembly. The one had enjoined the powers to remove the barriers which had obstructed European international relations since the war; the other announced that the Germans' slowness to meet the obligations of the settlement did not entitle them to lecture to others.[54] Now, face to face, Müller argued for unconditional evacuation. He cited article 431 and Allied assurances of 1919; he spoke of Locarno and peaceful conciliation, pointing out that evacuation was politics, not favoritism. It was the familiar German brief, now embroidered with a hint of blackmail—the dire consequences that might befall not only Franco-German relations but also the conciliatory republican government in Germany.

Briand, seconded by Cushendun and Paul Hymans (the Belgian foreign minister), argued that evacuation and financial compensation had been linked ever since Thoiry. Then as now, the French wanted to settle the financial question, for the Dawes plan left them uncertain as to whether they should ever be able to free themselves of the financial burdens imposed by the war. He suggested that the powers might delegate experts to open negotiations on reparations, which might run parallel to negotiations on evacuation. If the German government wanted to make proposals for the discussion of reparations, the French government was willing to listen. Briand then reverted to a point he had raised with Stresemann in December 1926: that the Germans agree to a "commission of conciliation and verification" to deal with violations in the demilitarized zone after evacuation had been completed. He promised that the second zone would be evacuated the moment the Germans agreed to this commission.[55]

Before meeting Briand again, Müller was in touch with Berlin. His conversations had succeeded in their intent, he reported, and the evacuation of the Rhineland was on the agenda to stay. He had also found the powers prepared to discuss a final settlement of reparations. He asked that the cabinet endorse the line he proposed to take: that he insist upon prompt and unconditional evacuation of the second zone and offer no compensation; that he insist upon assurance of an international conference to discuss reparations, but that these discussions be kept separate from evacuation; that, if necessary, he concede a commission of conciliation to come into power after the Rhineland had been evacuated and to be dissolved no later than 1935.[56] The cabinet met to discuss Müller's report on 15 September. In general, the ministers were satisfied. However, they were taken with the prospect of reparations negotiations, and this prompted them to shift emphasis and depart from established policy. They instructed the delegation in Geneva to give priority to a settlement of reparations. It should not permit the discussion for such a settlement to break off and therefore should not be unduly intransigent in negotiating the evacuation and Briand's commission.[57]

When the statesmen reconvened on the sixteenth, Müller presented his position. Briand replied that his government had endorsed official negotiations on early evacuation in order to settle the financial differences that still clouded relations with Germany. He considered this a major step forward, one which even Stresemann had not managed to achieve. Germany's position on the conciliation commission puzzled him, he said; surely, to bypass the League's cumbersome investigation procedures was in the interest of both parties, and therefore it made no sense to limit the life of the commission. In any case, he concluded confidently, "a satisfactory solution" would come once negotiations got under way.[58]

The communiqué which announced this ambiguous consensus was correspondingly vague: a committee of financial experts would be appointed to discuss a definitive settlement of reparations; negotiations would begin on Germany's demand for early evacuation; a conciliation commission had been accepted in principle.[59] Still, the communiqué was a milestone: years of discussion culminated here; from this point future negotiations took their departure. The Germans were assured that the occupation would be negotiated; the French were assured that their financial difficulties would be settled. The communiqué made no mention of partial evacuation or partial financial settlements, or of the unresolved differences over the conciliation commission.

Stresemann, to whom Müller reported in Baden-Baden on 17 September, was elated: he had not expected so much. In the cabinet, in the Foreign Affairs Committee, and among the state premiers there was some disappointment at the lack of immediate practical results, but in general these groups, too, were pleased. All were satisfied that Germany, as Müller observed, had succeeded in keeping reparations and evacuation distinct and independent of one another. If the reparations talks failed to reach an acceptable conclusion, or if they encountered unexpected obstacles, the negotiations on evacuation would not be affected.[60] The French, too, considered the discussions an achievement. Briand was quoted in the *Frankfurter Zeitung* as saying that he expected reparations to be settled in a few weeks or months, and that then evacuation could begin. Indeed, Hoesch was to report in November that for the French the September conversations represented a tacit agreement that evacuation was linked to a satisfactory financial solution.[61]

These differences in interpretation surfaced in the difficulties which arose over the implementation of the September accord. The Germans had assumed all along that the conference of experts would explore Germany's capacity to pay and would lower the annuities set by the Dawes plan. From this assumption they inferred that the experts appointed by the respective governments would be of independent judgment. The French argued that the smooth functioning of the Dawes arrangements amply demonstrated Germany's capacity to pay. They wanted a conference to set up new patterns of payment, bound this time to the interallied debts and the indemnities resulting from the war, and they thought the experts should be appointed by the reparations commission. The British, Belgians, and Italians concurred.[62]

In Germany the hopes which had sprung up after the Geneva discussions were fading. It now appeared that the Germans would have to pay for what they deemed their legal and moral right. This disappointment contributed to an ominous change in domestic politics. The election in May, which had strengthened the Left, had brought grief to the parties of the middle and the Right. Their electoral setbacks had intensified the parties' internal strife, which over the months came to be resolved by a shift toward the Right, away from cooperation with the republic. The Nationalists, demoralized after losing about one-third of their parliamentary seats, became receptive to arguments attributing their losses to their repeated collaboration with the republican government. At the party congress in October the radical wing, under Alfred Hugenberg, triumphed over the moderates, and the party swung back to uncompromising opposition to the "Weimar system." Changes in the Center party, a firm supporter of Stresemann's policy from the beginning, were of even greater consequence. Long divided over its political orientation, the party had provoked further controversy by entering Müller's coalition in June, and when its chairman, Wilhelm Marx, resigned in October, the party composed its differences by electing a clergyman, prelate Ludwig Kaas, as his successor. Under Kaas, the party adopted a conservative and generally more authoritarian outlook. These parties now joined the ranks of those who found fault with the government and its foreign policy.[63]

Stresemann himself began to express doubts publicly about a strategy that had failed to produce results. When he returned to Berlin early in November, the "comprehensive solution" seemed more distant than at Thoiry in September 1926. The Western powers clearly wanted to predetermine the outcome of the conference and to leave only technical details to the experts. There had been no further mention of the promised negotiations about the Rhineland. Frustrated and upset, not least of all at the criticism in the press, Stresemann struck a strident note before the Reichstag. The Rhineland, he reminded the deputies, was to be evacuated unconditionally; Germany contemplated no financial compensation and no conciliation commission beyond 1935. He defended his foreign policy as correct and realistic, and played up to public resentment by suggesting that the Western powers were not acting in good faith. The Reichstag, however, was not entirely assuaged. The Nationalists berated Stresemann for the collapse of the Locarno policy, and the Center reproached him for the "undeniable failure" of that policy. The Nazis introduced a motion of no confidence. The motion did not pass, but there was a significant number of abstentions.[64]

Stresemann's unrequited optimism now backfired. On the eve of the December session of the council, the party leaders received him coldly, and he left Berlin to the snide comments of the right-wing press and the skepticism of the liberal papers.[65] At Lugano (where the session was held in consideration of Stresemann's health), he was in ill humor: at the council table he ostentatiously lost his temper with the Polish foreign minister over minority questions—an unprecedented scene. His meetings with Briand and Chamberlain were exceptionally disharmonious. He reproached them bitterly for the collapse of their Locarno collaboration. He dwelt on the fierceness of his domestic opposition: even his backers in the Center and Socialist parties had deserted him. How could he persuade anyone of the validity of his policy if 60,000 Allied troops still garrisoned German soil? If international accommodation should fail, Briand and Chamberlain would have only themselves to blame. Briand and Chamberlain tried to minimize the remaining differences and to comfort Stresemann with assurances that evacuation was imminent. For all their apparent sympathy, however, both insisted on linking evacuation to compensation. Once the experts had convened, the diplomats could open talks on evacuation and on the projected conciliation commission. Evacuation would begin the moment a settlement had been reached on the basis of the experts' report and the diplomats had agreed on the commission.[66]

By the time Stresemann met with the Foreign Affairs Committee on 25 January 1929, a compromise favorable to the Germans had been worked out regarding the committee of experts, but there was no progress whatever on evacuation. Hoetzsch, of the Nationalists, asserted that Stresemann had not made good on his promises of the previous year and that he had forfeited an opportunity to invoke Germany's legal claim. Freytagh-Loringhoven, a radical Nationalist, accused Stresemann of persisting in a fruitless policy: Germany would get results only by threatening to leave the League. Stöcker of the Communists joined in the denunciation: to presume that evacuation would precede a reparations settlement was self-delusion. The Socialist Breitscheid came to Stresemann's defense, but he could only reiterate his belief in the wisdom of established policy. Everyone knew only too well that the achievements of 1928 were small.[67]

This stormy meeting was a fitting introduction to the year 1929. Foreign and domestic affairs were tense. The Locarnites were at odds. Briand seemed to back down from his assurances at Lugano. He told Hoesch that the reparations talks would have to be well under way before the governments could even consider the ways and means of evacuation. Chamberlain was aloof and declined to press Briand.[68] Ill and ill-tempered, Stresemann complained of British and French intransigence to his old friend D'Abernon. "Unless a miracle happens," he wrote, it would be too late to return to the spirit of Locarno. By May he had given up pressing for evacuation and resigned himself to waiting for the experts' report.[69]

In Paris, meanwhile, the deliberations of the experts—the Young committee made up of two delegates from each country involved in reparations plus two from the United States—struggled to find an acceptable solution. From the start it was clear that the independence of the experts was a fiction and that the Western powers had not given up their claim to damages and debts. Their representatives now proposed that Germany pay thirty-seven annuities beginning at 1.8 billion marks and rising progressively to 2.4 billion, and another twenty-one annuities at 1.7 billion each. The Germans offered thirty-seven annuities at 1.65 billion each on the condition that the transfers continue to be protected and that the Allies make certain political concessions. This proposal the committee would not entertain.[70]

Germany could not afford to withdraw from the negotiations. By spring of 1929, a new settlement of reparations had become indispensable to a deteriorating German economy. Failure to secure such a settlement would oblige Germany to retain the Dawes plan, whose high annuities put a strain on the national budget; failure would also cut off the flow of foreign loans to Germany. Statistics showed that since 1924 Germany had experienced a steady increase in investment and production, in national income and consumption, but what they did not show was that the economy had not had enough time to consolidate and that the prosperity was induced chiefly by foreign credits. When the volume of foreign credits diminished in the summer of 1928, the market narrowed, industry began to cut back investment and production, and workers were put on lower wages or laid off altogether. This recession revived antagonisms between labor and management (most dramatically in a major dispute in the steel industry in western Germany in the fall of 1928), and it appeared that management had deliberately intensified the crisis in order to weaken trade unionism and roll back the restrictions imposed on industry in 1918–19. The government looked for ways to stabilize the economy, but its options were few and its resources limited. In January 1929 the government reached the brink of bankruptcy, and only a last-minute loan from a German banking consortium allowed it to meet its obligations. The government was also beset by political troubles. In February and March, Müller's coalition—and with it Stresemann's hopes for a settlement with the Western powers—threatened to collapse. A dispute over the reorganization of the cabinet, during which the Center party went so far as to recall its ministers, was finally patched up in April. In the first week of May, the Communists staged demonstrations in Berlin, which led to bloody battles with the police. All these were symptoms of general dissatisfaction. Clearly the government could not withstand the economic, social, and political repercussions of withdrawing from the Young committee. On 21 June it accepted the committee's compromise plan as a basis for discussion.[71]

Shortly beforehand, at a session of the League council in Madrid, Briand and Stresemann had discussed the political consequences of the Young report. The French cabinet, Briand said, had accepted his proposal that a major conference should convene to settle not only reparations but also the other outstanding issues between France and Germany. The conference would make good what Thoiry had failed to do. The time had come, he emphasized repeatedly, to work energetically for "the general liquidation of the war" and to inaugurate an era of peace. But neither then nor at Paris, where Stresemann met later with Poincaré and several of his ministers, was there any indication that evacuation would be a binding consequence of a reparations settlement.[72]

The conference on reparations was scheduled to meet at The Hague the first week in August. The German delegation arrived with a firm mandate: liquidation of the war meant evacuation of the Rhineland and restoration of the Saar, and there was to be no conciliation commission, or at least none beyond 1935.[73] In the Reichstag, where foreign policy once again dominated the discussion and the Right was agitating vigorously against the Young report (and against Müller's coalition), Stresemann had implied that he would sooner see the negotiations fail and settle for the Dawes plan with all its imperfections than forgo the political settlement. He assured the cabinet that the delegation would not accept the Young settlement until there was "full clarity about the political questions." Evacuation was practically certain, he said: Briand had "as much as agreed" to it, and there could be no doubt about Belgium and Britain, where Labour had replaced the Conservative government in June and appeared to abandon Chamberlain's policy.[74]

At The Hague the delegations decided to divide their labors between a financial and a political committee. Before long, both ran into trouble. The financial committee quarrelled over the Young scheme: thirty-seven annuities rising from 1.7 to 2.4 billion marks and subsequently twenty-two annuities of 1.6 to 1.7 billion, to derive from Germany's railway and tax receipts and to be disbursed by a Bank of International Settlements according to a set scheme of distribution. Philip Snowden, chancellor of the exchequer in the new Labour government, claimed that Britain had been shortchanged. Under the agreement of 1920, which regulated the distribution of the reparations annuities, the British Empire had received 23 percent; now it was to receive only 20.5 percent of a considerably smaller sum. Furthermore, most of the money for the British was to come from that part of the annuities which the German government could withhold in case of financial difficulties. Snowden tried to have the scheme altered, only to find that the other creditors opposed him. The committee deadlocked and fell to bickering. Some three weeks later, on 27 August, a compromise emerged: that part of the annuities which had to be paid unconditionally was to be increased, and Britain was to receive a larger share of it. The compromise was subject to German consent.

The Germans were willing to give their consent only after the political committee had reached agreement. It too was at an impasse, for the German position that evacuation had to be guaranteed before Germany would accept the reparations scheme flatly contradicted the French position that evacuation could only follow Germany's firm guarantees to execute the plan. Stresemann had also requested a general discussion on the Saar, but Briand—and Arthur Henderson, the new British foreign secretary—wanted to relegate this subject to discussions between the French and the Germans. The committee had suspended its sessions on 12 August. In informal discussions among the chief delegates, Stresemann and Briand clashed, and Stresemann turned to Henderson. Henderson represented a change from Chamberlain's pro-French orientation. Upon coming into office he had made it clear that he did not want to estrange France, but he would try to promote conciliation with Germany by early evacuation. On the thirteenth he assured Stresemann that the British would begin to withdraw their troops in September regardless of what the French did. At the same time, Hymans announced Belgium's decision to withdraw by the end of the year.[75]

It took another week and several wearisome meetings before Briand gave Stresemann similar assurance. If Germany ratified the Young plan, French troops would leave the Rhineland within a year, by 30 September 1930. Stresemann refused to accept this date. He sent Briand a letter, the first (and the last) in their association, describing the growing opposition in Germany to the new reparations plan and emphasizing the "devastating" impression such a year's delay would make on the Germans. Without early evacuation, he wrote, he could not sign the Young plan, nor could he continue the policy to which they were both committed, the reconciliation between Germany and France. For Briand, it was a familiar dilemma. If Germany regained her economic and territorial sovereignty, she would be that much closer to restoring her power in Europe. If Germany were denied her economic and territorial sovereignty, and if the Hague Conference consequently collapsed, Weimar democracy would suffer a serious injury. Ten days later, Briand and Stresemann compromised on the date of evacuation.[76]

On the morning of 29 August, the powers reached an agreement on evacuation; the evening of the same day brought an agreement on reparations. On the thirtieth, the Rhineland accord was incorporated into letters from the three occupying powers to Stresemann. The British and the Belgians promised to withdraw within three months, the French after the Young plan had been ratified (but no later than 30 June 1930). The conciliation commission was given up in favor of the tribunals of Locarno, which were empowered to supervise the demilitarized status.[77] Briand promised that negotiations on the Saar would begin shortly in Paris. On 31 August, a final protocol set forth the new financial arrangements, and the delegates left The Hague. Within four days, Stresemann had received the approval of the cabinet.[78]

Stresemann had achieved his goal—though he was not to live to see its execution. The Rhineland was evacuated some four and one-half years ahead of schedule. The British and Belgians had withdrawn by mid-December. French troops were transferred from the second to the third zone, as was the Inter-Allied Rhineland High Commission. The Young plan went into effect on 17 May 1930. On 30 June, the last French soldier left the Rhineland. Germany now had more freedom of movement than at any time since the war. It was left to Stresemann's successors to put this new freedom to use.

In 1919, when the peacemakers redrew the map of Europe, millions of Germans had come under alien rule. Most of them were scattered through western Poland—in Posnania, Pomerelia (the "Polish Corridor"), and Upper Silesia—an area where Germans and Slavs had long intermingled. The Germans were different not only in language and culture (and usually in religion); but they were different also in being overwhelmingly urban, prominent in business and the professions, or, as in Upper Silesia, in control of the coal and iron industries they had built up before the war. A small though influential number lived on great estates, raising cash crops which they had sold in western Germany before the border went up. Smaller and more compact German settlements were in Danzig and Memel, two Baltic seaports situated on either side of East Prussia. Danzig was an independent city-state in close treaty relations with Poland; Memel, originally taken over by the Allies, had become part of Lithuania in 1923. The exact number of the German minorities cannot be ascertained; we have no reliable statistics. Of the estimated 3.5 million Germans in eastern Europe in 1920, when the peace treaty came into effect, perhaps about a third had emigrated (or been expelled) by the time Germany joined the League.[1]

The peacemakers had not left the fate of these German minorities—or of other national minorities—to the discretion of the "minority states" (as they were called). History had taught them that disaffected minorities could be disruptive, and they had concluded that the minorities would have to be assured protection if the postwar order were to endure. They had therefore compelled the new states to accept certain obligations, embodied in formal "minority treaties." These treaties contained elaborate provisions for equality "in law and in fact," laying particular emphasis on the minorities' right to use their own languages as they wished, especially in the schools, the press, and in legal and commercial transactions. The treaties were guaranteed by the League. The Germans in Danzig, Memel, and Upper Silesia were covered by special conventions, which adopted many of the provisions of the minority treaties.[2]

The new states were not always punctilious in observing their treaty obligations. They could not but resent them as infringements on their sovereignty (especially as they had not been imposed equally on all states with minority populations). Nor could they readily forget the past, when their own populations had been minorities and subject to harassment. Perhaps most important, as a British diplomat remarked of the Poles, these new states—like the old—were wont to regard minorities "as an unstable and potentially dangerous element," particularly in the border regions, and wished to reduce their number and influence.[3] The German minorities, for their part, promptly began a litany of complaint. In Poland, they accused the government of restricting the use of their mother tongue and of depriving them of their schools and their land. In Danzig and Memel, they charged that their local autonomy was being subverted. And German minorities everywhere claimed that the ostracism and boycotts they encountered were inspired (or at least condoned) by the authorities. They were not satisfied either with the redress offered by the League. They considered the League's procedures of adjudication cumbersome, secretive, and weighted in favor of the state and against the minorities.[4]

The League regarded the protection of minorities as a political problem. Therefore it had devised procedures to minimize frictions that might arise over the ill treatment of minorities. According to these procedures, a minority (or other interested party) could initiate proceedings by setting forth its complaint in a petition to the League secretariat. The minorities section of the secretariat first determined the validity of a petition according to certain set criteria. Having found the petition valid, the secretariat would forward it to the accused state for comment. Petition and comment were then submitted to the council, which set up an ad hoc committee composed of the president and two council members—the so-called committee of three. The committee usually settled its cases by "benevolent and informal" negotiations (often conducted by members of the minorities section). If it was satisfied with the concessions or remedies offered by the offending government, the committee would close the proceedings, communicating the outcome summarily to the council. Article 12 of the minority treaties gave members of the council the authority to place before the council "any infraction, or danger of infraction" of the minorities' rights. If a member invoked the article, the council was obliged to take immediate action. The article was invoked only once (by Germany in 1929). All knew that, in a council where at least one seat was always occupied by a minority state and where decisions had to be unanimous, an eventual decision would be bland to the point of meaninglessness.[5]

The protection that Germany could extend to her minorities abroad was one of Stresemann's (and the government's) major arguments for joining the League. It numbered among the reasons the cabinet adduced for its interest in membership in September 1924 and pervaded public debate until the very eve of entry two years later. At the core of the argument was the simple assertion that in the League Germany would be the champion of minorities, especially of course of German minorities. Germany would be the minorities' "refuge" and their "attorney," Stresemann claimed; she would "represent" their interests and "defend their welfare." Stresemann went so far as to imply that the minorities were pleading with Germany to join the League.[6]

Stresemann's insistence sprang from his awareness of popular interest in the fate of German minorities—in the "minorities problem" as it came to be called. Stresemann's generation had absorbed the enthusiasm for *Auslandsdeutschtum* stirred up before the war and had witnessed the ethnic struggles in Prussia's eastern provinces, where successive German governments had tried to reduce Polish influence. After the defeat, these memories became entangled with the indignation at the loss of territory and population under the peace settlement. Various patriotic associations—the so-called *Deutschtum* organizations, which now proliferated—stoked solicitude for the "lost" brethren and directed it primarily at the minorities in eastern Europe, where the subjection of Germans to Slavic rule was deemed a perversion of the natural order of things. The solicitude turned to anger whenever it appeared that the minorities were being persecuted or tormented, whenever it seemed that they might be forced to choose between emigration and assimilation. No German could reconcile himself to the thought that these minorities might be "lost" forever, and assimilation into the majority culture was a public bugbear.[7]

From the very beginning the Weimar governments had been under pressure to do something for the "oppressed" minorities in eastern Europe.[8] Representatives of the political parties, which themselves were beleaguered by their counterparts in the ceded territories, voiced their concern privately or in debate in the Reichstag. The Deutschtum organizations never ceased importuning the government. The minorities themselves established lobbies in Germany (amalgamated in 1923 into the Ausschuss der deutschen Minderheiten im Ausland), and their leaders appeared in Berlin to take up their problems with the government directly—Kurt Graebe and Eugen Naumann from the Corridor, Otto Ulitz from Upper Silesia, Heinrich Sahm from Danzig.[9] The government had granted these appeals a sympathetic hearing. It had a lively interest in the self-conscious and well-organized minorities in the areas contiguous to Germany's eastern borders. The notion that central Europe was Germany's rightful sphere of influence was still very much alive in the official mind. In the immediate postwar years the government had no precise plans for restoring these areas; for the moment it intended to preserve in them a German presence—and thereby an irredenta. Accordingly, it was prepared to assist the minorities in their efforts to resist "polonization."[10]

But the government had been able to offer only small assistance. The new states in eastern Europe would brook no German interference into what they regarded as their domestic affairs. On occasion the German government could offer these states diplomatic or economic concessions in exchange for the curtailment of some particularly noxious measure against the minorities. Otherwise Germany could only protest in the Western capitals when the Poles evicted German settlers from their land or put pressure on the Free City of Danzig, and when the Lithuanians seized Memel in 1923. In the ceded areas, German consular officials could intervene informally with League minority administrators or high commissioners. Or the Deutsche Liga für Völkerbund could plead the minorities' case at international congresses of League of Nations societies.

The most effective form of German intervention was financial aid to the minorities, for this strengthened them where they were most vulnerable. Germans in the Corridor and Upper Silesia, in Danzig and Memel received clandestine subsidies and economic concessions—either directly or through front organizations such as the Deutsche Stiftung, which had been set up in 1920 to disburse money. In this way schools were maintained, farmers given credit, small businesses and industries saved from bankruptcy. Through the consulates in Danzig, Memel, Poznań, and Katowice, the Foreign Ministry furnished the minority associations with legal advice and with funds for their petitions to Geneva. Such petitions were encouraged, not only because they exposed the "persecution" of the minorities and led to better protection, but also because they dramatized the "senseless" territorial settlement. To the same end the government financed extensive propaganda campaigns, carried out largely by the Deutschtum organizations. The propaganda acquainted the world with the "intolerable conditions" among the minorities, reproached the minority states, and generated public pressure for change.[11]

When Germany entered the League, Stresemann implied that the government would shift from a defensive to an offensive policy on minorities. Germany would now share the League's responsibility for guarding the rights of the minorities. She would see to it that the states bound by minority treaties would henceforth "respect" the autonomy these treaties accorded the minorities. She would also try to influence the minority adjudication of the League itself.[12]

But those who had expected dramatic changes were to be disappointed. For one thing, it became apparent that Stresemann had described the new opportunities too optimistically. Over the years, the League had constructed minority procedures that balanced the just claims of minorities against the prerogatives of sovereign states, and it had a firm interest in preventing anyone from tampering with these procedures. In fact, anticipating the likely consequences of Germany's entry, the council had approved specific measures to guarantee impartial adjudication. Thus, in June 1925, it had resolved that neither representatives of a nation kin to the petitioning minority nor those of a state neighbor to the accused was eligible for a committee of three. This effectively curtailed Germany's chances of intervening in the disputes of her minorities in eastern Europe. A newcomer to the League was not likely to challenge these procedures successfully.[13]

Even apart from these practical obstacles, the Germans were at pains to walk softly. Erik Colban, a Norwegian diplomat who headed the minorities section from 1920 to 1928 and whose commitment to compromise inspired the League's procedure, persuaded the Germans to work within the system for at least a year before trying to change it. Gottfried Aschmann, the German consul in Geneva (and not one of Colban's admirers) endorsed this course of action; a year of practical experience, Aschmann commented, would facilitate Germany's efforts to reform the system later on.[14] The Foreign Ministry agreed. When it reviewed its involvement in the League's procedures in 1927 and again in 1928, it concluded that "the time for revision will come when Germany's chances to appear in the League as the successful advocate of minorities have been improved."[15] Such restraint was practiced consistently. The Germans refrained from raising minority issues on the floor of the assembly. Until 1925 the assembly's annual debate on the League's activities had customarily referred particular questions on minorities to its sixth committee (Political Questions), where they were discussed openly. While Stresemann was alive, this practice was abandoned (to be revived by his successor in 1930).[16]

In the disputes over the German minorities, the delegation moved cautiously, evaded confrontations, and insisted on no unusual concessions. The Germans were prepared to compromise when an early settlement would profit the minority directly, and they encouraged direct private negotiations between the principals, exploiting the minority states' dread of publicity. In public sessions, the Germans remained within the boundaries of League custom. In dealing with the grievances submitted by Danzigers or Memellanders, for example, the Germans were content to search the text of existing treaties for a solution—and were reproached for casuistry at home. In a case involving minority schools in Polish Upper Silesia, which occupied the League machinery for several years, Stresemann endured severe criticism for acceding to postponements and compromise solutions.[17] Even in an issue as inflammable as the expropriation of Germans in the Corridor during the Polish land reform, the Foreign Ministry refrained from public outcry and accepted a quiet settlement from the League's secretariat.[18] What aid the Germans did give the minorities was inconspicuous and inoffensive. The delegation at Geneva never failed to express Germany's interest in the principles of minority protection and in the welfare of the German minorities. The representative on the council followed all minority cases attentively—also those not concerned with German minorities, which might become precedent—and objected to any unnecessary delay or obfuscation. The Foreign Ministry continued to encourage petitions from aggrieved minority groups, and the delegation assisted the petitioners when they came to Geneva. In keeping with the rising expectations which accompanied Germany's entry into the League, the number of petitions increased dramatically.[19]

To the German government, however, the matter of minorities meant nothing quite so simple as the rectification of grievances. The government supported the minorities, as Gaus was to say, "in the interest of territorial revision."[20] Forcible revision, whether unilateral or with Soviet assistance, was out of the question (though the Germans never entirely dismissed such possibilities). Revision could be accomplished only by means of severe political and economic pressure. And whether forcible or peaceable, it was unthinkable without the agreement of the Western powers.[21] In securing such agreement, the minorities served a useful purpose. The restoration of a sizable minority which had retained its ethnic and cultural identity could be justified as a matter of self-determination; in the absence of such a minority, restoration became expansionism. Furthermore, a restive minority was a challenge to the stability of the peace settlement and of the successor states. At home and before the council, Stresemann suggested repeatedly that such unrest warranted invocation of article 19 of the covenant, by which the League could consider the revision of treaties whose consequences were a threat to the peace.[22] His actual plan was probably more complicated. Once concerted international pressure had brought territorial revision within reach, he could use article 19 as a face-saving formula to justify depriving Poland of land.[23]

For the moment, however, territorial revision was not urgent.

In December 1926 Stresemann told the cabinet that "it was not time to open the problems in the east until the western questions had been settled."[24] Germany should concentrate first on regaining her sovereignty over the Rhineland and achieving a final reparations settlement. The "Colban system," in which the Germans acquiesced at Geneva, was fully consistent with this carefully paced strategy. In the Foreign Ministry it was axiomatic that "the revision of minority obligations" was "linked inextricably with the question of the borders." The Colban system served to keep the minorities problem in the public eye and allowed the Germans to protect the minorities from absorption. At the same time, the system prevented the minorities problem from becoming merely a domestic affair of the minority states and thus preserved a diplomatically useful tension between Germany and the successor states.[25] The Germans supplemented these efforts on one level by diplomatic conversations in the Western capitals and in Geneva, in which they argued that as long as the borders remained unrevised, there would be no peace in eastern Europe.[26] On another level, they argued their case in the propaganda of the Deutschtum organizations and minority groups, especially at the Congress of European Minorities, whose annual conference at Geneva was financed in part by the Foreign Ministry.[27]

This strategy obliged the Germans to intercept any attempt to open the question of revision prematurely. The government helped the minorities maintain themselves; in return it gained control over them. It obliged them to exercise restraint in their petitions and their demands at Geneva. In 1927, for example, Schubert made it clear to the Danzig government that any great number of appeals to Geneva was undesirable and that Danzig's policy would have to be carefully coordinated with that of the Foreign Ministry.[28] The Germans were bent also on averting untimely initiatives in eastern Europe. In 1927, when Stresemann intervened in a particularly acrimonious dispute between Lithuania and Poland, he was motivated to no small extent by fear that political convulsions in eastern Europe would make the question of the eastern borders acute.[29]

A stagnant foreign policy never excites much popular enthusiasm, and by the summer of 1928 the Foreign Ministry began to experience the consequences of pursuing dilatory tactics after it had raised public expectations. Reproach came from the Deutschtum organizations and from various minority lobbies, among them the Ausschuss der deutschen Minderheiten, to the irritation of the ministry which subsidized them. The center and right-wing parties complained in the Reichstag and in the press. The parties were not mollified when Stresemann and Schubert, who were engaged in hunting bigger game, resorted to equivocation, blaming the minorities' "exaggerated demands" for what had failed to happen at Geneva.[30]

The criticism was directed primarily at the procedures of the League and at Germany's failure to change them. The critics argued that these procedures were predicated upon the notion that the protection of minorities was a temporary measure and a means to assimilation, as a minorities rapporteur had said in 1925. In June 1928, when the Greek delegate in the council explained his government's treatment of minorities in terms of this notion, the minorities and their advocates were indignant.[31] At the annual conference of League of Nations societies in June, the Deutsche Liga für Völkerbund proposed that the League revise its procedure and, in particular, that it establish a permanent minorities commission to watch over the proper execution of the minority provisions. The Congress of European Minorities, meeting in Geneva on the eve of the League Assembly, also attacked the League's procedures and demanded a standing commission. In October the Reichstag Foreign Affairs Committee urged the government to give greater care and attention to the protection of minority rights before the League.[32]

The clamor had not abated when Stresemann left for the council session in Lugano in December 1928. Seven petitions from Polish Upper Silesia crowded the agenda, and Stresemann had promised the cabinet that the delegation would take emphatic action.[33] In Lugano, however, Colban and Adatci (the minorities rapporteur) negotiated a settlement satisfactory to both Germans and Poles, and the parties agreed to dispose of the cases without fanfare. Nevertheless, when Adatci reported the settlement to the council, Polish foreign minister Zaleski launched into a tirade. The council, he said, was being deluged by petty and trivial complaints from Upper Silesia. These were meant to give the impression that the German minority was oppressed. In fact, Upper Silesia prospered under Polish administration. Such unrest as existed was manufactured by the German minority association and its leader, whose activities bordered on treason. Their agitation was an abuse of the provisions for their protection and a trial to the council; ultimately the agitation might endanger the peace.

Stresemann, who had grown restless at these words, now lost his temper spectacularly. Pounding the council table, he rejoined that Zaleski's remarks were inspired by hatred of the German minority. In appealing to the League, the minority in Upper Silesia was exercising its accorded rights; to say that such appeals were a waste of the council's time vitiated the protection that the League afforded the minorities. If the League were to countenance such remarks, it would lose the support of those who placed their hopes in it. He therefore requested that the council review the entire question of minority rights and the League's responsibilities for the minorities at its next session.[34]

Stresemann's spontaneous outburst was not meant to open a campaign on the minorities problem. It was motivated in large part by political exigencies. Stresemann knew that the German press would feature a "Polish provocation" as front-page news, and that he could not afford to let Zaleski's remarks pass without challenge. In fact, in another move to shore up his position, he was about to inform the press of his bitter dissatisfaction with the inconclusive results of the latest Locarnite conversations. He also wished to head off untoward moves by the refractory minority lobby at home. Over the past months, pressure had been mounting for some kind of campaign, which, he feared, might disrupt his revisionist strategy. He therefore topped a suggestion that the council examine the possibility of specific, limited reforms of the minority procedures, made earlier that day by Raoul Dandurand, the Canadian delegate. By demanding a general review, Stresemann tried to regain the initiative.[35]

Stresemann had committed his government to the issue and a strategy had to be worked out. The German officials in the secretariat recommended that Germany propose a "maximum program" of minority protection.[36] In Berlin, Otto Reinebeck, the minorities expert of the ministry's cultural department, produced a more moderate strategy in consultation with the representatives of the minorities. He warned against trying to extend the rights of the minorities; the existing "constellation" in the League would hamper any attempt to change the minority treaties. On the other hand, Germany should not limit her initiative to a mere review of the provisions and procedures for protecting the minorities. Rather, the Germans should address themselves to the question of principle and should "change the spirit" in the council.[37]

The prospect of a major debate before the council created a stir. Minority associations and pressure groups besieged the Foreign Ministry with demands and proposals. They poured forth propaganda, whose unambiguously revisionist slant led Hoesch to warn the Foreign Ministry against a backlash.[38] The Poles denounced the German initiative as an irredentist plot. They bore down hard on the German minority and tried (unsuccessfully) to have the council debate on whether to subject all states to minority obligations. The German ambassadors reported that the British (because of India) and the French (because of Alsace) opposed extending minority obligations and were determined not to permit an irredentist campaign in the guise of a minority debate. When Stresemann arrived in Geneva, trailed by journalists and observers from the minorities, he found none of the great powers enthusiastic about the impending debate.[39]

The debate opened the morning of 6 March in a crowded council chamber. Dandurand suggested that the League remove the "atmosphere of mystery and silence" which attended its treatment of minority petitions. Minorities should submit their petitions directly to the council, and the entire council should sit in committee to determine how the petitions should be treated. Stresemann placed his proposals in the context of the League's responsibilities in the postwar world. His concern, he said, was not with individual minorities and their grievances, but with the League's attitude toward minorities as such, for, he argued, it was the attitude which informed the procedure. In 1920, the council had agreed that "the League must ascertain that the provisions for the protection of the minorities are always observed." The League's practices over the past decade seemed no longer to correspond to these principles. Stresemann therefore proposed that a "special committee of investigation" be appointed to examine how the formal procedures could be improved. The committee might examine the very nature and extent of the League's guarantee and in particular the possibility of permanent supervision of the minority provisions.[40]

The opposition had its say in the afternoon. The debate was not nearly as sensational as many had expected. Zaleski argued against any and all extensions of the minority provisions and called for a committee to examine whether the proposals made that morning did not in fact exceed the treaty obligations. Titulescu, the Rumanian foreign minister, seconded this suggestion. Chamberlain defended the existing system but conceded that there was room for improvement. Briand sermonized. The rights of minorities were sacred to the council; these rights would have to be reconciled with the sovereignty of states; solutions were difficult because there were some who exploited minorities for nefarious political purposes; no change was possible without the consent of the minority states. The League's intent should be to promote a "kind of assimilation" of the "small family" into the "larger family" without destroying the unique characteristics of the minority.[41]

The council came up with a compromise. A committee of three (composed of the representatives of Britain, Japan, and Spain) would examine the League's procedures and whatever comments members of the League might care to submit, and it would present its recommendations in June, when the council was to meet in Madrid. Then a "committee of the whole council," meeting in camera before the official session, would canvass the recommendations and prepare a final report for the council.[42] The German delegation was pleased with the compromise. The debate would continue, and the Germans would have another chance to take up the minorities' cause. Stresemann, who had kept in constant touch with the press, told German journalists that Germany had done well in the preliminary skirmish, and in an anonymous article in the *Kölnische Zeitung*, he lauded his delegation's achievements. The German press was not persuaded: it denounced the compromise as evidence that the council cared little about minorities and that it had dismissed Germany's initiative.[43]

The committee's recommendations—the London report—seemed to vindicate the press. The committee rejected both the Canadian and the German proposals and ignored almost all the comments it received from other powers. It upheld existing procedures and suggested only minor improvements for publicizing the actions of the secretariat and the committees of three. The Foreign Ministry was "surprised and disappointed"; the German press labeled the report a "catastrophe."[44]

The committee of the whole council was scheduled to convene on 6 June, four days before the council was to meet. Because Stresemann was delayed, Schubert represented Germany in the committee. He believed there was little chance that the committee would adopt Germany's proposals, and he intended therefore to have the committee postpone a final decision until the assembly in September. Stresemann agreed with this tactic. He thought that the Labour government, which had just come into power in Britain, might abandon the position taken by its predecessor, so that Germany could hope for British support in September. And he did not want a quarrel over minorities to spoil an impending settlement of evacuation and reparations.[45]

The council committee devoted its first meeting to reading the London report. The following day, 7 June, Dandurand opened the proceedings by suggesting that the entire issue be adjourned until September, since several governments had not had opportunity to examine the report. Schubert ignored what seemed an excellent chance for closing the proceedings at once. He believed that adjournment should come after he had argued Germany's case at length and then with the proper éclat.[46] Instead of supporting Dandurand's request, therefore, he turned to his prepared speech and opened fire on the report. The report, he said, was overwhelmingly "negative." It was narrow in conception and unconstructive in its proposals. He warned that the council committee would be unable to reach agreement if it accepted the report as a basis of discussion. As if disregarding Schubert's speech, Briand asked whether the committee wished to accede to Dandurand's suggestion and terminate discussion. No one wished to, and all save the German representative agreed to accept the report as a basis for discussion. Schubert, making a fine legalistic distinction, said that he would take part in the discussion without accepting its premises.[47] The German delegation interpreted this outcome as a victory. Schubert had succeeded in preventing the committee from simply adopting the London report; its decision to accept the report as a basis for discussion was a mere formality. In consequence the committee would be obliged to "fabricate a new report."[48] But the Germans were soon to be enlightened. In the session of 8 June, the committee discussed the procedural changes proposed by the report. It ignored Schubert's reiterated reservations, disregarded both his and Dandurand's emendations, and adopted the report's recommendations with minor alterations.[49]

Stresemann arrived in Madrid the evening of that day, studied the minutes of the past meetings, and by Monday, 10 June, was distressed and puzzled. Why had Schubert not taken up Dandurand's proposal for adjournment? The delegation rallied to Schubert's defense. If Schubert had agreed to prompt adjournment, he would have provoked the reproaches of the minorities and "the opposition." The Germans would still be able to adjourn the debate, for the committee had yet to discuss principles, and this discussion would lead to deadlock.[50] In the committee meeting on the eleventh Stresemann briefly acknowledged the improvement in procedure and then turned to the question of principle. The committee's failure to agree on the principles underlying minority protection would spill over into the council meeting, he said. The League could not admit to such "désaccord" in public. He suggested therefore that the discussion of principle be left to the assembly. The tactic did not work. The committee had already decided not to adjourn its work, Briand said. If it were to adjourn now, it would abandon all the improvements made in earlier meetings. Briand insisted that the committee must present the council with a unanimous report. The other members lined up behind Briand; Dandurand begged Stresemann not to jeopardize what had been achieved. The meeting adjourned without settling the issue.[51]

Shortly before the final meeting of the committee, Stresemann met with Briand to discuss the ramifications of the new reparations report, which had just been issued in Paris. Briand was optimistic: a general conference would settle the differences that remained between their countries. His remarks carried unspoken assumptions, and Stresemann responded.[52] Though dissatisfied to the last, he accepted the committee's report, which contained the procedural changes agreed upon and appended the London report and the minutes of the committee meetings. As he was to tell a press conference afterwards, the committee's report merely communicated the London report to the council, and the question of principle was therefore still open. The battle, he said, would continue; the issue would doubtless surface in the assembly in September. To Berlin the delegation cabled that the outcome was "entirely satisfactory": Germany had not surrendered the least of its principles, nor by any stretch of the imagination could she be said to have struck a compromise.[53] The public did not see it that way. The press attacked the delegation's tactics. The minorities expressed their dissatisfaction with mere procedural changes. All sides of the Reichstag protested that Stresemann had reneged on his promises—there was no reorientation in League attitudes, no new spirit of justice and compassion. For many, the episode was yet another confirmation of the League's partiality—and of the folly of Germany's membership.[54]

By September the international atmosphere had changed. The conference at The Hague had settled reparations and guaranteed the evacuation of the Rhineland. At Geneva, Briand created a small sensation by proposing a European federal union, which would enhance European security by stimulating economic growth and promoting political cooperation. Stresemann took up the idea. In what was his last address before the League, he urged Europeans to break down economic barriers and to encourage economic interdependence.[55] There was no minorities debate in the assembly, no move in the council—in fact, no general minorities debate ever came before the council again. Stresemann's great initiative, pursued with much oratory if little finesse, had focused the world's attention on the problem of minorities—and accomplished little else. The overt resistance of the minority states, and especially the reluctance of European statesmen to tackle what they deemed a delicate issue, proved too obdurate. Stresemann seems to have shared this reluctance: as long as he was preoccupied with evacuation and reparations, minorities remained a secondary issue.

Stresemann's habit of allowing minority grievances to be settled in committee prevailed also among his successors. At the council meeting in May 1930, Julius Curtius, the new German foreign minister, forwent a council debate because the Poles had remedied certain objections about minority schools in Upper Silesia; he acceded to the adjournment of several other Upper Silesian complaints. In September, he was relieved when a brief debate before the council brought a seemingly irresolvable Memel dispute to a private conclusion. Only reluctantly did he initiate the discussion on the protection of minorities, which Stresemann had predicted would take place the previous year and which the minorities had lobbied for. In this debate the Germans refrained from pressing their challenge to the League principles. They restricted themselves to reviewing the League's practice over the previous year and to urging a more conscientious application of the Madrid procedures.[56] As before, the Germans combined practical solutions with economic subsidies.[57] In fact, on more than one occasion the Foreign Ministry adopted an attitude of benign neglect. It gave Danzig's complaints about the Polish port at nearby Gdynia no more than formal sponsorship and sat by while the petition meandered through committee for three years—three years during which Gdynia prospered and Danzig's economy steadily declined. In an effort to save some remnant of their trade, the Danzigers finally resorted to direct negotiation with Warsaw in 1933.[58]

After the Reichstag elections in September 1930, a new tactic appeared in an essentially unchanged policy—a tactic that was in evidence until the Germans withdrew from the League three years later. The election campaign had been a chauvinist riot. Its tone was set by the radical parties of the Right, which had joined together in battling the Young plan in 1929. They appealed to those who suffered under the depression and despaired of parliamentary politics and who could be mobilized to oppose the republic and its foreign policy. They belittled the external accomplishments of the republic and denounced the policy of accommodation, demanding immediate and full-scale revision of the remaining restrictions of the peace treaty. Their propaganda concentrated on reparations and disarmament. It was directed also at the eastern borders with the argument that revision could begin now that the Rhineland had been evacuated.[59] As part of this propaganda the fate of the German minorities became a rallying point. Their "unabated sufferings" and their "helplessness" were adduced to call for intervention and restoration. The minorities themselves, already excited, became militant. Minority delegations and petitions arrived in Berlin in increasing number. The Verband der deutschen Volksgruppen (formerly Ausschuss der deutschen Minderheiten) asked accusingly whether the government had abandoned Stresemann's concern for minorities.[60]

The campaign, capped by spectacular gains of the extremist parties in the election, brought about certain tactical modifications in the government's foreign policy. Under the conservative Heinrich Brüning, who had formed a government in March 1930, this policy had already undergone considerable change. Parallel to a retreat from parliamentary practices at home, where Brüning had taken to governing by presidential decree, there was a retreat from accommodation abroad.[61] In fact, the new diplomatic style was reminiscent of that in vogue before Stresemann, when the government had ignored the effect of its policy upon international sensibilities. At the very moment of the final evacuation of the Rhineland, Brüning had shocked foreign opinion by raising fresh demands. He was determined to secure relief from reparations and equality in armaments. Like Stresemann, however, he considered the revision of the eastern borders a secondary objective.[62]

Unlike Stresemann, however, Brüning was not reluctant to adopt a harsh tone. Stresemann had tried to be moderate in order to protect his options in a grand diplomatic design. Brüning had chosen another course, and he had another way of protecting his options: he diverted the public from the sacrifices entailed in pursuing his major aims by prosecuting minor aims noisily. Therefore, again unlike Stresemann, he had a free hand to defuse the public discontent that had also troubled Stresemann in his last year in office.[63] His delegation to Geneva became more strident, turning certain minority cases into public spectacles. By staging dramatic displays at Geneva, the government could make a gesture toward gratifying the demand for the revision of the borders. By being rhetorically aggressive, it could afford to ignore the calls for retaliatory measures against Poland. By being rhetorically uncompromising, it could avoid acting for the minorities and their problems. On another level, the government hoped that this bluster would strengthen its hand in the contest with National Socialism. Bravado abroad might restore some political unity at home.[64]

The Germans demonstrated their new tactics in 1931, in a dispute over the Polish election campaign of the fall of 1930. In this campaign, the Poles had responded to the revisionist rhetoric in Germany by harassing the German minority. In Upper Silesia, members of the minority had been "terrorized" during an "anti-German week" in October.[65] Indignation in Germany was almost unanimous, especially after the minority lost most of its parliamentary representation in the election. The German government had protested repeatedly to Warsaw, and on 27 November, not two weeks after the election, it protested to the League. It accused the Upper Silesian authorities of having permitted a "premeditated wave of terror" against the minority. Early in December, the Germans supplemented this protest with a letter full of further details. On 17 December, the government disregarded the Foreign Ministry's misgivings and, gratifying those who called for firm action to recover the "lost territories," protested election abuses in the Corridor as well. Thus, before the minorities themselves had appealed to Geneva even once, Germany had sent three major protests.[66]

The council put Germany's protests on the agenda in January 1931. The Foreign Ministry prepared for the meeting by having its ambassadors tell the governments represented on the council that Germany could accept no adjournment on the issue and that the council would have to condemn Poland's conduct openly. The German press characterized the issue as a test case for Germany's further membership in the League.[67] Curtius and Zaleski addressed the council on 21 January amidst "absorbed attentiveness." Curtius spoke belligerently about "election terrorism" as a systematic exploitation of "national passions" which broke "all records of victimization." Twice he took occasion to assert that the German government was as determined as ever to revise the borders with Poland. Zaleski, in a speech full of irony and telling jabs, denied systematic persecution, but he did not deny that disorders had taken place. These he described as spontaneous reactions to developments in Germany, and he informed the council that the incidents were being investigated by the police. The issue was therefore not one of politics but of law.[68]

On 24 January the rapporteur (Yoshizawa) presented the council with the outcome of difficult negotiations behind the scenes. He asked the Polish government to report to the council in May on the measures it had taken to punish the perpetrators and compensate the victims. He asked further that it inform the council of the steps it had taken to revive the minority's "feeling of confidence," which had been "profoundly shaken." The council adopted the report unanimously—and with relief. Poland was satisfied because the League had not instituted an inquiry of its own; Germany was satisfied because, as the Foreign Ministry put it, never before had the council censured a member so severely.[69] In May, after the Poles had submitted their report, Curtius obliged the council to adjourn the discussion till September. Over the summer the Germans continued to exploit the case, contending that the situation in Upper Silesia was as tense as ever. Their contrived concern was meant to distract attention from the country's political and economic misfortunes. In September, they agreed to desist, but only after the council had adopted a resolution which in effect admonished the Poles to maintain normal relations with the minority. According to Curtius, the Polish government was bound to respect minority rights in the future and the German government (or the minority) was privileged to raise the "terrorism issue" again at any time.[70]

In the terrorism issue Curtius had broken League tradition by submitting petitions in advance and independently of the aggrieved minority. He had found fault with the conduct of a national election and intervened in another state's internal affairs. He had exploited the issue openly to meet his government's domestic needs. In 1932, the Germans were to employ similar tactics with a minority petition about Poland's agrarian reforms and in a dispute with Lithuania over Memel.[71] Adolf Müller reported from Berne that the terrorism issue had led members of the League to believe that the German government considered the gratification of its public more important than "the League, our position in the League, our foreign policy or even the minorities problem."[72] Müller was exaggerating for effect, but he was not mistaken. After Stresemann, the German government used minority issues for political purposes regardless of the cost to the League. It squandered the fund of good will and sympathy Stresemann had carefully stored up at Geneva. In fact, the government's tactics undermined Germany's case for territorial revision. They brought the minorities only grief, prompting them to leave their homes for Germany. And ironically, activism in minority affairs, while applauded and approved, did not relieve the government of public pressure or stay the move toward radicalism.[73]

8   Equality of Rights, 1932

Germany's association with the League's efforts to promote general disarmament illustrates with unique clarity the nature of Germany's relationship with the League. The association—which was initiated by Stresemann and terminated by Hitler and which culminated in the disarmament conference of 1932–33—was Germany's deepest involvement in League affairs. Here, as elsewhere, the League subserved specific national interests. The value of Germany's membership was judged by how well the League advanced these interests. Germany's dubious fortunes in the protracted disarmament negotiations revived the notion, popular shortly after the war, that the League was a hindrance to revisionism. These fortunes also indicated the limits, already suggested, to which the League could accommodate or reconcile conflicting international interests.

Germany had been drawn into the League's disarmament negotiations in December 1925, even before she became a member, when the council invited her to join the Preparatory Commission for the Disarmament Conference. This commission, composed primarily of the member states of the council (joined by Germany, the United States, and the Soviet Union), was charged with examining the practical problems of disarmament and preparing concrete proposals for an eventual disarmament conference. By appointing it, the council was attempting to carry out the covenant's injunction to "formulate plans" for reducing national armaments to a level "consistent with national safety and the enforcement by common action of international obligations" (article 8). Earlier attempts had been unsuccessful. The European powers, lacking a sense of security, had refused to disarm.[1]

The Germans had seized upon the invitation to the commission, for the talks opened the possibility of arriving at a more equitable distribution of arms.[2] As long as they (and their wartime allies) were the only ones to be disarmed, they felt enfeebled and insecure—and of course their national pride had suffered. Germany's army was limited to 100,000 troops and officers (with no reserves), sparsely equipped, and deprived of certain weapons (tanks, heavy artillery, aircraft). Her navy consisted of six battleships and some two dozen smaller craft (but no submarines), and had an overall strength of 16,500.[3] The country was demilitarized in the west, lightly fortified in the east, and hemmed in by heavily armed neighbors. Largely because of its territorial losses, it found itself in an unfavorable strategical position, and it could not offset this disadvantage by means of a system of alliances as before the war (for no one, the argument ran, wanted to ally himself with a disarmed state). Germany's armed forces could neither deter nor resist invasion. Nor could they lend the support necessary for a forceful foreign policy. Nothing, complained one diplomat in 1931, had affected Germany's policy since the war as much as her defenseless borders.[4]

The Foreign Ministry and the Defense Ministry collaborated in defining the German objectives for the Preparatory Commission. The Foreign Ministry was repeatedly obliged to impose diplomatic restraint on the Defense Ministry's hopes and expectations. The diplomats pointed out that it was too early to demand the abrogation of the disarmament provisions of the peace treaty, at least until Germany's position in the League had become "absolutely firm." Germany's ultimate aim—equal rights in all respects with the other states—still belonged to the distant future. Nor could Germany press to have the other powers reduce their armaments to Germany's level and accept the stipulations of the peace treaty for themselves. Such "utopian" demands might break up the talks. Rather, Germany should try to reduce the disproportion in armaments, especially with her immediate neighbors to the east and west. Her inferiority could be corrected by a general leveling of armaments—on the one hand, by limiting the armaments of other states (to their prewar level, the representative of the Defense Ministry thought), on the other, perhaps by "some modest rearmament" (presumably to the level to which the others were prepared to reduce). Because Germany's political aims lay on the continent, the Germans would address themselves first to land armaments and to divesting France, then Poland, Czechoslovakia, and Belgium, and finally Italy, of military superiority.[5]

Count Johann von Bernstorff represented these aims in the

Preparatory Commission. A former ambassador to Washington and now a Democratic member of the Reichstag, he discharged his mission with an authority bordering on self-righteousness and a "certain stiff courtesy."[6] His basic argument was that, since the peace treaty had assured the Germans that their own disarmament made possible the "general limitation of the armaments of all nations" (an assurance reiterated in the Allies' response to the official German protests in June 1919), the other states had a legal and moral obligation to disarm.[7] Now Germany had disarmed, he declared, and she expected the others to follow suit. In the covenant as well as at Locarno, he observed, the major powers had committed themselves to bringing about a disarmament agreement, and he pointed out that since both the League and the Locarno pact offered a full measure of security, nothing stood in the way of disarmament. The German delegation never deviated from this legalistic approach, citing with tiresome ingenuousness Wilson speeches, Versailles pledges, and League resolutions to establish the legitimacy of its demand for general and equal disarmament.[8]

The approach was not unlike that adopted by the German government in 1919. As in 1919, the Germans argued that they had been given contractual assurances of just and equitable treatment, and, again as in 1919, they set out to gain moral advantage by demonstrating that they had been deceived. After 1919, the legalistic posture had served to justify the Germans' intention to revise the peace treaty. After 1926, it served to justify eventual rearmament. Not infrequently Bernstorff would hint that if the disarmament commission failed in its purpose, Germany might no longer feel bound by the military restrictions of Versailles.[9]

The legalistic posture also gave the Germans certain immediate advantages. Bernstorff could act, in Bülow's words, as the "conscience of the commission." He could cut short discussions that strayed to what he termed side issues and focus attention on disarmament; he could remind the commission of universal expectations of rapid progress and urge it to wind up the preliminaries and summon a general conference.[10] He could also intercept developments that might prejudice German interests. Time and again he announced that Germany's commitment to disarmament would not permit him to endorse "partial solutions" or those which, merely by stabilizing the status quo, were "factitious." And by declining any part in the action, he also retained the freedom to dissociate himself from an outcome Germany might find unacceptable.[11] Most important, a legal posture kept the Germans out of conflicts. As long as the government professed to adhere to the principles of the League, it could not disrupt one of the League's chief activities. The Foreign Ministry repeatedly instructed the delegation to practice "great reserve," to leave the initiative to others, and to avoid "duels" with the French. If the talks miscarried, the blame should not fall on Germany.[12]

The Foreign Ministry believed it could afford such legal posturing. It attached less importance to the Preparatory Commission than to the future disarmament conference, where it supposed all the significant decisions would be made. As long as the commission did nothing to impair Germany's chances or burden her case, the Germans were content to see it produce little meaningful work. The posturing and dawdling were possible also because the German public was not nearly as interested in the problems of disarmament as it was in minorities; most of the comments in the Reichstag and the press (which brought steady if often confusing reports on the commission's deliberations) were fairly perfunctory—or slightly disdainful. The government therefore was under no great pressure to act.[13]

The commission labored for five years. It canvassed the political and technical issues involved; debated principles, priorities, and methods; and examined a number of disarmament schemes. Its sessions foreshadowed most of the tactics, expedients, alliances, and, above all, divisions of opinion that were to plague the disarmament conference. The French and their allies, for example, refused to consider any reduction of armaments unless they were given firm assurances of support in case they were attacked, while the British, usually seconded by the Americans and other non-European delegations, balked at extending their military commitments, insisting that security would follow automatically upon disarmament.[14] More often than not, the Germans' efforts were frustrated. They found themselves outvoted on issues they considered crucial, and the conference, originally projected for 1927, was postponed from one year to the next. But aside from repudiating an unsatisfactory disarmament scheme in 1929—probably in order to exert pressure on the commission—the Germans did not force the issue during Stresemann's lifetime. They only toyed with the notion of expressing their displeasure by resigning from the commission, and they usually gave vent to their vexation without foreclosing further participation.[15]

The commission concluded its work by adopting a draft for a disarmament convention in December 1930. Inevitably, the document was a compromise, containing broad criteria but no actual figures, and hedged with reservations and exceptions. It provided qualified agreement on the number of active troops, on tenure of service, and on money to be spent on troops and equipment; it prohibited chemical and bacteriological warfare; it proposed that a reasonably independent permanent disarmament commission be established to safeguard the terms on which the conference would settle. In fact, the draft convention did little more than record the apparently irreconcilable differences on disarmament with which the conference would have to contend.[16]

The draft convention did not have Germany's approval. Bernstorff had disassociated himself from it when it came up for second reading in May 1929. His government, he said, could not accept a scheme which failed to bring about an "appreciable reduction in the excessive armaments of the present." During the final session of the commission in December 1930, he condemned the convention outright: the draft would "serve only to conceal the real state of world armaments or even allow armaments to be increased."[17] The Germans were dissatisfied because the convention emphasized limitation, not reduction of armaments. Many items were not even limited or were limited only indirectly. And the convention stipulated that its provisions were binding only if earlier arms limitations were heeded—for the Germans an unmistakable allusion to Versailles.[18]

Curtius underscored Bernstorff's condemnation in the council session in January 1931, the same in which he denounced the Poles so fiercely for their "election terror." The convention draft, he declared, did not bind Germany. He warned that Germany would accept the proposals of the projected conference only if they were a great improvement upon those of the Preparatory Commission. Back in Berlin, he went a step further, telling the Reichstag that his government would be deeply influenced in its attitude toward the League if the League failed to secure general disarmament.[19]

The Germans' condemnation was but the logical outcome of the legalistic course they had followed all along. It also reflected developments at home. The election campaign of the previous summer, in which the extremist parties had attacked the government's foreign policy, had left a legacy of open antagonism toward the League and toward the League's disarmament commission. Newspapers of all political persuasions, reported the British ambassador in November, were "practically unanimous in voicing Germany's dissatisfaction at the failure of other countries to carry out the obligation to reduce armaments contained in article 8 of the Covenant."[20] Voices from the Right—an open telegram to the chancellor from Hugenberg, a resolution of the Nationalverband deutscher Offiziere—demanded that Germany leave the League if she were denied freedom and equality in military affairs. In December, as it became apparent that the delegation would not have its way, the Nazis managed to have the Foreign Affairs Committee adopt a resolution, 13–12, to recall the delegation from Geneva. Other radical resolutions were sidetracked in the committee by moderates in the Nationalist and Center parties, who introduced their own resolutions asking for firm action.[21] The military had also become restive. Just before the final session of the commission, it asked the delegation to demand that the convention guarantee "qualitative equality"—Germany's right to possess all kinds of weapons kept by the other powers. Bernstorff replied that a sudden change of tactic was inappropriate. A demand of this magnitude was best reserved for the conference itself. Not rearmament but "parity in security" was to be the demand that Bernstorff insisted upon.[22]

The tone of the Germans' remarks about disarmament was not unlike the new tone in their defense of minorities. But here the tone was used in a matter of great consequence in German foreign policy and implied a change in substance as well. Curtius's uncompromising position on a draft convention tailored largely to French needs was an outright challenge to the French; his declaration that the conference must revise the commission's labors was an invitation to battle. Curtius, who had stayed on as foreign minister under Brüning, was not sufficiently secure in the new cabinet to pursue an independent policy. He also spoke for Brüning, who believed that Stresemann's policies had been too trusting and too accommodating and that they were not attuned to the requirements of the German public. Brüning himself had no grand design, carefully graduated to achieve one objective after another in concert with the Western powers. Rather, he wished to pursue a number of specific objectives at an accelerated pace. Foremost among his objectives was the abolition of reparations. To this end, he deliberately exploited the economic depression, for he was convinced that the creditor powers would cancel reparations if they believed that the German economy, and with it the world economy, was about to collapse. He knew that the European powers were reluctant to cancel reparations as long as they were saddled with war debts to the United States. Therefore the American government would have to be induced to cancel these debts. Brüning believed that the American government would be able to do so if the European powers achieved some measure of disarmament. Thus, while Brüning began to work toward the abolition of reparations, he also began to urge progress in disarmament.[23]

The professionals in the Foreign Ministry supported this change in outlook and style at Geneva. Germany's membership had not turned them into admirers of the League. They were willing to concede only that it had yielded results through great-power diplomacy "en marge de l'Assemblée." In August 1929, on the eve of the Hague conference, Bülow had summed up the lessons of three years of membership: nothing had changed. The peace treaty still shaped Europe, and the Allies still dominated the League, which they had shaped for their own purposes. The League denied the Germans equality and restricted them in the exercise of their natural powers. This re-emergent skepticism superseded the Foreign Ministry's assessment in November 1927, when it had appeared as if Germany's entry had brought on decisive changes in the League.[24] In April 1930, Ernst von Weizsäcker, Bülow's successor in the ministry's League section, analyzed the implications of the settlement of evacuation and reparations for Germany's policy at Geneva. Germany could leave the League, but he thought she would be well advised not to.[25] Even if one regarded the League as no more than a "unique international diplomatic club" which offered a setting for political negotiations, there were still enough issues—such as territorial revision—which might be discussed. On issues for which the League was directly responsible, the Germans might now become more active and stop condoning the League method of bland harmony. They might press for progress in disarmament and for better protection of minorities, expand their involvement in economic affairs and the League's technical services, and exploit the covenant to improve their international position.[26]

These notions were reminiscent of the unsentimental opinions put forward by Bülow before Germany entered the League. After Bülow became state secretary in June 1930, these views gained currency. Stresemann's practice of achieving his goals by promoting good will at Geneva and cordial relations with the Western powers fell into disuse, as did his sensitivity to the rules of partnership and the need for reciprocity. Curtius told Secretary-General Drummond that Germany's attitude had changed. At Geneva Stresemann had concentrated on the Rhineland and reparations; he himself hoped to "bring Germany more completely into the regular domain of League work."[27] To the cabinet Curtius described Germany's role in the League as that of the "loyal opposition."[28]

The new orientation appeared in the government's preparations in 1931 for the disarmament conference. The time for moralizing and self-righteous posturing was over; the disarmament issue would have to be resolved. The Germans knew from the Preparatory Commission that any sort of effective scheme for reducing armaments depended upon France. Since Stresemann's death, however, the French had become even more unyielding—disturbed, according to Hoesch, by the resurgence of German nationalism and the government's apparent intent to use aggressive tactics abroad to appease domestic critics. In 1931 their strong opposition to the project of a German-Austrian customs union, which they regarded as a step toward renewed German dominance in central Europe, showed the extent to which they had retreated from the Briand-Stresemann détente. Consequently, the Germans would have to reach the French indirectly.[29] They began to look for allies. To the small and the revisionist powers they proposed concerted action at the conference. Among the great powers (other than France) they solicited good will and sympathy for the German case, and they urged that the French be pressed. More often, and with greater persistence, they tried blackmail. To the British ambassador, Curtius explained that unless the conference discarded the draft convention, it would deadlock, and such a deadlock would encourage those in Germany who wanted to rearm. Worse, if the conference failed to meet Germany's claims, the republican regime would be discredited and no longer able to withstand the pressure to leave the League and renounce Versailles and Locarno.[30] The Germans also launched a large and well-financed propaganda campaign in the Western countries. Its message was direct and unvaried: Germany, disarmed and uncompromisingly committed to disarmament, was being denied her moral right.[31]

Meantime the Germans worked out a program for the conference itself. They wanted the conference to redress what Bülow called the *Deklassierung* (or, with moral overtones, the *Diffamierung*) of the German army.[32] This demand was subsumed in the slogan *Gleichberechtigung*—equality of rights or, more felicitously, equal rights. The term itself was not new; it had been part of the German political vocabulary since Germany entered the League. On more than one occasion Stresemann had decried the double standard at Geneva and demanded that Germany enjoy equality in all respects with the other members of the League. Now *Gleichberechtigung* came to mean specifically that Germany be treated equally with the other powers in military affairs.[33]

As in years past, the Foreign Ministry and the Defense Ministry cooperated in working out the practical aspects of this demand. This time, however, the cooperation presented some difficulties. Above all, the strategy at the conference had to be harmonized with the military's planning for modernization and expansion. By 1930 the military was mapping out plans that would transform the existing ten divisions into twenty-one in case of war—adding 200,000 men to the army together with armaments forbidden by the peace treaty, and relaxing the system of organization imposed at Versailles. Its minimum demand, therefore, would be full freedom within the budgetary limits the conference was to set, so that it could dispose of funds for armaments and organizational purposes as it saw fit—a demand the diplomats saw as the very most the Germans might hope to achieve.[34] The Foreign Ministry also had to contend with the rather extreme position of a small lobby of officers, mostly young colonels, who hoped to gain freedom to rearm by breaking up the conference with unrealizable demands (including military parity with France).[35]

The program which emerged after some six months of preparation, and which Nadolny, the new head of the delegation, presented to the cabinet in January 1932, appeared to meet the interests of both the Foreign Ministry and the Defense Ministry. Germany should set her sights for a disarmament scheme that applied equally to all and released Germany from the discriminatory stipulations of Versailles. If the scheme failed to abolish everywhere the armaments now prohibited to Germany, the Germans should themselves acquire the right to such armaments, and they should in fact equip themselves with a small number, if only to document their equality. Germany also wanted "parity in security," a demand Bernstorff had introduced in the commission in 1930. Then it had been an argument against discrimination in the draft convention. Now it represented the practical side of equal rights. It empowered Germany to demand that her neighbors reduce their armaments "extensively and effectively" and at the same time to claim for herself the rights bestowed by article 8 of the covenant, which provided for a level of armaments "consistent with national safety." In time such parallel action might lead to some kind of proportion between levels of national armaments; for the time being it accommodated the army's plans for expansion.[36]

The disarmament conference opened at Geneva on 2 February 1932. It was the biggest international gathering since the peace conference of 1919, with some sixty states in attendance. Journalists, advocates of disarmament, and, less obtrusively, the representatives of arms manufacturers, flocked to Geneva to join hundreds of delegates. The conference itself attracted massive public attention; thousands of petitions and telegrams poured in, expressing hopes for a favorable outcome. The president of the conference, Arthur Henderson, former foreign secretary of Britain's Labour government, defined its purpose as "substantial reduction and limitation of all national armaments."[37]

The conference convened in a world considerably changed since the Preparatory Commission had last met in December 1930. The economic crisis had begun to affect nearly every country in Europe. Instead of drawing the countries into economic cooperation, it led to recrimination and protectionism. Domestic politics had become radicalized, and suspicion eroded what confidence remained between European states. None could overlook the growing agitation in Germany for withdrawal from the League. Finally, the League itself was struggling with the Manchurian crisis, which was to leave it deeply divided. In fact, the opening of the conference was delayed for an hour because the council met in emergency session to discuss the latest war news from the Far East. In this setting, the obligatory optimism in the opening speeches, as one contemporary remarked, "sounded singularly unconvincing."[38]

The first weeks of the conference were given over to general debate. The draft convention seemed almost forgotten amid the welter of other proposals, old and new. On the whole the delegates were restrained, maneuvering for position and confining themselves to formal approval or polite criticism. No one expected resolutions or compromises before the spring, when elections were scheduled in both Germany and France. And all seemed conscious of the possible consequences, should the conference collapse.[39]

The proposals put forward by the non-revisionist powers fell into two categories. The British and Americans favored "qualitative disarmament"—the reduction or abolition of weapons clearly suited more for attack than defense. This was endorsed by Italy and the Soviet Union, and by most smaller states, who saw it as a means of strengthening their own security. The French, supported by their East European allies and by Belgium, reiterated the arguments they had made in the Preparatory Commission. Represented by War Minister André Tardieu, one of the architects of the peace treaty, they were not inclined to grant concessions to Germany. Their case culminated in the proposal that the conference strengthen the covenant by providing for compulsory arbitration and watertight sanctions, which would be enforced by a permanent international police force. They made no mention of general disarmament.[40]

Brüning addressed the conference on 9 February. His theme was Germany's legal and moral claim to general disarmament. The conference's "greatest responsibility" was to secure disarmament "on the basis of equal rights and equal security for all peoples." Brüning's arguments, delivered grandiloquently and in measured tones, were well received.[41] The delegation advanced Germany's concrete proposals on 18 February. The spokesman, Rudolf Nadolny, the ambassador to Turkey, was the perfect representative of Germany's new orientation. A diplomat of the old school whose professional intransigence made him popular in military circles in Berlin (and unpopular among his colleagues in the foreign service), he had been Brüning's choice to succeed Bernstorff as head of the delegation.[42] He no longer asked for prompt general disarmament. He demanded in effect that the disarmament standards set by the peace treaty apply equally to all—certain "offensive weapons" (military aircraft, tanks, heavy artillery) were to be proscribed altogether; all other armaments were to be reduced.[43]

The general debate was concluded by the end of February, and the conference turned over the proposals that had been put before it to its technical commissions. Work proceeded by fits and starts. Frequently it bogged down in theoretical discussions and plain wrangling. It was interrupted for more than a week by a special session of the assembly called to deal with Manchuria and, shortly thereafter, by an Easter recess of three weeks. It stopped altogether as attention turned to the presidential elections in Germany. In mid-April an impatient American delegation proposed that the conference concentrate on abolishing "aggressive" land armaments. On 22 April the conference resolved to accept the proposal in principle. It instructed the technical commissions to work out practical definitions of what constituted "aggressive" weapons and adjourned to await their reports.[44]

From the very beginning the delegations had made private contact. As expected, the Germans found the Americans, the British, and the Italians sympathetic.[45] The French would be the greatest obstacle and therefore became the object of Germany's most careful attention. Nadolny's conversations in Geneva were paralleled by ambassadorial talks in Paris and Berlin. Tardieu, however, proved evasive, citing the coming elections and public mistrust of developments in Germany. Nadolny responded with a promise to mind the tone of his public statements. After several weeks the talks reached a point at which, for the sake of discussion, the French were willing to postulate German equality and the Germans to regard as feasible French proposals for expanding security within the framework of the League.[46] Nadolny now professed a certain optimism. He was convinced, he wrote to Bülow in mid-March, that the conference would grant Germany not merely equality in methods of disarmament but also some flexibility in her level of armament. Tardieu's evasiveness indicated, he assumed, that the French wanted to avoid confrontation in order to bring the conference to such a "positive outcome."[47]

In April the presence of American Secretary of State Henry Stimson in Geneva provided an opportunity for the European statesmen to confer. At Prime Minister MacDonald's suggestion, Stimson invited Brüning and Tardieu to his villa at Bessinge on the twenty-sixth for a frank exchange of views. It was an important meeting for Brüning, for he was in a tight corner. His position in Germany, apparently strengthened by Hindenburg's reelection on 10 April, was in fact precarious. Brüning had lost Hindenburg's favor. Hindenburg had been reelected by the parties on the Left, toward which he was antipathetic, and he blamed Brüning's policies for the loss of support on the Right. He also resented the government's decision on 13 April to ban the Nazi storm troopers but not the left-wing associations. The elections on 24 April, which had boosted Nazi representation in the state diets, made the government's decision appear even more dubious. Brüning believed that his government and his policies would be saved only by a "striking success" at Geneva.[48] The meeting at Bessinge, which MacDonald and various members of the American delegation attended but Tardieu declined, seemed an opportunity to prepare such a success.

Brüning and Bülow explained Germany's position at length. In practice, they protested, equal treatment meant neither German rearmament nor an arms race. Germany was quite prepared to keep her forces at their present level for eight or ten years, or until a second disarmament conference. She asked only to be permitted to make some "adjustments" in her military organization (reduce the twelve-year enlistments for part of the army or establish a militia on the Swiss model) and to alter the procurement of matériel, which the provisions of Versailles made unduly costly. Never before had the Germans said so specifically what they meant by equal rights.[49]

Contemporaries have regarded this meeting as a lost opportunity in the history of the disarmament conference, for Tardieu (prime minister since February) had gone to Paris for the election campaign and pleaded laryngitis when Stimson invited him to return to Geneva for the discussion.[50] It has been argued that the combined pressure of the Americans and British might have induced Tardieu to make concessions, which would not only have promoted disarmament but also would have helped Brüning fortify his position at home. However, there is no evidence in the documents that the Americans or the British were committed to anything more than good will,[51] and even if we assume that they had agreed firmly to Brüning's plans, Tardieu could hardly have afforded an arrangement with the Germans only a few days before the French elections. The French opposed concessions to a radicalized Germany, and they had never given much credence to the claim that support for Brüning was the only way to prevent further radicalization.[52]

Bülow—and apparently Brüning—considered the meeting a significant achievement. MacDonald and Stimson, as Bülow was subsequently to say, had conceded equal rights in principle.[53] Another summit meeting was planned for 17 or 18 May, at which the French would also be present, and all but Tardieu promptly agreed to attend.[54] The meeting never took place. On 8 May Tardieu lost the election. Hoesch reported that the new government being formed by Herriot was incapable of decisive action before June.[55] At the end of the month Hindenburg replaced Brüning with Franz von Papen, who promptly dissolved the Reichstag and governed by the extraparliamentary powers given him by the president.

Brüning's policy did not fall with Brüning's government. On 2 June Bülow submitted a draft of guidelines for further negotiations to his new foreign minister, Konstantin von Neurath. Bülow believed that disarmament should be on the agenda when the European statesmen met at Lausanne on 16 June to discuss reparations. The statesmen should try to revive the disarmament conference, which had stalled when its technical commissions could not agree on what constituted "aggressive" weapons. The Germans should use the opportunity to pursue their objectives. They would have to induce the French to accept what the British and Americans had accepted at Bessinge. Once the French had done so, the talks at Geneva would proceed without difficulty. In order to gain France's consent, Bülow suggested that Germany offer her a separate accord, in which Germany agreed to keep practical equality within limits acceptable to France. Neurath, phlegmatic by nature and only just arrived from the embassy in London to accept his new post, was ill-equipped to challenge these proposals. Two days later Papen, also new to the subject, approved them as well.[56]

Not so Kurt von Schleicher, the minister of defense and the most influential figure in the new cabinet. He did not want the Germans to concede explicitly that they would be satisfied with minimal equality in armaments. Germany should insist upon "full equality," which might be limited in practice by an accord with the French. Schleicher made this point particularly baldly in a memorandum on disarmament policy sent to Neurath on 15 June. To assure equality of security Germany should insist that the conference insert into the disarmament convention precise figures which made Germany's armaments numerically equal to France's or at least to those of Poland and Czechoslovakia combined. The conference might enter further figures to indicate the numerical limits which Germany was prepared to accept for the duration of the convention (not to exceed five years). These figures would correspond to her present military establishment—with some slight alterations. The army would increase troop strength to 160,000 men (the navy from 16,500 to 27,000) and augment border and coast guards with a small militia of three-months service. For this larger army the military would require heavy artillery, heavy armor, aircraft, and anti-aircraft weapons. If these conditions were not met, the army's interest required that Germany leave the talks and undertake expansion on her own.[57]

Bülow represented the established position of juridical equality, based politically and morally on membership in the League;[58] Schleicher thought in terms of practical military equality, to be limited only by temporary accords or by fiscal stringency. The military had expressed an interest in practical equality all along, but never before with such insistence. The sense of urgency was prompted in part by military considerations. Plans for expansion, underway since 1929–30, were taking definite shape. The first modest increases in personnel and armaments were to be effected within the coming months. The urgency was also motivated in part by the domestic situation. Since the fall of the Müller government in 1930, the military (and the president) had promoted a trend toward authoritarian government. The rapidly growing Nazi party and the civil strife the party incited would have to be checked before they undermined the regime. The military believed that it could "tame" the Nazi movement by gathering the storm troopers into a militia under the auspices of the army. The disarmament talks offered an opportunity to implement such measures legally, but only if the government abandoned Bülow's accommodating program.[59]

International developments strengthened Schleicher's hand. Brüning's abrupt dismissal had aroused suspicions abroad. The Western powers were reluctant to treat with a government that lost little time in repealing the ban on Nazi storm troops and which might become a "Kerensky government" (as Nadolny put it), unable to conclude lasting agreements.[60] At Lausanne late in June, Herriot rebuffed all attempts to discuss equality with the remark that these issues belonged to the disarmament conference. The powers also rejected Papen's attempt to buy equal rights with a final payment in reparations—"it reeked of bad faith," commented Herriot. Papen left Lausanne with a settlement that all but canceled reparations (mainly the result of Brüning's spadework), but with no more than assurances of good will for the disarmament negotiations.[61] At Geneva, meanwhile, German delegates had carried on fruitless conversations with the French and British, while the conference itself stagnated. The technical commissions were once again locked in disagreement, and a new American plan, which called for specific numerical reductions in land and sea armaments, came to nothing.[62] On 10 July Nadolny sent distressing news. The conference would recess with a resolution summarizing its progress and setting forth specific tasks for the next session. The resolution, to be worked out by the British foreign secretary in consultation with the major armed powers, would not mention German equality.[63]

This was an outcome Germany could not countenance. Schleicher argued that Germany should withdraw from the conference and declare her freedom from the disarmament provisions of Versailles unless the conference reached a satisfactory decision on equality. Without consulting the Foreign Ministry, he instructed the military representative on the Geneva delegation to assume this position.[64] The German diplomats were too conscious of the uses of force, or the threat of force, in foreign affairs to be unsympathetic to rearmament. However, they took exception to this challenge to their prerogatives. Bülow warned against attempting to coerce the conference into a decision on equality. He believed that the various delegations were too intent on having France disarm to entertain a German resolution on this issue. To leave the conference was pointless; the gesture would not be understood abroad. To break up the conference was impossible. Bülow came up with a compromise: the Germans could present a resolution of their own, protesting the official line, and then wait for developments.[65]

The Foreign Ministry drafted a protest, which Nadolny was to read at the final session. The German government, he was to say, was prepared to continue participating in the work of the conference, but it could do so only if the determinations of the conference would apply equally to all. It was ready to negotiate this claim to equality at any time. However, it would face "serious decisions" if its claim had not been settled satisfactorily by the time the talks resumed. After a discussion between Neurath and Schleicher "serious decisions" was changed to read that Germany could not continue collaborating in the conference.[66] On 22 July Nadolny presented this declaration to the conference. On the twenty-third he—and the Soviet delegate—voted against the official resolution. The German press was almost unanimous in its approval.[67]

On the question of tactics, the Foreign Ministry had prevailed. Germany had not walked out of the conference and had not turned her back on negotiation. But the method of diplomacy had changed, for Germany had gone over to open rebellion against the disarmament stipulations of Versailles. From a draft which had left open the consequences of an unacceptable resolution emerged a declaration in which Germany threatened openly. Germany now removed the question of German armaments from the competence of the conference and decided that equal rights would be negotiated diplomatically.

Schleicher was bent on influencing the course of these negotiations, and he took occasion more than once to pronounce publicly on Germany's policy toward the conference. His motives, as before, were political—nothing was to take place in foreign policy that did not bear on Germany's "domestic needs," he told the cabinet. His concern, also as before, was the Nazis, who had become the strongest party in the Reichstag in the elections on 31 July and now were bidding for power. To deal with them, Schleicher believed that his policy on armaments had to prevail.[68] He was encroaching even further on Neurath's province, and Neurath seemed to yield. On 29 August, Neurath (with Schleicher in attendance) received the French ambassador François-Poncet and transmitted a memorandum which set forth Germany's position on equality. Germany must insist that a future disarmament convention bind all powers equally and for the same length of time, thus releasing Germany from the discriminating terms of the peace treaty. The convention would have to grant Germany explicitly the "right to national security" and would have to allow Germany "in principle" those arms not proscribed for all. However, Germany did not insist on material equality: for the duration of the convention she would be satisfied with "certain modifications" of her present armaments.[69]

When news of the meeting broke on 31 August, the French public was incensed. The press spoke of government by a clique of barons and generals, of a revival of the old war spirit, and of Germany's intentions to rearm.[70] The French government was offended at the "aggressive manner" in which the Germans had presented their claims and was in no mood to make concessions. Its reply, transmitted by François-Poncet the morning of 11 September, was bland in form and general in content. The French accepted Germany's right to national security (through compulsory arbitration and arms control) and did not expressly deny the claim to equal rights. They rejected the notion that the convention should replace the stipulations of Versailles. Neither the peace treaty nor the covenant provided legal basis for a claim that general disarmament should lead to the abrogation of special stipulations. They referred "modifications" of Germany's army, which Schleicher's pronouncements obliged them to treat as rearmament, to the Council of the League, where the peace treaty had placed competence over such matters.[71]

The Germans reacted promptly and uncompromisingly. Within twenty-four hours the cabinet had authorized Neurath to inform the powers that Germany would not be represented when the bureau of the conference convened on 21 September. However, Neurath was asked to point out that his government would welcome results of the conference which would enable Germany to return. At the same time, Neurath instructed his ambassadors to tell the governments to which they were accredited that Germany's attempt to settle the impasse had "miscarried." The French reply, they were to explain, had evaded Germany's arguments and distorted her case. The French had "discredited" the modest modifications the Germans requested as a "sudden and arbitrary" demand to rearm. They had claimed that general disarmament was independent of and separate from Germany and her disarmament and that the conference was not obliged to deal with Germany's equality. "As long as France maintains this untenable position," he wrote, "a reasonable, practical understanding on this problem is unthinkable."[72] On 14 September, Neurath notified Henderson at Geneva that Germany would not be present on the twenty-first.[73]

The German government had made good its threat and walked out of the conference. Now it waited to see what reaction it would get. Early in October the British invited the European prime ministers to London to discuss the impasse. Bülow interpreted this as a sign that Germany's stubbornness was working; the British were now coming around to Germany's wish for negotiation. Yet he believed that Germany might be forced into a compromise at such a conference and he advised reserve, persuading Papen, who favored accommodation.[74] Bülow told the British that his government would accept only if it were assured in advance that the talks would reach satisfactory conclusions. And the Foreign Ministry sabotaged the talks by refusing a change of venue to Geneva, to which Herriot had won over the British.[75]

By the end of the month the British and the French began to worry about the consequences of Germany's continued absence from the conference. They were afraid that the Germans might rearm in defiance of the peace treaty and conference if no one acted.[76] In the Chamber of Deputies on 28 October, Herriot presented a new scheme for disarmament. Abandoning Tardieu's February program, it proposed to standardize Europe's armies into national short-service conscript armies, without professionals and with no heavy armaments. These armies would be under international control, and their essentially defensive nature would be complemented by compulsory arbitration and mutual assistance pacts. The German Foreign Ministry realized that implicitly the scheme provided a framework for equality, yet publicly it characterized the scheme as utopian and far removed from true disarmament.[77] On 10 November the British offered their solution to the impasse. Foreign Secretary Sir John Simon told an approving House of Commons that the government accepted Germany's claim to equal rights and a common convention (superseding the peace treaty), but in order to allay anxieties about the practical ramifications of this claim, all European powers should declare that they would not resolve differences by resorting to force. The Foreign Ministry responded warmly, asserting that Simon's scheme "accepted German claims and made them, within limitations, its own."[78] The ministry now informed London, Paris, and Rome that Neurath would be in Geneva when the council met about Manchuria on 21 November, and that this would be an occasion for "preparatory talks." In the cabinet Neurath announced that Germany's position remained that of the August memorandum: equality in principle and in practice.[79]

At Geneva Neurath found Simon the moving force toward a resolution of the impasse. Leaving aside questions of detail (on which agreement was difficult), Simon concentrated on questions of principle. He first assured himself that the Germans were agreed to negotiate on the terms he had outlined in the Commons and then secured the agreement of the American and the Italian delegation. He now dispatched a special emissary to Paris to enquire whether Herriot would also accept the British proposals. If Herriot accepted, Simon told Neurath, the powers could meet the following week to draw up the declaration necessary to ensure Germany's return to the conference. Should Herriot refuse, Simon would announce that everything possible had been done and that responsibility for the failure rested with

France. By 22 November, then, Neurath had achieved his first aim: "to create a front of the three chief powers against France." By the twenty-fourth Simon informed Neurath that Herriot was coming to Geneva to take part in conversations—though it appeared, Neurath observed, that Herriot had evaded Simon's question.[80]

The statesmen assembled in the first week of December. MacDonald came from London, Herriot from Paris. Neurath, who had been back in Berlin to secure his position in the new cabinet when Schleicher succeeded Papen as chancellor, arrived on the fifth. He returned to Geneva intent upon obtaining from the powers an "unambiguous and binding declaration" that equal rights must be conceded before Germany could participate in the conference and that equality was to be the guiding principle of the convention. He would accept no formula that might prejudice the practical terms of equality.[81]

At the first meeting, on 6 December, Norman Davis of the American delegation proposed that the conference be adjourned and that in its place a permanent disarmament commission try to arrive at a disarmament convention and settle the questions of German equality and French security. Neurath immediately rejected postponement and announced that he could participate only in talks on German equality. He was more interested in Herriot's proposal, submitted that same day, that the powers agree "that one of the aims of the conference of disarmament is to accord to Germany and the other disarmed powers equal rights in a system which would provide security for all nations," and that Germany return to the conference on that basis. The French in effect declared that the disarmament negotiations could provide Germany with equality. To Neurath, this looked like progress. "Last July," he telegraphed Bülow, "such a declaration would probably have made our withdrawal from the conference unnecessary." Now it no longer met all of Germany's desires. So as not to forfeit these gains, however, he suggested that the French should be urged to accept an interpretation that would satisfy the Germans. He asked Bülow to get the cabinet's opinion.[82]

Bülow presented the case to the cabinet on 7 December. Germany could hardly expect to improve on Herriot's formula, he explained. It went beyond Germany's claims at Lausanne and Geneva, for it settled a matter still officially on the agenda of the

conference. Could the cabinet agree to the formula? Schleicher
was not satisfied. He argued that Germany would be settling for
something she had in effect been offered before she withdrew
from the conference. At this stage, Germany could not accept
equal rights merely as the *aim* of the conference, and she could
not make it conditional by permitting it to be tied to security.
Bülow asked whether Neurath might not press for an interpretation which would satisfy these reservations. The cabinet
deemed this expedient insufficient for domestic reasons.
Schleicher suggested that Neurath ask instead for express
confirmation that equal rights would be an essential part of the
future disarmament convention.[83]

With these instructions Neurath now worked for a clear
definition of Herriot's formula. On 8 December he put specific
questions to the others. Notably, was German equality to have
"practical effect" in the convention in every respect and, in consequence, to be the "starting point" of the conference's future
discussions? By the evening of the ninth, Minister of War Paul-
Boncour (representing Herriot) declared that the French could
not go beyond their formula. MacDonald undertook to find a
formula which would meet the objections on both sides.[84] The
formula, presented the morning of the tenth, satisfied neither
Germans nor French. However, they managed to agree on certain parts, and in the afternoon, the statesmen went to work on a
revised (and truncated) version. They debated, drafted, and revised for nearly six hours. The French argued that they could
not accept a principle without knowing its application and that
only the conference could decide on application. The Germans
insisted that they must know whether the decisions of the conference applied to them as to others. Neurath remained firm,
and ultimately Paul-Boncour yielded to MacDonald and Davis.
In the evening a formula was found to which both Schleicher
and Herriot promptly gave their consent. Released to the public
the following day, it acknowledged that as "one of the guiding
principles" of the conference Germany was to be given equality
within "a system which would provide security for all nations";
that this principle was to be embodied in the future convention;
and that Germany would return to the conference on this basis.
The disarmament conference accepted these terms at a meeting
on the fourteenth.[85]

To the cabinet Neurath explained that Germany had har-

vested the "maximum effect" of her July departure and that her
position for future negotiations was "immensely improved," and
he received Schleicher's thanks for his energetic and tenacious
negotiating. To the press Bülow reported in cautiously optimistic tones. Much progress had been achieved since July: at that
time German equality had been an item on the agenda of the
conference, now it was recognized by the great powers. Its practical application would be discussed at the conference. The principle itself was established "whether the conference succeeded
or failed." If it failed, the Germans were legally entitled to
rearm. Speaking on the radio on 15 December, Schleicher said
that the League would receive new impetus and stimulus for its
work if it succeeded in its attempt at disarmament. And he
warned that the fate of the disarmament conference would be of
great consequence in Germany's continued participation in the
League.[86]

The December accord fell short of what Schleicher had demanded in the summer, coming closer to what Brüning had
asked for in the spring. The Western powers in effect conceded
to the intransigent Schleicher what they had denied the more
moderate Brüning. The diplomacy of intransigence, though
never pursued quite as rigorously as Schleicher would have
wished, had been vindicated. Its success sanctioned a course
both diplomats and military officers were now inclined to follow.

9   Germany Leaves the League, 1933

Germany's relations with the League in 1933, the year Hitler became chancellor, were shaped by the interplay of Hitler's interests with those of the Foreign Ministry. Thus the year saw not only the beginning of something new but also the end of something old.

Hitler had no respect for the principles of the League and no use for its practice of adjustment and compromise. He perceived international politics as a perpetual "struggle for existence," for living space, in which force prevailed. If Germany was to survive in this struggle, if she was to be able to guarantee the future of her "racially superior" people, she would have to restore her "racial integrity" and extend her territory. This she could not accomplish by acquiring colonies or by abrogating the peace treaty and returning to her prewar boundaries. Hitler intended to acquire territory for the "master race" in eastern Europe and to establish hegemony over the continent—and ultimately the world. And he intended to attain these goals by war or the threat of war, at first perhaps in alliance with Britain and Italy, and equipped with a powerful army.[1]

The League was an obstacle to these ambitions. As long as Germany was a member, she was bound in a web of relationships that obliged her to accommodate her national interests to those of her fellow members and to maneuver among a multitude of pressures. As long as she participated in the disarmament conference, she was engaged in an enterprise incompatible with the vast rearmament program Hitler's purposes required. If the conference arrived at a binding convention, such a convention would never suit his requirements. If Germany accepted a convention, she might be subject to international inspection and penalties.[2]

Hitler, however, was in no hurry to turn to these problems.

Before he embarked on his imperialist policy, he would have to make himself master in his own house. In 1933 he wanted to secure full control of the government and extend his party's influence over every facet of domestic life. He also wanted to reorganize the economy, build up the armed forces, and prepare the nation for the tasks that lay ahead. He realized that certain powers might decide to interfere, if only to forestall the aggressive ventures he had announced so freely before he came to power. His foreign policy was intended to protect him against such interference. It was therefore cautious and flexible, and it preserved at least the pretense of continuity with the past. Hitler was content to let relations with the League remain the province of the Foreign Ministry.[3]

The Foreign Ministry was still in the hands of Weimar diplomats. They tended to dismiss Hitler's pronouncements on foreign affairs and to assume that he, like other chancellors before him, would heed their advice and adopt their policy.[4] This policy, which Neurath described at length to the cabinet in April, was little changed. Its principal objective was still the revision of the peace treaty; all else was secondary. Reparations had practically been eliminated, Neurath reported, and, since the accord on equal rights in December, the abolition of unilateral disarmament was simply a matter of time. Once these issues had been settled, Germany could take up territorial revision, first on the eastern borders, then in Memel, Eupen-Malmédy, and Alsace-Lorraine. Later she could seek union with Austria and recover her colonies, perhaps even acquire new ones. However, until she had regained her military and economic strength, Germany would have to work in concert with the great powers, concentrating on one objective at a time. Nothing would be gained by precipitate action or by attempts to revise the remaining clauses all at once.[5]

Toward the League, the ministry's attitude was a mixture of resignation and pessimism. Neurath told the cabinet that Germany might consider leaving the League if she would gain some "direct advantage" or if she found continued membership to be incompatible with her dignity. German diplomats in Geneva complained about the growing ineptitude of the League in dealing with vital political problems. Tellingly, German representation at Geneva, once led by Stresemann, was now in the hands of

August von Keller, an agreeable but not outstanding diplomat. The German government had appointed him "permanent representative on the council" in November 1932, imitating a practice followed chiefly by states which found the expense of regular delegations prohibitive. All of this implied that the Foreign Ministry believed that the League had outlived its usefulness for the prosecution of German foreign policy.[6]

The most important contact Germany had with the League in 1933 was the disarmament conference.[7] Here the interests of Hitler and the Foreign Ministry coincided, but their strategies diverged. Both Hitler and Neurath wanted rearmament, Hitler for the sake of conquest, Neurath because Germany could then act as a major power and might possibly begin to revise the eastern borders. Unlike Hitler, the Foreign Ministry was impatient for results, so that it could get on with its plans. It wanted the conference to produce a convention that would translate theoretical into practical equality, and in short order—or it would not scruple to risk the collapse of the conference.[8] In this respect the diplomats had now approached the position of the military, and Neurath maintained much better relations with the new minister of defense, Werner von Blomberg, than he had with Schleicher the year before. Blomberg, apparently eager to promote the army's role under the new regime, was intent on pursuing the rearmament program planned the previous year and scheduled to be launched in April. His attitude toward the conference was determined by how the conference could help or hinder this program.[9] Hitler did not not want decisive action of any kind—neither the conclusion of a convention nor the collapse of the conference, nor other crises that would compel him to make choices or limit his options. Therefore he became a moderating force, obliged to repair the emergencies that the Foreign Ministry manufactured or allowed to arise.

The conference reconvened at Geneva early in February. As in 1932, Germany's claim to equality dominated the proceedings. Nadolny and his delegation declared that Germany was entitled to the same measure of national security as other states and therefore to the armaments that other states considered necessary for their defense. She was also entitled to expect general and substantial disarmament, and she saw no reason why this could not be accomplished promptly and effectively. The French, on the other hand, were determined that the conference should adopt a scheme of security (pacts of mutual assistance or a system of arms control) before conceding equality, which would release Germany from the disarmament provisions of Versailles. The French gathered support for their view among the growing number of states which were apprehensive about the militant and revisionist new regime in Berlin. In consequence, the Germans found themselves in the minority time and again.[10]

The delegation pursued tactics that seemed "deliberately obstructive" to observers.[11] From the outset the Germans tried stubbornly to force the conference to discuss the limitation and reduction of armaments, for they believed that such a discussion would bring the conference to a decision on German equality. Aided and encouraged by the Italians, they tried repeatedly to dictate or, if a vote went against them, to reverse decisions on the order of business. When the conference debated a proposal that the European powers standardize their armies on the same model, a proposal the French pursued with great interest, Nadolny withheld his consent, saying he could reach no decision until he knew what the conference would decide on armaments.[12] In the Political Commission, the Germans rejected a no-force declaration that expressly left open the possibility of force in defending breaches of the Locarno agreements or the covenant; the issue had to be settled by private negotiation. And in the Air Commission they blocked all further progress when the other delegates declined to address themselves to the question of abolishing air forces until they had worked out effective means for preventing the military use of civil aircraft.[13] By the first week of March, the incessant quarreling suggested to the *Times* correspondent "that the conference may be dangerously near to the rocks."[14]

Troubled by the prospect of failure at Geneva, Prime Minister MacDonald announced that his government would try to break the stalemate. He and Simon would personally attend the conference and help resolve the differences. The announcement was greeted with "philosophic relief" in Geneva and with chagrin in Berlin.[15] Neurath seemed to have been working for a breakdown; both he and Nadolny had been steadily building up pressure and plotting to put France in the wrong. Neurath was not merely afraid that MacDonald's intervention might salvage the situation; even more he (and Blomberg) feared that it might bring about an interim convention which would fix the status quo. They promptly warned the great powers against such a convention and let it be known that no German minister would go to Geneva to meet with the British.[16] At the same time they recalled Rheinbaben, Nadolny's deputy, in order to coordinate action between the ministry and the delegation.[17]

When Rheinbaben reported to Hitler on 15 March, he found a remarkable contrast to the tactics of the Germans in Geneva. Hitler told Rheinbaben that the delegation was not to sabotage the conference, that in fact it could be accommodating on the question of standardization and on armaments.[18] The delegation was taken aback by these instructions, which so abruptly reversed past policy, but before it was obliged to heed them (and before they were canceled on the twenty-second at the behest of the Defense Ministry), the British delivered the Germans from a decision.[19] In a rambling and patently sincere speech on 16 March, MacDonald put a comprehensive disarmament plan before the delegations. The plan contained practical suggestions for strengthening European security, but its most remarkable feature was a specific and precise scheme for disarmament. Within a transition period of five years and under the supervision of a permanent disarmament commission, the highly armed states would gradually reduce their armaments and troops to prescribed levels, and all European states would transform their armies into short-service militias. At the end of the period, Germany's troops would equal those of France, Italy, and Poland (200,000 men); the other states (save Russia) would keep fewer. Armaments—except aviation and heavy artillery—would also be equal. It was the closest that Germany had yet come to equality.[20]

At the end of April Nadolny presented Germany's amendments to the MacDonald plan. In truculent tones, he charged that the plan failed to limit armaments to a level commensurate to national security and therefore did not meet the standards the conference had set for itself. Among other things, he proposed that offensive weapons and military aircraft be abolished, and that trained reserves and colonial troops (but not paramilitary formations) be included among the forces allotted to each country. The standardization of European armies, to which, as in February, he took especial exception, should be referred to the permanent disarmament commission, inasmuch as the matter was not yet ripe for discussion.[21]

Neither at the conference table nor in private conversation would other delegations concede this particular point. They were put off by Nadolny's rigidity, and their animus was inflamed by developments within Germany. They were troubled by the disregard for civil liberties, distressed by the tales the first refugees told of Nazi excesses, and indignant at the persecution of the Jews. They were agreed that standardization was at the heart of the British draft, and until this matter had been settled, the conference could not turn to the rest of the draft. The dispute crystallized in a question of procedure. The Americans, British, and French advocated a second reading of the section on personnel, which related to the problems of standardization. The Germans insisted on a first reading of the armaments section of the draft and announced that they could give no satisfaction on personnel until they knew what concessions the others would make on armaments. Both sides remained obdurate.[22]

The evidence suggests that Neurath may have been trying once again to break up the disarmament talks. For nearly two weeks he and his delegation waged a war of nerves. In private and public they expressed confidence that the impasse could be resolved, but from first to last they resisted all arguments and ignored all efforts at compromise. Their own offers at compromise, touted both in Berlin and Geneva, turned out on inspection to be spurious.[23] On 9 May, Nadolny put conditions tantamount to considerable German rearmament, and Anthony Eden, the British representative at the conference, concluded that, unless Nadolny moderated his terms, further negotiations were "useless."[24] Two days later Neurath fanned the flames by publishing an article that cast doubt on the good will of the armed states and declared that if the conference failed to produce a satisfactory convention, Germany would have to provide herself with the arms that these states possessed.[25] The article made an "extremely bad impression" in Geneva and was widely construed as an announcement that the Germans would rearm no matter what. At this point even such allies as the Italians began to defect, and Germany was isolated.[26]

On 12 May the German cabinet met over the crisis. Neurath canvassed the situation: Germany faced a closed and hostile front at Geneva, and the climate of opinion in the major countries was deteriorating. For the moment Hitler was not conciliatory. He denounced the conference, claiming that its purpose was not to bring on general disarmament but to disarm Germany yet further or, failing that, to accuse her of sabotaging the talks. These tactics could not be answered at Geneva, he maintained, but only by an official declaration at Berlin. He would demonstrate that the Germans were united on the issue of disarmament and that they were prepared to accept the "ultimate consequences" of a failure of the conference. He would indicate also that such tactics had made further membership in the League "exceedingly doubtful." Both Neurath and Blomberg suggested that the delegation withdraw from the talks, as it had in the summer of the previous year.[27]

The Reichstag was convened on 17 May to hear Hitler's message. It was milder than his statements in the cabinet. He could not have been unaffected by Mussolini's private counsel to be moderate and by Roosevelt's appeal on 16 May, calling upon the states represented in the conference to sweep away "petty obstacles" and make progress toward an agreement. More important, Hitler could not afford a spectacular setback. He was still consolidating his power and, in particular, his party was struggling with its Nationalist partner in the government.[28] According to the delegation, the French and their allies were about to engineer the collapse of the conference. They would lay the fault at Germany's doorstep and expose her rearmament. Germany would be bound once more to the provisions of Versailles and, as foreign politicians threatened even now, she could expect sanctions if she were found guilty of contravening them. Rumors of a preventive war against Germany that had made the rounds of Berlin in April now reappeared in the French press.[29]

To an excited Reichstag, Hitler poured out Germany's grievances over Versailles and the action of the powers. She had disarmed; she was defenseless; she had a moral and a legal claim to equality. She was willing to disband her entire military establishment, scrap all her weapons, and submit to international inspection of armament—if the neighboring countries did likewise. But as long as these retained armaments, she could not be deprived permanently of weapons of defense. She was prepared to negotiate the practical use she would make of her equal status and to participate in any solemn pact of non-aggression. "Germany has only one desire," he summed up, "to be able to preserve her independence and defend her frontiers." For all the protestations of good faith, Hitler's address had a menacing undertone. Germany would not sign a convention that perpetuated her inequality. If the conference attempted to impose a convention that discriminated against her, she would have to draw the "only possible conclusion." And it would be "difficult" for her to remain in the League as a "permanently defamed nation."[30]

But Hitler meant to placate and persuade. He was conciliatory, reasonable, and appeared sincere in pledging his cooperation. He disavowed his foreign minister's pugnacious intransigence and endorsed the MacDonald plan as a "possible" solution to the question of German equality (including its premise that equality would be attained, not immediately, but over a five-year transition period). The speech, soon to become known as the "Friedensrede," was repeatedly interrupted by prolonged applause. The Reichstag deputies, who at this time still represented all parties but the Communists, approved it unanimously.[31] This highly effective performance was the first instance of a stratagem that Hitler was to employ again and again in managing international crises.

The delegates to the disarmament conference had waited in "hopeful uncertainty" for Germany to take a position. They were visibly relieved to hear Nadolny accept the MacDonald plan as the basis not merely of discussion but of a future convention. Nadolny withdrew his amendments to standardization and cleared the way to further discussion. In the next weeks, the conference finished the first reading of the British draft. It could not, however, clear away all disagreement, and at the end of June, disregarding Nadolny's appeal to its historic role, it adjourned to mid-October. Meantime, Henderson would make the round of the European capitals and use private diplomacy to remove the persistent differences.[32]

By September, when the annual assembly met, the palliative effect of Hitler's Friedensrede had worn off and Germany's international position had deteriorated again. To be sure, over the summer the German government had concluded a concordat with the Vatican and encouraged the Nazi government in Danzig to resolve its differences with the Poles. Hitler had personally repudiated his Nationalist minister of economics, Alfred Hugenberg, who had produced a pan-German tirade at the League's Economic Conference in London that shocked the world. Nazi tactics elsewhere, however, had more than offset these conciliatory deeds. Europe was alarmed at Germany's attempt to subvert Austria. Germany's neighbors were troubled by the martial activities of the storm troopers and by rumors that the Germans were rearming on a large scale. Members of the League were dismayed when a German delegation under Robert Ley abruptly walked out of the International Labor Conference in June. Nazi Germany represented an undefined threat, and in the face of it the European powers drew together. The British and French settled many of their differences, and the French succeeded in improving their relations with Italy and with the Soviet Union.[33]

The Foreign Ministry expected that the new climate would be manifest when its delegation appeared at Geneva for the meeting of the assembly. Reaction to governmental policy toward the Jews would be especially troublesome.[34] The council meeting the previous May had been unpleasant: Franz Bernheim, a Jewish attorney in German Upper Silesia, had petitioned against the application of Germany's anti-Jewish legislation. Other Jewish complaints appeared on the agenda, and the German delegation thought it faced a "general offensive" against Germany, designed to undo the diplomatic gains of Hitler's speech. To prevent Germany from being publicly embarrassed, the delegation tried evasive legal tactics, innocuous explanations, change of venue, pressures on the rapporteur and even a counterreport. Squirming and evasion brought little relief. In the end Germany was put in the dock as the council debated the issue and, over the vote of the German and Italian delegates, adopted a resolution that bound Germany to observe the stipulations of the minority convention for Upper Silesia and to report to the rapporteur the measures taken to rectify the situation.[35] The day after the council debate, the League of Nations societies, meeting at Montreux, released a resolution expressing their concern over the treatment of German Jews.[36]

As the delegation prepared to leave for the assembly, Neurath urged that the Germans should brave it through. It would be a mistake, he argued in the cabinet, to yield so readily. The time for Germany to leave the League would come when the disarmament conference had collapsed (which he seemed to regard as inevitable) and the Saar had been restored—in other words, in a year's time, at the earliest. Until then the government could continue to use the League to advance its political interests.[37]

To improve their country's image and make the most of the opportunities for propaganda and publicity, the Germans sent a large delegation to Geneva, headed by Neurath and Goebbels and swelled with many young party functionaries.[38] Other delegations and members of the secretariat received the Nazis with distrust. Goebbels's conciliatory defense of the new Germany found little sympathy from a press corps that was accustomed to German delegations of another format. In their private conversations, the German ministers heard mostly protests. At the assembly the representatives of Norway, Sweden, Holland, and France directed barbs at Germany, and the plenum accorded Austrian chancellor Dollfuss "ostentatious applause."[39]

On 29 September the Dutch foreign minister deGraeff focused attention on life in Nazi Germany. Large numbers of German nationals had sought refuge in neighboring countries, he reported to the assembly, and the influx created immense "economic, financial, and social" difficulties. The matter fell within the purview of the League, and in a tactful but unambiguous resolution, deGraeff asked that the council arrange for rectification and relief. Ambassador von Keller challenged the League's authority to deal with the issue. The emigrés were still German citizens and had left Germany voluntarily, not a few of them because of "bad conscience." The ploy did not work, and the Germans accepted a compromise. The assembly would not discuss the issue but referred it to its second committee (Technical Questions) for examination.[40] The Germans were not to get off so lightly. In the sixth committee, where the Germans under Curtius and Brüning had chastized the League's "ineffectual" minority protection, discussion had also turned to the treatment of Jews in Germany. Keller, rather incautiously, delivered a brief lecture on Nazi racial theories. The Jews in Germany constituted a "special sort of racial problem," which was beyond the definition of minority and outside the competence of the

League. This provoked a reaction. The French delegate violated custom to hark back to the Bernheim case. Such cases ought to be raised in the assembly, he said. The committee applauded "demonstratively," and various speakers gave their support to a British draft resolution which expressed strong disapproval of the methods of Nazi Germany and presented the case for toleration, asking for greater publicity of minority petitions.[41]

The Germans also found themselves on the defensive over disarmament. On his visit to Berlin in July, Henderson had told them that the French, suspicious of German rearmament, wanted modifications in the MacDonald plan. The future disarmament convention was to last not five but eight years. In the first four years all powers would stop producing armaments for land warfare, and the continental powers would transform their armies as envisaged in the plan. A control mechanism would supervise these changes. If the control mechanism proved satisfactory, in the second four years the powers would reduce their armaments to the level set in the plan.[42] Not without reason, the Germans believed that these changes created a "probation period" for them (a "période de bonne conduite," Nadolny called it), and that in practice the mechanism would search for infractions of the peace treaty. Neurath—and Hitler himself—left Henderson in no doubt that Germany would resist this discrimination and insist on the original scheme. They gave him to understand that the Germans "would feel free to rearm" if a disarmament convention were not concluded.[43]

At Geneva Neurath conferred with various foreign ministers and leading delegates to the conference.[44] He found that they all favored the modifications proposed by France, insisting only that in return the French agree to substantial reductions in armaments. He apparently accepted (details subject to negotiation) the principle of dividing the convention into two periods; he also accepted automatic, periodic supervision applied to all without distinction (no specific probation period for Germany) and qualitative and quantitative disarmament in the second period. He could not accept the others' reluctance to undertake any disarmament in the first period and he protested vigorously against their refusal to grant Germany equality in types of weapons—or as Simon recorded it, grant Germany in the first period the right to "limited numbers" (or "samples") of weapons prohibited by the peace treaty but permitted to others, and in the second period the right to these in "adequate measure."[45] Simon and Neurath realized independently that the question of arms for Germany was the crux of the matter. Simon, making much of English public opinion, said positively that his government would not accept the notion that equal rights should be realized by raising the level of armaments. Neurath in turn made clear that Germany would have to insist on material equality (though he conceded that actual figures might be negotiated).[46] He told Simon that he intended to consult with his government and return to Geneva shortly and, in any case, communicate with him directly from Berlin. He left the impression that accommodation was still possible.[47]

Neurath arrived in Berlin in a black mood, conferred with Bülow, and then reported to Hitler. Again Hitler took a moderate line. He urged Neurath to continue negotiations. A disarmament convention, he said, "would be desirable in any case," even if it failed to meet all of Germany's wishes. Germany need not ask for more than she could absorb economically or financially. Neurath now instructed his ministry to draft a statement for Simon and then departed for a rest in the Bavarian alps.[48]

The statement, drafted in consultation with the Defense Ministry, represented a hard line. It stated Germany's demands explicitly as never before. Equal rights, it said, must be the basis of all negotiations. It followed from this that Germany would accept any prohibition of arms which applied equally to all. By the same token she would have to insist upon the right to acquire those land armaments which all others might acquire in limited number. The question of amount she was prepared to settle in further discussions. She would have to insist also on the right to acquire in unlimited number those armaments the convention would neither prohibit nor limit numerically. The Foreign Ministry instructed Weizsäcker, who as minister in Berne had easy access to Geneva, to deliver the terms orally to the delegations there; it sent copies of the statement to London, Rome, and Washington to be communicated there; and it began to prepare directives for the negotiations Nadolny was to conduct when he returned to the disarmament talks the following week.[49]

On 4 October Otto von Bismarck, the German chargé d'affaires in London, sent news of what Bülow termed a "new, much worse English disarmament plan." This draft reflected Simon's conversations with the various statesmen in Geneva and was meant as a compromise that would make a disarmament convention possible. According to Bismarck, it did not meet all the wishes of the French but neither did it meet Neurath's demand for "samples" in the first period—in effect postponing German equality for the length of that period. The British would present this plan to the bureau of the conference. They assumed, Bismarck added, that Germany—disarmed and politically isolated—would accept.[50] This telegram prompted another course of action to be superimposed on the first. Five days earlier Hitler had advised Neurath to be moderate, in the hope apparently that negotiations might be spun out until Germany had rearmed or that the MacDonald plan, as revised, might accommodate Germany's initial rearmament. In the news from London he saw this hope destroyed. He saw here also an opportunity to divest himself of the League, its obligations and embarrassments.

Domestic reasons probably contributed to the decision. Hitler needed a "patriotic foreign diversion." His own public defense of the departure implied as much; diplomats and journalists, seasoned observers, were convinced. National Socialism had entered a critical phase. Much of the initial "exhilaration and intoxication" seemed to have given way to grumbling. Rallies, parades, and speeches no longer evoked the same response. Diplomatic setbacks that summer had hampered the government's dynamism. At the trial on the Reichstag fire in Leipzig the government had been unable to produce proof of Communist conspiracy; a "parallel trial" at London, bent on proving that the Nazis had set the fire, was a humiliation.[51] The Nazis had not fulfilled their promises to improve the economic conditions—prices were up, wages down, and unemployment but little reduced. Nazi ecclesiastical policies distressed adherents of the church. There seemed to be rifts in the party ranks: party loyalists resented compromises with traditional institutions and were disgruntled about the spoils. Even in the upper echelons there was dissension, and a split between Göring on the one hand and Hitler and Goebbels on the other was rumored.[52] A well-managed coup could restore unity and revive popular enthusiasm. It could achieve with a "national" issue what the "socialist" program had failed to attain. It could also prepare for

the final steps of consolidation, especially in the state governments, which continued to show some independence.[53]

To quit the League, citing the developments at the disarmament conference as justification, seemed a small risk. The
Japanese had withdrawn from the League in March without
penalty. The Western powers were unlikely to agree on concerted action, much less on sanctions, as their reaction to Germany's pressure on Austria had shown.[54] In Germany there was
little love left for the League. Neurath and Blomberg, whose
rashness Hitler had been obliged to temper earlier, would favor
the move. The military had never really taken to the MacDonald
plan and would be hostile to the modifications. Hindenburg's
support was also assured, for he too had reservations about the
British plan.[55] Hitler could reduce his risk even further if he
could vaunt ostensibly legitimate grounds and cite popular support. He could manipulate the modified MacDonald plan—and
the apparent rigidity of the powers. In a manner analogous to
the use Germany had made of Wilson's fourteen points, he
could interpret the December accord and the MacDonald plan
as pledges made and broken.

Late in the afternoon of 4 October, Hitler and Blomberg discussed the Bismarck telegram. They agreed not to enter into any
negotiations on the British draft, since Germany might be outvoted and then expected to sign an unacceptable scheme. If the
Germans refused, they would be blamed for breaking up the
conference. Instead, Germany should confront the conference
with her original demands that the heavily armed states disarm
and that Germany be assured equal national security. If the
conference denied these demands or put up an unacceptable
draft for debate, Germany should leave the conference and the
League. Bülow, who had been summoned from a cabinet meeting to join this conversation, suggested less abrupt tactics. The
delegation should revert first to the MacDonald plan and then to
the original demands. He also suggested that the delegation
present an ultimatum to the leading delegates before Germany
announced her withdrawal.[56] In the directives for the delegation, worked out in a conference two days later between Hitler,
Blomberg, and Nadolny, the delegation was provisionally empowered to "intimate" that Germany might be obliged to withdraw from Geneva if the conference rejected her demands. The

directives expressly reserved for Hitler the decision whether the delegation should threaten openly to leave.[57]

The basic decision having been made and the tactics set, Hitler now looked for the proper moment. He anxiously awaited news of the details of the British plan; he could not exclude the possibility that the British might compromise and deprive him of his excuse. British reaction to Neurath's note already implied that Hitler need not worry. In London, Simon told Bismarck that Germany's demands differed from Neurath's accommodating attitude at Geneva and were not conducive to agreement. From Rome Ambassador Hassell reported a similar Italian reaction.[58] At Geneva, where the delegations gathered for the first meeting of the bureau, Nadolny privately defined Germany's position. He gained the impression from Davis and Paul-Boncour that the solid front of September was crumbling. He was mistaken. On 11 October the powers agreed to a common line, and Simon informed Nadolny that he would make no concession on essential points in his speech to the bureau. During the first period Germany would be asked to transform the army, but she would not be permitted to rearm. In the second period Germany would be granted equal rights in armaments, and the heavily armed states would disarm.[59]

For Berlin this was the decisive conversation. On 11 October Neurath had wired to Nadolny that Germany would "withdraw" from the conference if the British proposals remained irreconcilable with German demands. News of Nadolny's conversation with Simon reached Berlin the morning of the twelfth, and Hitler had Nadolny recalled immediately. When Nadolny stalled, eager for agreement and convinced that he could achieve a compromise, the order was repeated peremptorily.[60] Hitler wanted no further negotiation, and he did not want Nadolny in Geneva in case the powers came up with a compromise. He himself evaded Mussolini's offer to mediate, which the Italian ambassador had submitted to him that very day.[61]

Nadolny arrived at Tempelhof airport at 10:35 on the thirteenth, accompanied by his military adviser, and made his way directly to the chancellery. Hitler received him in the company of ministers and advisers. Nadolny's report made the situation at Geneva seem less critical and the British more accommodating than Berlin had assumed, and he found himself contradicted by

Neurath and Göring.[62] Hitler appears to have conferred with his ministers and with his legal and military experts all day. He consulted Hindenburg, who had unexpectedly returned that morning from his estate in East Prussia. At 2:00 in the afternoon, the Foreign Ministry heard from Rheinbaben in Geneva that the other delegations, especially the Americans and the Italians, were looking for ways to mollify Germany, so that negotiations might continue.[63] At 6:20 that evening Hitler convened the full cabinet to inform it of his decision. Germany would have to leave both the conference and the League. He proposed to dissolve the Reichstag and combine new elections with a plebiscite asking for support for the government's "policy of peace." He would announce the decision the following day—unless changes should occur that would make it possible for Germany to remain at the conference.[64] Later that evening a telegram instructed Hassell in Rome to inform Mussolini that Germany was about to withdraw from the conference; there was no mention of the League. That night Hitler prepared his proclamations for the morrow.[65]

The morning papers in Berlin carried "obviously inspired" articles on the disarmament conference: the British were being intransigent and obstructing progress.[66] At 11:00 A.M. the Foreign Ministry received by telegraph the text of the speech Simon was about to deliver in the bureau. Forty-five minutes later the delegation telephoned to say that on the way to the podium Simon had told Rheinbaben that the speech would be conciliatory and would leave the door open for negotiation. It made no difference: the speech, though obviously drafted with careful attention to tenor and nuance, conveyed the essentials of the modified British plan.[67] Before noon Bülow called Keller in Geneva to instruct him to leave before the council met again.[68] At noon Hitler informed the cabinet briefly that no change had taken place and the decisions of the previous day were now in effect.[69] Radio programs were now interrupted to announce the news. At 1:00 P.M. Goebbels personally communicated to an astonished press a government communiqué and a "manifesto of the Führer," both justifying the decision to leave the conference on the grounds that moral and material equality had been denied (but, significantly, making only passing reference to the

League). By 2:00 P.M. Swiss newspapers hawked the news in Geneva.[70] By 3:00 a telegram from Neurath reached Henderson:[71]

> In the light of the course which recent discussions of the powers concerned have taken in the matter of disarmament, it is now clear that the disarmament conference will not fulfill what is its sole object, namely, general disarmament. It is also clear that this failure of the conference is due solely to the unwillingness on the part of the highly armed states to carry out their contractual obligation to disarm. This renders impossible the satisfaction of Germany's recognized claim to equality of rights, and the condition on which the German government agreed at the beginning of this year again to take part in the work of the conference thus no longer exists. The German government is accordingly compelled to leave the Disarmament Conference.

That evening Hitler addressed the nation on radio. His speech was a subtle piece of antithetical rhetoric; its theme: Germany the creditor, the other powers the debtors. The Germans had met their obligation under the peace treaty; the other powers had not. Germany had disarmed with almost "fanatical fidelity"; the other powers had not. Germany was insecure, equipped only with defensive weapons and these in inadequate measure; the other powers were secure and highly armed with offensive weapons. Germany had taken part in the disarmament conference jointly and equally to seek ways to abolish armaments; the conference was determined to keep Germany in a state of perpetual inferiority. And—once again in passing reference—Germany had joined the League for conciliation and accommodation on the basis of equality; this had been denied her. To leave Geneva, therefore, was to escape an irremediable situation.[72]

The Foreign Ministry promptly instructed the German nationals to cease work in League committees and commissions and set out to secure the release of the leading German officials in the secretariat.[73] It was not until 21 October, however, that the German consul at Geneva presented notification of Germany's withdrawal (dated 19 October) to Secretary-General Avenol. The note, signed by Neurath, was brief and abrupt:[74]

In the name of the German government I have the honor to
inform you that Germany hereby declares her withdrawal
from the League in conformity with Article 1 §3 of the Covenant.

Some weeks later, in a public address on 6 November, Neurath
presented the official interpretation of these events. Germany
had been forced to leave the League. From the beginning the
League had rested on a contradiction. It had been founded in
the name of an everlasting peace of justice, but in practice it had
perpetuated the status quo of 1919, which assured the superiority of the victors and subjection of the vanquished. That
explained its treatment of Upper Silesia, Danzig, the Saar, German minorities, and the rest, and explained its inability to cope
with the problems that were its proper task. Germany withdrew
from the League in order to turn to a "genuine and fruitful
policy of peace." She could now render service to the idea of a
true association of nations.[75] German propaganda had come full
circle.

On 14 October the news struck the public in Berlin like a
bomb, as the French chargé d'affaires put it.[76] It shocked
Geneva: the second resignation within the year left the League
truncated, and without Germany the disarmament conference
was virtually meaningless. Foreign capitals were amazed—and
then indignant. Observers were agreed almost at once that the
Germans had seized upon Simon's speech as a pretext for realizing a decision long since taken. The press in the Soviet Union
proclaimed that Germany was preparing for war. The French
said the withdrawal confirmed their suspicion that Germany was
rearming and had no intention of observing international obligations. According to an American diplomat in Paris, the French
press adopted an "I-told-you-so" attitude. In Great Britain the
government and the press were irritated at the way Simon had
been used. Americans and Italians were both incensed:
Washington because the resignation reduced hopes for disarmament, Rome because its efforts at mediation had been ignored and because it had been notified of Germany's step to
leave the conference only at the last minute and had received no
word at all of the decision to leave the League.[77]

For all this fulminating, it was clear that no great power would apply sanctions. The French might have been willing, and they could have opened their dossier on secret German rearmament to invoke article 213 of the peace treaty.[78] But the Italians, themselves skeptical of Geneva, and the British, eager to settle the situation, intended to remain neutral. The United States promptly declared its indifference to "any purely European aspect of the picture." None of the great powers delivered a direct protest in Berlin. The disarmament conference confined itself to a telegram refuting Neurath's charges and then affirmed its intention to continue its deliberations.[79] On 17 October Hitler could assure his cabinet that the "critical moment" was past and that Germany had nothing to fear.[80]

Hitler had found his adversaries' weaknesses. The *Times* was inclined to concede that his justification contained "some obvious truths." The plebiscite on 12 November, which approved Hitler's policy by some 95 percent, intimidated the democratic states.[81] Each of these was uncertain of its own commitment to disarmament, and therefore they could not decide on a common course of action. Since they were all afraid of Germany's intentions to rearm, they had no choice but to approach Berlin individually. Turning his chosen isolation to advantage, Hitler now courted their interest. Ten days after he had shocked them with his abrupt withdrawal from the conference, he outlined to the British ambassador his idea of a progressive disarmament convention. Germany should be accorded equality of rights. The highly armed states should commit themselves not to increase their armaments, and Germany should be permitted a short-service army of 300,000 (which would absorb the Reichswehr) and "normal armament" with defensive weapons. In December the German government communicated an elaborated and refined version of this scheme to all the great powers.[82]

The French government was alarmed by the rearmament the scheme permitted and held fast to the revised British plan, which it was disposed to modify only slightly. It declared that it considered a settlement of disarmament possible only in cooperation with the other interested powers and therefore in the context of the League.[83] The Italians cast themselves in the role of mediator and proposed that the League be reformed to induce Germany to return. The covenant was to be separated from the peace treaty, League affairs were to be put in the hands of a great-power directorate, and the League's overall functions were to be curtailed. As a first step, the powers would conclude a disarmament convention that would reconcile Germany's ambitions with gradual disarmament.[84] The British government, worried that German rearmament would bring on an arms race, thought in terms of an international agreement on armaments, to which Germany would be a party. It was prepared to return to the original MacDonald plan, and for a while it seemed to entertain a reform of the League covenant "to win back League members who had resigned." In January 1934 it offered the Germans a scheme that came close to their wishes (falling short chiefly on air armaments), predicated upon their return to the League.[85]

Germany could parry or evade these approaches largely because the powers differed among themselves. The French were displeased both with the British concessions on rearmament and with the Italian proposals for reforming the League. The British approved neither the Italians' readiness to acquiesce in Germany's demands nor their scheme for altering the League.[86] Germany's tactic was to contribute to the confusion. The government exhausted the powers in long exchanges of memorandums and interviews, offering pledges, conditions, and justifications. To some, the Germans seemed compromising; to others, intransigent. At times they flatly refused to return to Geneva; at other times they held out prospects. Thus Neurath could tell the Italian Suvich that Germany had no intention of returning, and Hitler told Eden that the Germans were prepared to discuss the conditions of their return once practical equality was attained. At the same time, the Germans preserved an apparent interest in reforming the League and used the Deutsche Gesellschaft für Völkerbundfragen to propagate ideas that would turn the League into an international technical organization.[87] At bottom, Hitler no more wished to reach a disarmament convention than he wished to return to the League.

In the months after resignation, Germany's tactics had made withdrawal painless; her tactics thereafter also made withdrawal pay. As long as the powers believed Germany might be induced to return to Geneva, Germany could exploit their willingness to repair past wrongs.[88] After the Nazis attempted a putsch in Austria in the summer of 1934, rumors circulated in Paris that the

Germans were contemplating a return to Geneva. After Germany regained the Saar in January 1935, the rumors revived, and they multiplied two months later when Hitler seized upon British rearmament measures as a pretext for announcing general conscription. Simon and Eden visited Berlin at the end of March and urged Hitler to return to the League. Hitler replied that this was the "honest desire" of all Germans, but it was impossible unless Germany enjoyed equal rights. The next month, when the council was about to adopt a resolution condemning conscription in Germany and to take measures that would keep her from violating her treaty obligations again, Bülow informed the British ambassador in Hitler's name that such evidence of continued discrimination against Germany made her return to the League impossible. But in a defense of conscription before the Reichstag in May, Hitler responded to continued British interest and spoke of the possibility of returning to a League which assured "equal esteem and equal rights." In consequence of these carrot-and-stick tactics, the Western powers let pass what may have been the last chance of firm action—possibly even sanctions—against Germany. And then in June, after no more than nominal consultation with the French, the British concluded a fleet agreement with Germany which broke up the front of the victors of 1918 and to all intents and purposes destroyed the peace treaty.[89]

By October the statutory two years had elapsed and Germany's resignation from the League took effect.[90]

10   Conclusions

When Germany had sued for peace in 1918–19, the Germans had been enthusiastic about Wilson's proposal for an association of nations. They had endorsed their government's efforts to join the new organization and hailed the postwar order of equal nations united by a commitment to peace and to a better life. In 1933 the Germans overwhelmingly approved their government's decision to withdraw from the League. The League, they said, had disappointed them. Instead of promoting international conciliation and adjusting outstanding differences in an amicable and impartial spirit, it had protected the Versailles settlement and perpetuated Germany's inequality among nations.

Between those years, the League figured in both Germany's external and internal affairs. In the early 1920s, after Germany had been denied admission to the League, the Germans had bewailed the "betrayal" of their idealistic hopes and looked on the League with a mixture of hostility and fear as an instrument of the victorious powers. Being outside became a virtue, and many thought eventual membership would lock Germany even tighter into the shackles of Versailles. Germany's diplomats, who set policy toward the League, displayed mistrust and preserved distance. Only when Germany teetered on the edge of disintegration in the summer of 1923 did they move beyond purely formal cooperation with the League's technical services and conferences—and they did so mainly because they needed Britain's backing in the contest over the Ruhr.

In the Stresemann era, the Germans fastened on membership in the League as an expeditious means for dismantling the peace treaty. At Geneva, Stresemann acquiesced in the League's conventions and attended to its tasks, especially those that happened to touch on German interests. When the occasion arose, he admonished his fellow members to live up to the ideals on which the League had been founded and, by implication, to stop discriminating against one of their own. And all the while he strove to convince Western statesmen that removing Germany's disabilities served the interests of peace and international understanding. His achievements, orchestrated by his optimistic rhetoric, gained him a following among the liberal and socialist Left, who welcomed the prestige and respect he brought the republic. By the end of 1929, however, as the approaching economic collapse first cast its shadows, neither achievements nor rhetoric could protect his policy from the destructive critics on the Right.

In the early 1930s, as Weimar democracy crumbled, the Germans increasingly treated the League with open contempt and abused their government for the "failure" of its League policy. Under Brüning no less than under Papen and Schleicher, the government did little to defend Germany's presence at Geneva. Without the least qualms about damage to the League, the government became uncompromising at council sessions in order to appease its domestic critics. And it was prepared to threaten withdrawal in order to get its way at the disarmament conference. By the time Hitler acceded to power, both the public and the government had come to believe that the League's usefulness was exhausted. Hitler, who had denounced the League from the beginning and who regarded membership as an impediment to his plans, could withdraw without fear of unfavorable domestic repercussions. His withdrawal signaled the beginning of National Socialist foreign policy.

During seven years of active membership, the German government pursued two distinct policies toward the League, each lasting about the same length of time. These policies reflected different revisionist strategies and different diplomatic styles. The first was predicated on the assumption that by joining the League, Germany could promote conditions which would facilitate her recovery of power and eminence. It was characterized by emphasis on form and appearance (in the council and assembly as well as in the secretariat), and it tried to convey an impression of loyal collaboration. The second was predicated on the assumption that unless membership netted tangible revisionist returns, there was no point in submitting to the League's cooperative ethic and limiting Germany's freedom of action. It conceded loyalty only in exchange for results.

The first policy was Stresemann's. Like his predecessors, Stresemann intended to revise the peace treaty, but unlike them, he forswore confrontation and defiance. He believed that Germany could revise the treaty only in concert with the powers which had made it. He would concentrate his efforts on France, which for reasons of geography, national interest, and historical memory, was the greatest obstacle to revision. He would enlist the aid of Britain, with which he could establish common political interests, for the British could influence and restrain France. He would secure the good will and support of the United States, whose economic involvement in Germany he might be able to exploit in dealing with the European powers. The League offered Germany access to the Western powers—and the opportunity to cultivate the relationship inaugurated at Locarno. Active membership would reassure the security-conscious European states and create a climate in which the Germans could press for revision. It would demonstrate to the United States that Germany was committed to keeping Europe on a stable course and therefore deserved favor. Not least of all, membership with a permanent seat on the council was incontrovertible evidence of Germany's status as a great power, and Stresemann knew that Germany would profit from the prestige such status conferred.

This policy, belittled by the German public (and by subsequent historians), yielded substantial results. It took Germany to Geneva where she could work for her objectives in cooperation with the powers, rather than by trying to divide them. It released Germany from her "moral probation" and restored her to a place among the great powers.[1] It delivered her from supervision of her military status. It enabled her to persuade the Allies to reduce and then to withdraw their troops from the Rhineland, and to induce the French to recall their garrison from the Saar. It led to a reparations settlement that lowered annuities and named a fixed sum and a method of payment. All these achievements removed sources of national unrest and annoyance and deprived the Allies of direct control of Germany and German affairs. Stresemann's policy also hastened Germany's economic recovery: large investments from abroad allowed the Germans to modernize their industry, improve their production, and raise their standard of living. The policy helped bring about the few years of relative internal tranquility the republic enjoyed.

Stresemann did not achieve these results the way he had expected—and certainly not the way the German public had expected. The Western powers made no elegant *geste de magnificence*, meeting German claims promptly and generously in return for a display of good will and for promises of good behavior in the future. Stresemann's achievements were slow in coming, and they came at a price. Military supervision was removed and the occupation forces reduced only in 1927, after Germany had met the last of the Allies' objections about German disarmament. In return for the final evacuation of the Rhineland in 1929, Stresemann committed Germany to paying reparations for some sixty years (and acceded at The Hague to last-minute adjustments unfavorable to Germany). According to his party colleague Rheinbaben, Stresemann said in September 1929 that he would not have signed the Locarno agreements had he known that the results would be realized so slowly.[2]

Germany could not avoid having to pay a price, for the parties to the Locarno settlement, while agreed on diplomatic method, were not agreed on their diplomatic policies. Basic differences persisted, especially over Germany's place in Europe. The French, wrote the British ambassador in Paris in July 1927, were "not convinced that the gap between the political institutions and practice of the Germany of 1914 and those of the Germany of today is necessarily a wide one"[3]—and their anxieties were not alleviated by Germany's opposition to an "eastern Locarno" or by intelligence about Germany's secret rearmament. Briand might be accommodating and sanguine when he conversed with Stresemann, but he was as determined as Poincaré not to surrender the rights France held under the peace treaty and to guard France against possible German aggression. The British, especially the francophile Chamberlain, found the Germans irritatingly ungracious and grasping. They were pleased to have assumed no more than limited responsibility for continental affairs at Locarno, and they intended no more than to restore Germany to "her rightful place" in Europe, that is, to make her a member of the League.[4] Like the French, they were reluctant to grant concessions without firm guarantees to a country where anti-republican Nationalists might come to power and repudiate the policy of détente. They were therefore not inclined to intervene on Germany's behalf as Stresemann had envisioned. The United States, at least at the time of Thoiry, indicated that she would not let the Germans use her economic resources for revisionist purposes.[5]

Not least, Germany had to pay a price because her membership in the League did not become the "heart of conciliation," as Stresemann had planned.[6] Even though Stresemann gave much time and effort to the League's affairs and did not stint his staff's technical assistance and expertise; even though he did not press for revision within the League itself, but walked softly, especially in contentious matters such as minorities and disarmament, and restrained his delegation—nevertheless, his commitment to revisionist objectives necessarily limited his commitment to the League. He could not give Germany's full support to the League's schemes to strengthen international security, whether these were projects to reinforce the League's investigative powers, proposals to widen the application of sanctions, or general non-aggression pacts.[7] Such schemes, the Germans believed, would limit possibilities for revision. But it was precisely such schemes which might have made the French, on whom revision ultimately depended, less hostile to revision, less afraid of Germany. Had the Germans been less evasive, the French might have been persuaded that Germany had reconciled herself to her postwar status, or, put differently, had been integrated successfully into the system which the League was meant to protect. In any event, the Germans' evasiveness merely confirmed the French in their suspicions of Germany's intentions. The League therefore could not become the instrument of conciliation for which Stresemann had hoped. Inevitably, Stresemann's plans interfered with the functioning of the League.

Stresemann's successors pursued the second policy. They considered the League incidental to their revisionist strategy. They preferred to negotiate with other states directly and separately, and they conducted a campaign to isolate France and constrain her to accept the abolition of reparations and of unilateral disarmament, perhaps even a customs union with Austria that would prepare the way for boundary changes in the East.[8] They threw off the restraint Stresemann had practiced at Geneva, spurned the language of compromise, and moved to extract whatever revisionist advantages membership might yield. Their tactics served only to stifle the last possibility of reconciliation. Their attempt to gain the League's consent to the customs union ended in humiliation. Their aggressive minority litigation, far from advancing territorial revision legally or even morally, served only to dissipate sympathy for Germany's claims. And their intransigence at the disarmament talks foreclosed any hope of realizing their demand for equal rights.

They were unsuccessful because the League and the objectives of German revisionism were irreconcilable. The covenant specifically guaranteed the members' political independence and territorial integrity (article 10), and its provisions for corrective change (article 19) remained a dead letter. The organization itself was weighted in favor of the existing order. In the young years of the League, when France exercised strong influence, this conservative tendency had become iron-clad policy. Germany's diplomats sensed the contradiction between the possibilities of the League and the intent of their foreign policy. At Geneva, one contemporary records, they displayed a "chronic discontent."[9] They never put aside their misgivings, and they regarded membership in the League with resignation and growing pessimism. The notion that Germany would have to redirect the League's orientation was a recurrent theme in their memorandums.[10]

Throughout, Germany's relationship with the League was burdened. The German government and the public had no commitment to the League. They thought not in terms of what they could contribute by supporting the covenant and limiting German sovereignty but in terms of the use they might make of membership. By the very nature of the things they wanted, they gave greater attention to the League's incidental functions (such as Danzig or the Saar) than to its proper tasks. The public thought that the League ought to make good past wrongs. Their own peculiar vision of Germany's relationship to the League found expression in their behavior toward the League—in their conviction that they had been done badly and their great display of self-pity.[11] Because the League failed to give the Germans what they had expected of it, membership in the League, indispensable to Stresemann's policy, became yet another weakness in the body politic of the republic.

When Germany acceded to membership in 1926, the League had already lost much of its original inspiration and impetus. The obvious reluctance of the member states to subordinate their sovereign prerogatives to the common cause had cast doubt upon its capacity to preserve the peace, generally considered its most important responsibility. Even as the covenant was being drafted, the member states had insisted that all but procedural decisions be unanimous (articles 5, 15), that arbitration be voluntary and, in any case, confined to juridical disputes (article 13), and that force not be ruled out, even though war was proscribed (article 16). Once the League was established, its members had retreated from their covenanted obligations. They had resolved, more or less formally, that each member could decide for himself both whether aggression had taken place and warranted sanctions and what action to take if fellow members were threatened or attacked.[12] And they had rejected various proposals, usually sponsored by France and her allies, to tighten the provisions of the covenant in order to make its guarantees effective.

The League suffered also because the secret diplomacy and power politics it was supposed to supersede continued to flourish. Issues of moment, especially those involving the great powers, were decided with little regard to the League. The Supreme Council and the Conference of Ambassadors in Paris dealt with problems arising from the peace treaties, over which Woodrow Wilson had wanted to give the League jurisdiction. The major naval powers negotiated and concluded a disarmament accord in Washington, though all but one of the signatories belonged to the League. In 1923 both the occupation of the Ruhr and the bombardment of Corfu proved that the League was helpless to intervene when great powers chose to ignore the injunctions of the covenant. Perhaps most discreditable, even in instances when the League was powerful to act, it rarely defied the wishes of its dominant members, so that preserving the peace became tantamount to defending the status quo.[13]

Germany seemed ideally suited to give the League a renewed

sense of purpose. As the principal victim of the peace settlement, she could be expected to seek redress by invoking the League's principles and turning to its procedures, thus bringing problems of major import before that body. Disarmed and virtually defenseless, she would be motivated to press for reduction of armaments, long an item on the League's agenda, and to advocate the development of international law and peaceful arbitration. In pursuing her national interest, she would in effect pursue the League's interest. In the process, she might galvanize other states loyal to the covenant, and together they might offset the preponderance of the great powers and their client states, introduce greater flexibility and, in consequence, greater practical importance into the League.[14] In time, the League might evolve a dynamic of its own and come to assume the role that proponents of the new diplomacy had long hoped for.

Nothing of the kind ensued. The Germans did not make the League's cause their own. Contemporaries have argued that the Germans were incapable of participating constructively in the work of the League because they were ever conscious of being treated as a "nation of inferior status." Whenever "the others" spoke of justice and equity, Rheinbaben recalls, the German delegation turned its thoughts to "evacuation, the burden of war tributes, the threat of highly-armed neighbors, Danzig, and the bitter lot of the minorities in eastern Europe."[15] The argument is true as far as it goes: on the one hand, League rhetoric was not without its shot of hypocrisy; on the other, the Germans deliberately styled their obligations under the treaty as rank injustice. This does not mean that the converse is necessarily true—that is, that the Germans would have supported the League, had they been treated differently, had their claims been satisfied.

Germany and the League were incompatible; the very concept of the League was alien to German thinking. The League represented an attempt to apply the lessons of the democratic experience to relations between states and place international politics into a setting in which member states could settle their differences peaceably and openly. The Germans, steeped in Wilhelmine traditions, thought of international relations as a competition for dominance in which armies and alliances played important roles and the decision went to the stronger. Only in the realm of pure ideas could they conceive of such a revolutionary approach to international relations. They cited Kant's notion of "permanent peace" and thought in terms of obligatory arbitration and automatic punishment for transgressors. Significantly, whenever they found cause to denigrate the League, they contrasted it unfavorably with a "true" League, whose principles of justice and equality brooked no compromise.[16]

The Germans were blind to the advantages that the League could offer them, for all its constitutional and political imperfections. The League could deliver Germany from international isolation such as she had known in the early twenties and remove the peril of renewed confrontation. It could offer security to a country at odds with its neighbors and without means to defend itself, for its international guarantees would also protect Germany—perhaps better than she had been able to protect herself when she had relied on armaments and alliances. The League could also provide a framework for achieving political goals. As a member, Germany could shed the restrictions imposed by the treaty and rebuild her international position. Working through the League, she would be obliged to adjust her interests to those of the other members and she would not realize her full revisionist program—but what she lost in this respect, she would gain by seeing the results accepted and therefore made permanent and effective. As an integral part of a stable international organization, a restored Germany could exercise her power without creating the tensions that had troubled and threatened Europe since her national unification in the nineteenth century.

The Germans were also uncomprehending of a great power's responsibility to promote peace and stability—in this instance, to promote an organization which might bring some order into international politics. Stresemann knew that when Germany had entered the League, the international atmosphere would improve (and Germany would benefit from this improvement). There is no evidence that he, like Brüning, contemplated leaving the League and severing Germany's multilateral ties once she had gained her revisionist aims. But even Stresemann did not think in such wide terms as to ask how Germany might help the League resolve disputes, enhance the authority of international law, or strengthen the security of its members. "The main purpose of the League is the prevention of new wars," Bülow wrote, "an objective in which we have less interest than the others, especially the allied powers."[17]

Germany's membership did not help the League. In the negotiations for her admission to the League, she had explicitly limited her commitment, insisting that she be exempt from the obligations of article 16. After she entered, she joined the other great powers in using the League's regular sessions as a setting for private diplomacy, resolving the issues of the day behind closed doors rather than around the council table. In fact, far from helping the League, Germany's membership damaged it. Her policy differed too greatly from that of the organization at large. The revisionist ambitions of the potentially strongest European power undermined the League's attempt at cooperation for collective security and disarmament. The League's supporters began to retreat from internationalism; its critics found their prejudices confirmed. In the Balkans, governments canvassed the idea of regional security pacts, even the possibility of confederation. Briand's proposal for a European federal union sprang in part from a sense that the League was insufficient.[18] And Germany's revisionism was contagious. Her example encouraged other discontent countries. When Hungary and Poland, and ultimately Italy, came to defy their contractual obligations, the League was not able to withstand the onslaught.

Over the last ten years historians have studied the style and substance of German foreign policy from Bismarck to Hitler with growing sophistication.[19] They have searched for traditions that remained alive and operative beyond war and revolution and beyond the various changes of regime. Their interest is part of a larger and older question: whether Hitler and his war policy were a natural development or an aberration in German history. This question became particularly immediate and provocative when Fritz Fischer suggested in his study of Germany's bid for world power in 1914 that the Germans may have also brought about the First World War. In this perspective, the continuities that suggest themselves in the reigning attitudes of the Weimar Republic and in the consequent (and counterposed) policies toward the League are illuminating and instructive.

Few would argue today that the upheaval of 1918–19 produced a decisive break with the past, even though it may have encouraged new departures. The revolution ushered in a new

form of government, precipitated reforms, and loosened an os-
sified social and economic order; the peace treaty deprived
Germany of territory, stripped her of military power, and imposed heavy economic and financial burdens. But neither revolution nor peace treaty altered traditional ways of thinking or
abolished institutions that fostered such thinking. Conservatives,
frustrated in their nationalist ambitions and frightened by the
specter of social revolution, clung to inherited orthodoxy. The
liberals who rallied to the republic put down the radicals on the
Left and later supported Hindenburg's candidacy to show that
they too had not abandoned time-honored sentiments. Conservatives and liberals alike were unable to see that Germany's
changed situation offered certain opportunities. They saw nothing but humiliation and deprivation—and perhaps a distant
hope that Germany would not be permanently crippled. They
might differ on the means, but they were at one in their determination to revise the peace terms. Germany would be restored,
and restoration abroad would necessarily effect far-reaching
changes 'at home—an implication to which moderates seemed
oblivious.

Stresemann's revisionist policy, the most distinctive policy of
the republic, was rooted in the past. Stresemann had been a
National Liberal, a member of the patriotic, moderately liberal
party of the educated and propertied bourgeoisie of imperial
Germany. The National Liberals, caught up in Wilhelmine
confidence, had urged that Germany use her economic power in
world affairs. They supported the government's colonial ventures, its military and naval programs, and, during the war, its
annexationist plans. They assumed that political expansion
would automatically follow economic expansion. Much like the
advocates of social imperialism in Britain, they believed that a
vigorous policy abroad would be conducive to tranquility at
home, draining tensions and lessening class conflict.[20]

Stresemann never discarded the National Liberal legacy altogether. Like his quondam colleagues, he tried to strengthen
Germany—or, in the context of Weimar, to restore her strength
and make her once again a member of the system of great powers. He founded his strategy on available political and economic
opportunities, rejecting the possibility of military action as wishful thinking. In the League, Stresemann combined the advantages of open diplomacy, with emphasis on world opinion and

international justice, with those of a traditional diplomacy of confidential negotiations, pressures, and concessions. He deliberately exploited Germany's economic potential—the direction of her foreign trade and the development of her international cartelization no less than her attractiveness as a market for goods and credit. He believed that in time Germany's economic strength and her place in an international system would become a lever comparable in certain circumstances to the military power she lacked.[21]

Stresemann was also an exponent of the National Liberal theory of *Mitteleuropa*. The National Liberals had regarded central Europe as Germany's proper and foremost sphere of influence, as a source of raw materials and an outlet for trade. Stresemann always kept open the possibility of revising the status quo in the East, whether by altering the borders with the successor states or by merging with Austria. His concern for German minorities in eastern Europe, his defense of their cultural autonomy and their right to domicile, motivated no doubt by genuine patriotic sentiment, was founded also in national tradition and prompted by political consideration. More than once he implied that the Germans' right to self-determination, as he spoke of it, meant the right to dominance warranted by their history and superiority.[22] In this larger perspective, Stresemann's intent is not fundamentally inconsistent with the germanization of Prussia's eastern provinces before 1914 and the nazification of eastern Europe in the early 1940s.

Finally, Stresemann retained the National Liberals' concern for internal stability. He believed that an active and successful foreign policy would help integrate society, that revisionism, like imperialism before the war, would bridge the differences both between social classes and between political parties. He spoke and wrote about his policy tirelessly, suggesting progress, voicing expectations, asking for support and discipline until he had achieved his aims. He appealed constantly for a "united national will," which he claimed was a source of political strength for his dealings with foreign statesmen. At the same time, he hoped that such solidarity would help consolidate the republic, to which he had committed himself, and that it would consolidate the liberal-bourgeois order on the prewar pattern, in what he thought was Germany's best interest.[23]

Stresemann's policy never came to fruition. It has been argued that the great depression vitiated his efforts, for by depriving Germany of her economic leverage and encouraging a vociferous nationalism, it destroyed the good will she had accumulated abroad. The Western powers have also been blamed: had they responded promptly and generously to Stresemann's claims, his critics would have remained inconsequential and he could have shaped a stable and peaceful Germany. These arguments ignore the injury that Stresemann did his own policy. For tactical reasons and in his fixation upon his ultimate aim, he belittled his great achievements—the Locarno pact, membership in the League, withdrawal of the military control commission, and even evacuation of the Rhineland. In so doing, he fostered domestic discontent and played into the hands of his most dangerous enemies, the conservative Right and the petit-bourgeois radical Right.

These antagonists represented another line of continuity— "the continuity of error," as Waldemar Besson has called it. In imperial days they had misjudged Germany's position and potential and in trying to improve her situation had "run blindly against realities." To secure a "proper share of world hegemony," they had at one and the same time challenged Britain's supremacy on the seas and risked a two-front war with the continental powers.[24] Revolution and democratization had not changed them; they contrived explanations that obscured the reasons for collapse and defeat. They wanted no mere revision of the peace treaty but a return to the world of 1914; some even dreamed of advancing to the world projected in Germany's war aims of 1914–18. They refused to accept any modification of their goals, so that even Stresemann's commitment not to resort to war to regain Alsace-Lorraine seemed to them a "betrayal of national interests." They made false historical analogies their guide, comparing Prussia's preparation for the wars of liberation in the early nineteenth century with their own activities in the early 1920s. Thus for them Rapallo could become a crusade with Russia against the defenders of Versailles.[25]

These notions were common in the Defense Ministry, whose members speculated that Germany might recover power and status by military means. Many thought the disarmament talks served no purpose beyond lifting the military restrictions upon Germany. Once freed, Germany could court allies, regain territory, establish hegemony over the continent, and gird herself once again for the struggle for world power.[26] This interpretation also had adherents in the Foreign Ministry. Diplomats such as Bülow were more sophisticated than the ambitious military but no less convinced that a conciliatory policy was idle. For these diplomats, membership in the League was never more than a tactical maneuver, and their adherence to the League's basic principles and formal tasks was a masquerade.[27] Even Stresemann's plans implied a League quite different from the one at Geneva.

This line of continuity with the empire, latent in Stresemann's time, became pronounced again in German foreign policy after Stresemann. As the government moved to the Right, departing from parliamentary principles at home, it abandoned conciliation and accommodation abroad. Brüning worked for the abolition of reparations and for legal equality in armaments in order to prepare a truly right-wing government, perhaps even a restored monarchy. Papen and Schleicher, both on the course charted by the military, held out for practical equality in armaments irrespective of the interests of the other powers. Their policies and tactics were carried into the Nazi era by Neurath and Blomberg, who were disposed toward vast rearmament and willing to sabotage the disarmament conference in a play for traditional great-power status.

Hitler's program brought certain innovations. Hitler practiced unorthodox methods of diplomacy which competed and often conflicted with those of the Foreign Ministry. He wanted to rearm Germany, not because military power would improve Germany's prestige and strengthen her diplomacy, but because he intended to expand into the East. Above all, Hitler embroidered traditional imperialist thinking with anti-Semitic mythmaking. Nonetheless there is an eerie continuity here: Hitler's public plans appealed because they answered old ambitions of German foreign policy; specifically, his expansionist program and his commitment to conquest have much in common with schemes of Ludendorff's High Command in 1917–18. And while conservative diplomats and generals may have discounted what they considered Hitler's fantasies, they readily believed that his course coincided with what they had wanted since the shocking defeat of 1918.

Abbreviations

ADAP	*Akten zur deutschen Auswärtigen Politik 1918–1945*
BAK	Bundesarchiv, Koblenz
DBFP	*Documents on British Foreign Policy 1919–1939*
DDB	*Documents diplomatiques belges 1920–40*
DDF	*Documents diplomatiques français 1932–1939*
DGFP	*Documents on German Foreign Policy 1918–1945*
FRUS	*Foreign Relations of the United States*
LNOJ	*League of Nations Official Journal*
PAB	Politisches Archiv, Bonn
Schulthess	*Schulthess' Europäischer Geschichtskalender*
Survey	*Survey of International Affairs*
Verhandlungen	*Verhandlungen des Deutschen Reichstags, Stenographische Berichte*
Vermächtnis	Gustav Stresemann, *Vermächtnis: Der Nachlass in drei Bänden*

Notes

Chapter 1

1. F. P. Walters, *A History of the League of Nations* (London, 1960), chap. 2; F. H. Hinsley, *Power and the Pursuit of Peace* (Cambridge, 1963).

2. Walters, chap. 3. See also Theodore Marburg and J. H. Latané, *The Development of the League of Nations Idea*, 2 vols. (New York, 1932), and Henry R. Winkler, *The League of Nations Movement in Great Britain 1914–1919* (New Brunswick, 1952). In Germany, such interest was confined to pacifist intellectuals, who labored under very restrictive consorship (Ernst Jäckh, *Der Völkerbundgedanke in Deutschland während des Weltkrieges* [Berlin, 1929]).

3. A convenient collection of documents concerned with the peace negotiations is in Ferdinand Czernin, ed., *Versailles 1919* (New York, 1965). Wilson's various messages, pp. 10–22.

4. See Arno J. Mayer, *Wilson vs. Lenin: The Political Origins of the New Diplomacy 1917–1918* (Cleveland, 1964), especially chap. 9.

5. Ibid., pp. 326–27, 332, 383–88; Max Beloff, *Imperial Sunset*, I (New York, 1970), pp. 233–50.

6. Mayer, pp. 332–33; Beloff, pp. 264–73; Walters, pp. 22–23.

7. Klaus Schwabe, *Deutsche Revolution und Wilson-Frieden: Die amerikanische und deutsche Friedensstrategie zwischen Ideologie und Machtpolitik 1918/19* (Düsseldorf, 1971), pp. 300–301, 318–19, 440. The debates of the League of Nations Commission at Paris are in Czernin, pp. 86–103, 115; for the attitudes of the British dominions, see Beloff, pp. 292–96.

8. The two versions are in Czernin, pp. 140–63. See also Felix Morley, *The Society of Nations* (Washington, 1932), chaps. 1–6.

9. Fritz Fischer, *Griff nach der Weltmacht* (Düsseldorf, 1964), pp. 831–33.

10. Both of 10 Jan. 1918.

11. 11 Jan. 1918.

12. Fischer, pp. 525–29; Wilhelm Stahl, ed., *Schulthess' Europäischer Geschichtskalender, 1918* (henceforth *Schulthess*) I, pp. 27–29, 40–41.

13. *Schulthess, 1918*, I, pp. 19–25, 38, 86–91; Ernst Fraenkel, "Das deutsche Wilsonbild," in *Jahrbuch für Amerikastudien* (1960), p. 74.

14. *Frankfurter Zeitung*, 2, 3, 4, 18 Aug.; *Berliner Tageblatt*, 1 Sept. 1918.

15. *Deutsche Tageszeitung*, 13, 17, 23 Aug.; *Rheinisch-Westfälische Zeitung*, 21, 30 Sept. 1918.

16. Klaus Schwabe, "Die amerikanische und die deutsche Geheimdiplomatie und das Problem eines Verständigungsfriedens im Jahre 1918," in *Viertel-*

jahrshefte für Zeitgeschichte XIX (1971), pp. 1–32. Draft of the constitution in Politisches Archiv, Bonn (henceforth PAB): Handakten von Simson, Völkerbund.

17. Schwabe, *Wilson-Frieden,* pp. 95–98, 101–4; Walter Schücking, ed., *Das Werk des Untersuchungsausschusses der Deutschen Verfassunggebenden Nationalversammlung und des Deutschen Reichstags 1919–1926,* 4th ser. II (Berlin, 1925), pp. 399–401, 407–9, 422; Auswärtiges Amt, ed., *Amtliche Urkunden zur Vorgeschichte des Waffenstillstandes 1918,* 2d ed. (Berlin, 1924), nos. 12, 20, 21.

18. Schwabe, *Wilson-Frieden,* pp. 99–101; Schücking, *Werk des Untersuchungsausschusses,* pp. 298–300.

19. Erich Matthias and Rudolf Morsey, eds., *Der Interfraktionelle Ausschuss 1917/18* (Düsseldorf, 1959), II, pp. 520–50, 779–88; Erich Matthias and Rudolf Morsey, eds., *Die Regierung des Prinzen Max von Baden* (Düsseldorf, 1962), pp. 65–68, 139.

20. *Verhandlungen des Reichstags, Stenographische Berichte,* 314:6151 (henceforth *Verhandlungen*).

21. Compare, for example, *Berliner Tageblatt,* 10 Jan. and 5 Oct. 1918; also, *Frankfurter Zeitung,* 8, 13 Oct. 1918.

22. Matthias and Morsey, *Regierung Max von Baden,* pp. 87, 99; *Berliner Tageblatt,* 8 Oct.; Hugo Preuss to Walter Schücking, 14 Oct. 1918, Bundesarchiv, Koblenz (henceforth BAK): Nachlass Schücking, 88. Privately, German politicians admitted that a Wilsonian peace would not be easy (Annelise Thimme, *Flucht in den Mythos* [Göttingen, 1969], p. 74).

23. *Berliner Tageblatt,* 28 Oct., 3 Nov.; *Frankfurter Zeitung,* 3 Nov. 1918.

24. *Verhandlungen,* 314:6157.

25. Erich Matthias and Susanne Miller, eds., *Die Regierung der Volksbeauftragten* (Düsseldorf, 1969), I, pp. 100, 152–54; Schwabe, *Wilson-Frieden,* pp. 232–34.

26. The conclusions of recent research are summarized in Reinhard Rürup, "Problems of the German Revolution 1918–19," *Journal of Contemporary History* III (1968), pp. 109–35. See also, Eberhard Kolb, ed., *Vom Kaiserreich zur Weimarer Republik* (Cologne, 1972).

27. Matthias and Miller, *Regierung der Volksbeauftragten,* I, pp. 198, lxix–lxx; Wolfgang Elben, *Das Problem der Kontinuität in der deutschen Revolution* (Düsseldorf, 1965), pp. 111–12.

28. Schwabe, *Wilson-Frieden,* pp. 239–40; Arno J. Mayer, *Politics and Diplomacy of Peacemaking* (New York, 1967), pp. 99–101.

29. Matthias and Miller, *Regierung der Volksbeauftragten,* I, pp. 155–60.

30. Ibid., I, pp. 161, 164, 166–68, 170.

31. Ibid., II, pp. 281–82; *Verhandlungen,* 326:66–72; Schwabe, *Wilson-Frieden,* pp. 346–52.

32. Matthias and Miller, *Regierung der Volksbeauftragten,* II, pp. 268–69, 282, 293–300; Schwabe, *Wilson-Frieden,* pp. 253, 284, 322–23, 351–52.

33. *Deutsche Allgemeine Zeitung,* 23 Jan. 1919.

34. Ulrich von Brockdorff-Rantzau, *Dokumente und Gedanken um Versailles,* 3d ed. (Berlin, 1925), p. 37.

35. Ibid., pp. 36, 42, 48–49; Matthias and Miller, *Regierung der Volksbeauftragten,* II, p. 268.

36. Matthias and Miller, *Regierung der Volksbeauftragten,* I, 90–92; *Frankfurter*

Zeitung, 23 Nov., 20 Dec. 1918; *Berliner Tageblatt*, 22 Nov. 1918; *Deutsche Allgemeine Zeitung*, 3, 18 Feb. 1919.

37. Mayer, *Politics and Diplomacy*, pp. 101–2.

38. Matthias and Miller, *Regierung der Volksbeauftragten*, II, pp. 268, 282, 297–300; Schwabe, *Wilson-Frieden*, pp. 323, 347–54; Hagen Schulze, ed., *Das Kabinett Scheidemann* (Boppard, 1970), pp. 41–42.

39. Schwabe, *Wilson-Frieden*, pp. 241, 292–96, 327–32, 396–99, 532–39; Mayer, *Politics and Diplomacy*, pp. 281–82, 493–97, 759–62.

40. *Deutscher Geschichtskalender, 1919*, ed. Friedrich Purlitz, I, pp. 127–30, 229–35, 373–76; Schulze, *Kabinett Scheidemann*, pp. 87–91; Hans Wehberg, "Das deutsche Volk und der Völkerbund," in P. Munch, ed., *Les origines et l'oeuvre de la Société des Nations* (Copenhagen, 1923), I, pp. 448–49.

41. Brockdorff-Rantzau, pp. 38–39.

42. Schwabe, *Wilson-Frieden*, pp. 236, 348, 352–53; Schulze, *Kabinett Scheidemann*, pp. 94–95; *Berliner Tageblatt*, 16, 30 Dec. 1918, 17, 23 Mar. 1919.

43. Mayer, *Politics and Diplomacy*, p. 101. The original printing of Erzberger's book (50,000 copies) was sold out within weeks; it was translated as *The League of Nations* (New York, 1919).

44. Matthias and Miller, *Regierung der Volksbeauftragten*, I, p. 243; Ernst Jäckh to Hans Wehberg, 5 Dec. 1918, BAK: Nachlass Wehberg, 46; Wehberg, "Das deutsche Volk," pp. 444–45.

45. Ernst Jäckh, *Der goldene Pflug* (Stuttgart, 1954), pp. 352–54; Marianne Brink, "Deutschlands Stellung zum Völkerbund in den Jahren 1918/19 bis 1922 unter besonderer Berücksichtigung der politischen Parteien und der pazifistischen Vereinigungen" (diss., Berlin, 1968), pp. 185–86; Wehberg, "Das deutsche Volk," p. 445.

46. *Vorwärts*, 2 Nov. 1918; Brink, pp. 92–96.

47. *Freiheit*, 23 Dec. 1918, 28 Jan. 1919; Fraenkel, pp. 76–77.

48. *Germania*, 23 Nov. 1918, 3 Jan. 1919.

49. *Frankfurter Zeitung*, 24 Nov., 2, 14 Dec. 1918.

50. Brink, pp. 170–72; *Dokumente und Materialien zur Geschichte der deutschen Arbeiterbewegung*, ed. Institut für Marxismus-Leninismus, 2d ser. III (Berlin, 1958), p. 144.

51. *Kreuzzeitung*, 24 Nov. 1918.

52. Schwabe, *Wilson-Frieden*, p. 236; Wehberg, "Das deutsche Volk," pp. 440–42; Johann Bernstorff, *Erinnerungen und Briefe* (Zurich, 1936), p. 213; *Münchener Neueste Nachrichten*, 25 Jan. 1919.

53. Brink, pp. 175–84; Wehberg, "Das deutsche Volk," pp. 441–43.

54. The cynicism showed. In January, after Brockdorff-Rantzau had praised Germany's idealistic acceptance of the association of nations and had spoken of her moral commitment to a new order, Harry Kessler, an alert observer of the new scene, noted in his diary: "Who's to be fooled by that? Who's to believe that? Wilson perhaps? . . . Rantzau comes across like an old courtesan who wants to persuade herself and the world of her unsullied virginity" (*Tagebücher 1918–1937* [Frankfurt/Main, 1961], p. 105).

55. Schwabe, *Wilson-Frieden*, pp. 330–32, 444–46; Schulze, *Kabinett Scheidemann*, p. 26.

56. Schwabe, *Wilson-Frieden*, pp. 233–34, 243–44, 247–48, 275–76, 284–85,

321–24; *Deutsche Allgemeine Zeitung*, 18, 23 Feb.; *Neue Zeit*, 28 Feb. 1919; *Verhandlungen*, 326:184–85, 205, 263, 495.

57. *Frankfurter Zeitung*, 25 Feb.; *Deutsche Allgemeine Zeitung*, 17 Mar.; *Berliner Tageblatt*, 24 Mar. 1919; Schulze, *Kabinett Scheidemann*, pp. 94–95.

58. *Deutsche Allgemeine Zeitung*, 4, 6 Apr. 1919.

59. *Verhandlungen*, 327:914.

60. Schwabe, *Wilson-Frieden*, pp. 525–32; Schulze, *Kabinett Scheidemann*, pp. 75–91. Directives in Schulze, pp. 193–204; English translation in Alma Luckau, *The German Delegation at the Paris Peace Conference* (New York, 1941), pp. 199–209.

61. Matthias and Miller, *Regierung der Volksbeauftragten*, II, p. 322.

62. Memorandum by Simons, 4 Apr. 1919, PAB: 9105/H234933–4. The cabinet agreed that a German draft would be more effective in propaganda than mere criticism or emendation of the Allies' draft (Schulze, *Kabinett Scheidemann*, pp. 177–79).

63. Schücking was familiar with a draft drawn up by Harry Kessler, who was dismayed at the "bureaucratic" construct the Allies projected. Kessler envisioned an organization, not of states, but of international institutions already in existence—trade unions, religious bodies, commercial associations (*Tagebücher*, pp. 128, 136, 176–78).

64. *Deutsche Allgemeine Zeitung*, 18 Feb. 1919.

65. Luckau, pp. 226–33; the draft was published in *Deutsche Allgemeine Zeitung*, 24 Apr. 1919. It drew wide commentary in the press (*Vorwärts*, *Kreuzzeitung*, *Hamburger Nachrichten*, *Königsberger Hartungsche Zeitung*, all of 24 Apr. 1919).

66. *Deutsche Allgemeine Zeitung*, 23 Jan. 1919; *Verhandlungen*, 326:66; Kessler, p. 130.

67. Memorandum . by Simons, 4 Apr. 1919, PAB 9105/H234933–4; Schulze, *Kabinett Scheidemann*, pp. 205–6.

68. Schulze, *Kabinett Scheidemann*, p. 205.

69. Verhandlungen, 327:1108–10; general discussion of the peace treaty, 1082–1110.

70. Schulze, *Kabinett Scheidemann*, p. 311 n.

71. Luckau, pp. 314–15, 320–23. The peace delegation at Versailles rejected a proposal that Germany refuse to sign the treaty and place herself under the protection of the League: "It augured better for Germany's future eventually to sign the peace conditions under coercion than to surrender promptly to the League—that is, to our enemies" (Protokoll, 16 June 1919, BAK: 4662/E212613–5).

72. Luckau, pp. 418, 423–24.

73. Wehberg, "Das deutsche Volk," p. 451.

Chapter 2

1. Aside from the covenant, the League is mentioned in some two dozen articles of the peace treaty. An annotated copy of the treaty is in *Foreign Relations of the United States: The Paris Peace Conference 1919*, vol. XIII (Washington, 1947).

2. Bernhard Guttmann, *Soll Deutschland in den Völkerbund?* (Berlin, 1919); Hermann Kantorowicz, *Deutschlands Interesse am Völkerbund* (Berlin, 1919).

3. Nadolny (Stockholm) to Foreign Ministry, 4 Sept.; Sthamer (London) to Foreign Ministry, 27 Oct., PAB: L1837/L530650, L530662–3. Memorandums by Hudson and Drummond, 20, 21 Aug. 1920, League of Nations Archives, Geneva: 1919–27, 28/6426/1032; Wehberg, "Das deutsche Volk," p. 472.

4. *Verhandlungen*, 345:863–64; *Frankfurter Zeitung*, 17 Nov. 1920.

5. *Kreuzzeitung*, 25 Aug. 1919; *Deutsche Zeitung*, 13 Apr. 1920; Brink, p. 157; Wehberg, "Das deutsche Volk," pp. 456, 465.

6. *Verhandlungen*, 327:1410, 328:1851, 1894, 1987–88.

7. *Frankfurter Zeitung, Vossische Zeitung*, 10 Jan. 1920.

8. *Verhandlungen*, 345:907–9, 930, 996, 1023–26.

9. Alois Seiler, "Die Behandlung des Völkerbundes im Unterricht während der Weimarer Zeit," in *Geschichte in Wissenschaft und Unterricht* XXII (April 1971), pp. 193–211; Wehberg, "Das deutsche Volk," pp. 456–57.

10. Wehberg, "Das deutsche Volk," pp. 454–60, 474–76, 483–84; Brink, pp. 130–32, 178–84, 189; Hans Wehberg, *Die Völkerbundbewegung* (München-Gladbach, 1924).

11. *Deutsche Allgemeine Zeitung*, 24 Nov. 1920, 10 Sept. 1922; *Deutsche Zeitung*, 26 Sept. 1921; *Berliner Tageblatt*, 20 Dec. 1920, 13 Sept. 1921; Wehberg, "Das deutsche Volk," pp. 465–66. See also, Werner Becker, *Demokratie des sozialen Rechts* (Göttingen, 1971), pp. 106, 161, 216, 221.

12. *Verhandlungen*, 347:2304–5, 352:5888, 355:7681, 7958; Wehberg, "Das deutsche Volk," p. 476.

13. Wehberg, "Das deutsche Volk," pp. 453–54, 461–66.

14. Perceptive comments on this conservative mentality and its manifestations are in Ernst Troeltsch, *Spektator-Briefe* (Tübingen, 1924). See also, Johannes Erger, *Der Kapp-Lüttwitz Putsch* (Düsseldorf, 1967), chap. 2; Gotthard Schwarz, *Theodor Wolff und das "Berliner Tageblatt"* (Tübingen, 1968), chap. 4. The observations of foreign observers are in *Documents on British Foreign Policy*, 1st ser., vols. 6, 9 (London, 1956, 1960).

15. In addition to Troeltsch, see Thimme, *Flucht in den Mythos*, Kolb, *Vom Kaiserreich zur Weimarer Republik*, and Gerhard L. Weinberg, "The Defeat of Germany in 1918 and the European Balance of Power," *Central European History* II (Sept. 1969), pp. 248–60.

16. *Verhandlungen*, 328:1853.

17. Those in dominant positions in the republic's foreign service—state secretaries, division chiefs, ambassadors—had almost all entered the service before the war. In general, see Erich Kordt, *Nicht aus den Akten* (Stuttgart, 1950), the recollections of a German diplomat who entered the foreign service in the 1920s.

18. Several foreign ministers (Rosen, Rathenau, Rosenberg) had the reputation of being personally hostile to the League; the same was said of the pro-Russian professionals in the ministry. See Bernstorff, pp. 206, 219; Wehberg, "Das deutsche Volk," p. 493.

19. Seeckt to Simons, 18 Jan. 1921, PAB: 3147H/D653567–73.

20. Bernstorff, p. 218; *Mitteilungen der deutschen Liga für Völkerbund*, 19 Sept. 1921.

21. Müller (Berne) to Foreign Ministry, 19 July; Sthamer (London) to Foreign Ministry, 27 July 1921; Wiedfeldt (Washington) to Foreign Ministry, 16 May 1924, PAB: L1837/L530741–6, L530755–7, L531068–93. See also, Werner Link,

Die amerikanische Stabilisierungspolitik in Deutschland 1921–32 (Düsseldorf, 1970), pp. 44–100, 342–43.

22. The most recent of the numerous works on German-Soviet relations after World War I is Horst Günther Linke, *Deutsch-sowjetische Beziehungen bis Rapallo* (Cologne, 1970).

23. Wiedfeldt to Foreign Ministry, 16 Oct. 1922; Brockdorff-Rantzau to Foreign Ministry, 14 Aug. 1923, PAB: 3147H/D653700–2, D653937.

24. Müller to Foreign Ministry, 24 Nov. 1920, 3 Mar., 11 Mar., 25 Apr. 1922, PAB: L1837/L530717–24, L530803–17, L530818–25, L530862–81.

25. Müller to Foreign Ministry, 24 Nov. 1920, 3 Mar., 25 Apr., 2 June 1922, PAB: L1837/L530717–24, L530803–17, L530862–81, L530921–34.

26. Müller to Foreign Ministry, 3 Mar.; memorandum by Köpke, 3 May 1922, PAB: L1837/L530803–17, L530898–900.

27. Müller to Foreign Ministry, 3 Mar., 25 Apr. 1922, PAB: L1837/L530803–17, L530862–81.

28. Ibid.

29. Müller to Foreign Ministry, 13 Sept. 1921, PAB: Abteilung II, Völkerbund, Bd. 1.

30. Troeltsch, pp. 223–24; *Berliner Tageblatt*, 30 Apr. 1921. The Germans appear to have been no less obsessed with a "French menace" (*Verhandlungen*, 348:2858–65, 350:4275–78, 353:6622–32, 354:6638–43).

31. On France, the League, and Germany see Alfred E. Zimmern, *The League of Nations and the Rule of Law 1918–1935* (London, 1936), pt. 2, chap. 10; memorandums by Mantoux, Sept. 1920, League of Nations Archives: 1919–27, 28/7511/1032; *Records of the First Assembly, Plenary Meetings* (Geneva, 1920), p. 575.

32. Müller to Foreign Ministry, 16 Nov. 1920; Mayer (Paris) to Foreign Ministry, 25 Aug. 1922, PAB: L1837/L530713–6, L530990.

33. On British foreign policy toward Germany and the League, see F. S. Northedge, *The Troubled Giant: Britain among the Great Powers, 1916–39* (London, 1966), chaps. 7, 9; Hermann Graml, "Die Rapallo-Politik im Urteil der westdeutschen Forschung," *Vierteljahrshefte für Zeitgeschichte* XVIII (1970), pp. 366–91.

34. On these early travails and hopes, see Walters, *History of the League*, chaps. 10–16; Byron Dexter, *The Years of Opportunity: The League of Nations 1920–1926* (New York, 1967).

35. Müller to Foreign Ministry, 25 Apr.; memorandum by Köpke, 3 May 1922, PAB: L1837/L530862–81, L530898–900.

36. Simons to Sthamer (London), 20 Dec. 1920, PAB: L1837/L530689–90.

37. *Verhandlungen*, 351:4733–75.

38. Simons to Müller, 29 Nov. 1920; Foreign Ministry to Müller, 3 Feb.; memorandum by Nöldecke, 15 Dec. 1922, PAB: 3147H/D653516–8, L1837/L530792–4, L1511/L447418–23. The Foreign Ministry valued the Liga for the information it gathered and the appearances it preserved. Should the Liga become an embarrassment, the diplomats argued, the ministry could always disavow it.

39. Simons to Müller, 29 Nov.; memorandum by Simons, 14 Oct. 1920, PAB: 3147H/D653516–8, L1837/L530656–8.

40. Foreign Ministry to Müller, 8 July, 8 Aug. 1921, PAB: L1837/L530708–9, L530750–1.

41. For the origins of the Genoa conference, see David Felix, *Walther Rathenau and the Weimar Republic* (Baltimore, 1971), chap. 6.

42. Foreign Ministry to Müller, 3 Feb.; memorandum by Köpke, 3 May 1922, PAB: L1837/L530792–4, L53098–900; see Walters, pp. 164, 166.

43. This interpretation follows Graml, "Rapallo-Politik," which reviews the literature and reaches new conclusions.

44. Haniel to Rathenau, Rathenau to Haniel, memorandum by Köpke, all 3 May; Rathenau to Schiffer, 12 May 1922, PAB: L1837/L530887, L530888, L530898–900, L530903–4. *Verhandlungen*, 356:8056.

45. Haniel to Rathenau, 4 May; Haniel to D'Abernon, 6 May 1922, PAB: L1837/L530889, L530896–7.

46. Edgar Vincent D'Abernon, *An Ambassador of Peace* II (London, 1929), pp. 45–46; London *Times*, 26, 27 June 1922; *Westminster Gazette*, 28 June 1922.

47. Nasse (Geneva) to Foreign Ministry, 26 May; Sthamer (London) to Foreign Ministry, 15 June 1922, PAB: L1837/L530912–5, L530941–2. *Frankfurter Zeitung*, 29 June 1922; *Welt am Montag*, 6 June 1922; *Verhandlungen*, 355:7968–69; Wehberg, "Das deutsche Volk," p. 495.

48. The article did not appear in the *Berliner Tageblatt* until 20 July 1922. In September 1922 it appeared in *The Contemporary Review* CXXII, pp. 282–88.

49. Unsigned memorandum, 12 July 1922, PAB: L1837/L530980–1.

50. Maltzan to Haniel, 22 July 1922, PAB: L799/L235046–8.

51. Wirth to D'Abernon, 25 July 1922, PAB: L1837/L530975–9; D'Abernon, II, p. 78. Müller was the first to mention the idea of a permanent seat as a condition for membership. His original intent was to test the sincerity of Allied soundings (Müller to Foreign Ministry, 21 June 1921, 3 Mar. 1922, PAB: L1837/L530703–7, L530803–17).

52. *Vossische Zeitung*, 22 Sept. 1922.

53. Brink, pp. 102, 135–37, 163–64; Radbruch to Wirth, 15 Sept. 1922, PAB: L1837/L531023.

54. Suggested by Radbruch, 15 Sept. 1922, PAB: L1837/L531023.

55. *Der Versailler Völkerbund: Eine vorläufige Bilanz* (Stuttgart, 1923). See also, *Deutsche Nation*, April 1922, pp. 255–60; *Berliner Börsenzeitung*, 19 Oct. 1922.

56. Memorandum by Bülow, Sept. 1922, PAB: L1837/L531003–22; *Versailler Völkerbund*, pp. 4, 130, 548, 550, 566.

57. Memorandum by Bülow, Sept. 1922, PAB: L1837/L531003–22. Bülow suggested that Germany let the crisis in the League ripen, for she was bound to benefit from it.

58. Memorandums by Bülow, 2 May, 2 Aug. 1923, PAB: L1511/L447426–8, L447585–93; Rosting to Attolico, 28 July 1923, League of Nations Archives: Minorities Section Files, Box S. 348. A year later, on 17 Sept. 1924, Bülow claimed that the cooperation on non-political matters was intended to promote a closer relationship between Germany and the League (memorandum, PAB: 3147H/D654337–47).

59. Rosenberg (Berlin) to Legation Stockholm, 20 Jan.; Bülow to Kamphoevener (London), 11 May; memorandum by Bülow, 2 Aug. 1923, PAB: 3147H/D653719–20, L1511/L447517–8, L447585–93.

60. Rosenberg to Legation Stockholm, 20 Jan. 1923; Bülow to Embassy London, 14 May 1923, PAB: 3147H/D653719–20, L1511/L447519–23. See also *Frankfurter Zeitung*, 7 Feb.; *Vossische Zeitung*, 4, 11 Mar.; *Berliner Tageblatt*, 25 Mar.

1923. Ludwig Zimmermann, *Frankreichs Ruhrpolitik* (Göttingen, 1971), draws on French diplomatic archives for an interpretation of the Ruhr crisis.

61. On Germany in 1923, see Werner T. Angress, *Stillborn Revolution* (Princeton, 1963), chaps. 10–12; Karl-Heinz Harbeck, ed., *Das Kabinett Cuno* (Boppard, 1968).

62. Sthamer to Foreign Ministry, 13 June; Cuno to Sthamer, 15 June; Kessler to Foreign Ministry, 20 June; Kessler to Schubert, 21 June 1923, PAB: 4584H/ E177489–90, E177491–3, E177495–6, E177511–21.

63. Rosenberg to Sthamer, 22 June; Sthamer to Foreign Ministry, 23 June 1923, PAB: 4584H/E177499, E177584–8.

64. Memorandum by Bülow, 26 June; memorandum by Gaus, 27 June 1923, PAB: 4584H/E177592–5, E177596–603. Martin Walsdorff, *Westorientierung und Ostpolitik: Stresemanns Russlandpolitik in der Locarno-Ära* (Bremen, 1971), p. 44.

65. Rosenberg to Sthamer, 8 July 1923, PAB: 4584H/E177630–4. To Wiedfeldt, Cuno wired that the German government wanted to use the American proposal to encourage British advocates of German membership (11 July 1923, PAB: 4584H/E177468–9).

66. Sthamer to Foreign Ministry, 20 July; Rosenberg to Sthamer, 21 July 1923, PAB: L1511/L447550, L447551.

67. Memorandum by Bülow, 2 Aug. 1923, PAB: L1511/L447585–93; *Berliner Tageblatt*, 16 July; *Frankfurter Zeitung*, 17, 19 July 1923.

68. Memorandum by Bülow, July 1923; Müller to Foreign Ministry, 7 Aug. 1923, PAB: L1511/L447555–61, L447623–4.

69. Rosenberg to Sthamer, 29 July 1923, PAB: L1511/L447562–4. The Germans appear to have addressed themselves to no one else, though Bülow was to claim repeatedly in 1924 that, on the basis of British encouragement, German diplomats had sounded various states about Germany's admission (memorandum by Bülow, 17 Sept. 1924, PAB: 3147H/D654337–47).

70. Sthamer to Foreign Ministry, 30 July; memorandum by Bülow, 1 Aug.; Bülow to Poensgen (Geneva), 30 Aug. 1923, PAB: 4584H/E177652–4, E177655–6, L1511/L447599–602. On 7 August, the Foreign Ministry informed Sthamer that the government would not press its offer to join the League (4584H/E177689).

71. Pfeiffer (Vienna) to Foreign Ministry, 6 Aug.; Bülow to Missions, 26 Aug. 1923, PAB: L1511/L447603, L447685–90.

72. Müller to Foreign Ministry, 15 Sept.; Bülow to Missions, 30 Sept. 1923, PAB: L1511/L447750–1, L447758–9; Zimmermann, pp. 215–16.

Chapter 3

1. Arnold Wolfers, *Britain and France between Two Wars* (New York, 1940), pp. 57–59.

2. Henry A. Turner, Jr., *Stresemann and the Politics of the Weimar Republic* (Princeton, 1963), chaps. 1–3; Michael-Olaf Maxelon, *Stresemann und Frankreich: Deutsche Politik der Ost-West-Balance* (Düsseldorf, 1972), chaps. 2, 3.

3. *Verhandlungen*, 357:9423, 358:9976; Gustav Stresemann, *Vermächtnis: Der Nachlass in drei Bänden*, ed. Henry Bernhard et al. (Berlin, 1932–33), I, p. 56 (henceforth *Vermächtnis*). See also, Maxelon, pp. 125–34.

4. *Deutscher Geschichtskalender 1924*, I, p. 354, II, pp. 23–24, 204–5; *Vermächtnis*, I, p. 35; Maxelon, pp. 120–21, 129, 131–32, 134–36.

5. *Schulthess 1923*, pp. 158–60, 162–64, 404–5.

6. On the Dawes plan and on American interest in Germany, see Link, *Amerikanische Stabilisierungspolitik*, pp. 188–89, 203–8.

7. A detailed account of the diplomatic negotiations leading to Germany's entry into the League is in Jürgen Spenz, *Die diplomatische Vorgeschichte des Beitritts Deutschlands zum Völkerbund, 1924–1926* (Göttingen, 1966). His interpretation differs from mine in several respects.

8. The term "clearing house" in Bernstorff (London) to Bülow, 26 June 1924, PAB: L1837/L531146–9.

9. Sthamer to Foreign Ministry, 24 Jan., 21 Mar. 1924, PAB: L1511/L447831, L447929–35; *Manchester Guardian*, 13 Feb. 1924. See also, Dufour (London) to Bülow, 3 Apr. 1924, PAB: L1837/L531029.

10. *Verhandlungen*, 361:12471–72, 12530. Stresemann's references to the League and to Germany's interest aroused wide commentary in the press (*Vossische Zeitung; Kölnische Zeitung; Frankfurter Zeitung; Deutsche Tageszeitung*, all 29 Feb. 1924).

11. *Vermächtnis*, I, pp. 314–15. In Berlin there was a brief flurry of anxiety that Russia might respond to MacDonald's urging and join the League. The Foreign Ministry applied pressure on Moscow: by joining simultaneously, the two powers could either "paralyze" the League or "force it to change its political principles so radically that it could no longer be dangerous." See Maltzan to Embassy Moscow, 25 Mar.; Bülow to Rantzau, 27 Mar. 1924, PAB: K1908/K483364–71, K483384–8. Nine months later, when the Russians proposed joint entry, the Germans turned a deaf ear.

12. Memorandum by Bülow, 1 Mar. 1924, PAB: 4584H/E178145–8.

13. Müller to Foreign Ministry, 26 Mar. 1924, PAB: L1511/L447961–85.

14. Édouard Herriot, *Jadis* (Paris, 1952), II, p. 138; Maxelon, p. 155 n; memorandum by Bülow, 21 July 1924, PAB: 7171H/H156222–5.

15. Memorandums by Bülow, 5 June, 5 July 1924; Bernstorff to Bülow, 26 June 1924, PAB: L1837/L531036–41, L531175, L531146–9; *Manchester Guardian*, 25 June 1924.

16. Bülow suggested that article 19 (revision of inapplicable treaties) be invoked to invalidate article 10 (guarantee of territorial integrity) and that Germany be exempted from the obligation of article 16 (sanctions) as long as the League was not universal and world disarmament complete (memorandum by Bülow, 11 July 1924, PAB: L1837/L531184–95).

17. Wiedfeldt to Foreign Ministry, 16 May; Hoesch (Paris) to Foreign Ministry, 17 June; Hoffmann (Berne) to Foreign Ministry, 18 June 1924, PAB: L1837/L531068–93, L531118–22, L531104.

18. Maltzan to Missions, 6 July 1924, PAB: L1837/L531111–7. See also, Stresemann to Sthamer, 18 July; memorandum by Bülow, 21 July 1924, PAB: 4584H/E178042–6, 7171H/H156222–5.

19. *Der Nachlass des Reichskanzlers Wilhelm Marx*, ed. Hugo Stehkämper (Cologne, 1968), I, p. 343.

20. Memorandum by Schubert; Stresemann (London) to Foreign Ministry, both 11 Aug. 1924, PAB: L1837/L531202–6, 3147H/D654616–20.

21. Memorandum by Bülow, 17 Sept. 1924, PAB: 3147H/D654337–47. The Foreign Ministry, Bülow noted, had interpreted Britain's reticence at the London conference as support for a policy of "cooperation without membership."

22. *League of Nations Official Journal, Special Supplement 23* (henceforth *LNOJ*), pp. 42–43, 55; *Vossische Zeitung*, 4 Sept. 1924.

23. *Welt am Montag*, 9 Jan. 1922; *Vorwärts*, 6 Sept. 1924; *Verhandlungen*, 382, no. 295.

24. *Vorwärts*, 9 Sept. 1924; *Vermächtnis*, I, p. 570. The affair was a tempest in a teapot; Parmoor later admitted that he had been mistaken (*Vermächtnis*, I, pp. 573–75).

25. Kessler to Maltzan, 2, 3, 4 Sept.; Maltzan to Kessler, 3, 5 Sept. 1924, PAB: L1837/L531217–23, L531230–3, L531236–9.

26. Müller to Foreign Ministry, 10, 15 Sept. 1924, PAB: L1837/L531311–30, L531343–6.

27. Press conference, 12 Sept. 1924, PAB: 7177H/H157225–38; Günter Abramowski, ed., *Die Kabinette Marx I und II* (Boppard, 1973), pp. 1040–42.

28. Memorandums by Bülow, 17, 19 Sept.; Müller to Stresemann, 23 Sept. 1924, PAB: 3147H/D654337–47, D654348–57, D654377–80.

29. Abramowski, *Kabinette Marx*, pp. 1050–62; memorandum by Bülow, 22 Sept. 1924, PAB: L1837/L531386–9.

30. Stresemann to Missions, 25 Sept. 1924, PAB: 3147H/D654412–20 (memorandum reproduced in *Ursachen und Folgen*, ed. Herbert Michaelis and Ernst Schraepler VI [Berlin, n.d.], pp. 476–78); Abramowski, *Kabinette Marx*, p. 1065.

31. Maltzan to Missions, 6 July 1924, PAB: L1837/L531111–7.

32. To the Foreign Affairs Committee of the Reichstag Stresemann said, "We may no longer be a great power in the military sense, but we must not allow ourselves to be maneuvered into a place in the second rank politically" (*Vermächtnis*, II, p. 21).

33. For example, Maltzan to Missions, 6 July 1924, PAB: L1837/L531111–7.

34. Stresemann in Cabinet, 23 Sept. 1924, PAB: L1837/L531423–31.

35. Abramowski, *Kabinette Marx*, pp. 1050–62.

36. Radowitz (Moscow) to Foreign Ministry, 23 Sept.; Stresemann to Embassy Moscow, 21 Oct. 1924, PAB: 4584H/E177925–6, E177741–2.

37. Memorandum by Gaus, 25 Sept.; memorandum by Brückner, 22 Sept. 1924, PAB: L1837/L531417–8, L531434.

38. Müller to Foreign Ministry, 25 Sept., 10 Oct. 1924, PAB: L1837/L531449–50, 4584H/E177758–68.

39. Memorandum by Bülow, 8 Dec. 1924, PAB: L1837/L532019–21.

40. Stresemann to Drummond, 12 Dec. 1924, PAB: L1837/L531991–7; *Vermachtnis*, II, 22–23.

41. In fact the procedure resulted in wild speculation in the press (memorandum by Zechlin, 2 Feb. 1925, PAB: L1837/L532126–30). The two German memorandums were published on 23 December 1924.

42. Bülow to Rantzau, 18, 31 Dec. 1924, PAB: L1837/L532024–7, K1908/K483443–7. Bülow remarked that the note had been phrased in such a way that the League could offer a satisfactory reply only if it "jettisoned" all its "previous

principles." Little wonder that Köster, the German minister in Riga, thought that the ministry was deliberately sabotaging Germany's entry (Kessler, *Tagebücher*, p. 395).

43. Michael Salewski, *Entwaffnung und Militärkontrolle in Deutschland 1919– 1927* (Munich, 1966), pp. 240–68, 271–88. In this connection, Bülow explained to Brockdorff-Rantzau that a further reason for replying so promptly to the League was the need to argue Germany's military weakness "in these weeks of decision on the evacuation of the Cologne zone and the end of military control." The argument would take the teeth out of the IMCC's final report and, by implication, weaken the Allies' case for refusing to evacuate (Bülow to Rantzau, 18 Dec. 1924, PAB: L1837/L532024–7).

44. Salewski, pp. 268–70.

45. Müller to Foreign Ministry, 9 Oct.; memorandum by Gaus, 22 Nov. 1924; Bülow to Rantzau, 18 Dec. 1924, PAB: 4584H/E177773–90, E178381–3, L1837/L532024–7.

46. *Verhandlungen*, 385:1880.

47. *Vermächtnis*, I, pp. 598–99, 614–16; *Deutscher Geschichtskalender*, II, pp. 23–24, 204–5; Gustav Stresemann, *Nationale Realpolitik* (Berlin, 1924); Abramowski, *Kabinette Marx*, pp. 1255–56, 1277.

48. D'Abernon, *Ambassador of Peace*, III, p. 21. On D'Abernon's motives, see F. G. Stambrook, "*'Das Kind'*—Lord D'Abernon and the Origins of the Locarno Pact," *Central European History* I (1968), pp. 237–46; Northedge, pp. 254–55.

49. Memorandum by Schubert, 29 Dec. 1924, PAB: 4509H/E124822–3.

50. Stresemann to Rantzau, 19 Mar., in *Locarno-Konferenz 1925: Eine Dokumentensammlung*, ed. Ministerium für Auswärtige Angelegenheiten (Berlin, 1962), no. 9; Stresemann in Foreign Affairs Committee, 11 Mar. 1925, PAB: 7135H/ H148981–149010. On the various interpretations of Stresemann and his foreign policy, see Maxelon, pp. 9–14. For an almost exhaustive list of writings by and about Stresemann, partly annotated, see Martin Walsdorff, *Bibliographie Gustav Stresemann* (Düsseldorf, 1972).

51. German Memorandum, 9 Feb. 1925, *Locarno-Konferenz*, no. 5.

52. What the Germans wanted back was defined by Stresemann in June 1925; see Christoph M. Kimmich, *The Free City: Danzig and German Foreign Policy, 1919–1934* (New Haven, 1968), pp. 73–74.

53. *Vermächtnis*, II, p. 117.

54. Rantzau to Foreign Ministry, 25 Nov. 1924; Stresemann to Rantzau, 6 Mar. 1925, PAB: 3147H/D654603–5, 4509H/E125197–200. Stresemann to Rantzau, 19 Mar. 1925, in *Locarno-Konferenz*, no. 9.

55. Sthamer to Foreign Ministry, 30 Jan.; Hoesch to Foreign Ministry, 17 Feb. 1925, PAB: 4509H/E124679–81, E124982–7.

56. Memorandums by Schubert, 19 Feb., 10 Mar. 1925, PAB: 4509H/ E124954–9, E125472–83. Drummond to Stresemann, 14 Mar. 1925, PAB: L1837/L531548–52 (printed in *Ursachen und Folgen*, VI, pp. 483–85). Spenz's analysis of Allied motives (pp. 64–66) seems rather contrived.

57. Schubert to Rantzau, 16 Mar.; Schubert to Embassy London, 18 Mar. 1925, PAB: 4584H/E178197–8, 4509H/E125322–3.

58. Memorandum by Gaus, 7 Mar.; Schubert to Missions, 17 Mar. 1925, PAB:

4584H/E178265–7, E178190–3. The League's reply, the Germans claimed, left unresolved the issue of transporting troops across German territory and denied explicitly any exemption from economic sanctions.

59. Memorandum by Gaus, 16 Mar.; memorandum by Schubert, 21 Mar. 1925, PAB: 4509H/E125359–60, E125745–6; *Locarno-Konferenz*, p. 73.

60. Hoesch to Foreign Ministry, 10 Apr.; Sthamer to Foreign Ministry, 11 Apr. 1925, PAB: 3147H/D655072–9, D655089–96.

61. Stresemann to Rantzau, 19 Mar. 1925, in *Locarno-Konferenz*, no. 9. The Foreign Ministry was determined not to give in to Russian pressure (Bülow to Aschmann (Geneva), 5 May 1925, PAB: K1908/K483466–9).

62. Bülow to Aschmann (Geneva), 5 May; Stresemann to Consulate Geneva, 27 Mar. 1925, PAB: K1908/K483466–9, 4584H/E178428. Bülow, always candid, was to give away the ministry's ulterior motives for trying to keep the decision in abeyance. If the security pact were concluded first, he wrote to the consul in Geneva, the government could agree to join the League at its own price—perhaps in return for early (if not immediate) evacuation of the entire Rhineland. Evacuation in turn might lead to a prompt settlement in the Saar.

63. Press release, 16 Mar.; Schubert to Missions, 17 Mar. 1925, PAB: 4584H/E178200–2, E178190–3. For Schubert's conversations see memorandums, 17, 21 Mar., 20 Apr. 1925, PAB: 4509H/E125333–6, E125740–4, E125995–7.

64. Memorandum by Schubert, 30 Apr. 1925, PAB: 4509H/E126098–100. The idea of a formula (drawn from the Geneva Protocol) had emerged in conversation between Schubert and D'Abernon two days *before* the reply arrived from the League (memorandum by Schubert, 12 Mar. 1925, PAB: 4509H/E125431–9). Stresemann later recalled that the government had originally raised reservations on article 16 because Bülow had argued that the sanctions were legally binding. Gaus disputed this interpretation subsequently, arguing that member states were bound morally, not legally (Henry A. Turner, Jr., "Eine Rede Stresemanns über seine Locarnopolitik," in *Vierteljahrshefte für Zeitgeschichte* XV [1967], p. 421).

65. Hoesch summed up his impression of Herriot's first reaction as "unexpectedly favorable" (Hoesch to Foreign Ministry, 17 Feb. 1925, PAB: 4509H/E124982–7).

66. The phrase in William J. Newman, *The Balance of Power in the Interwar Years, 1919–1939* (New York, 1968), p. 64.

67. On French policy, see Wolfers, pp. 258–59, 261 n; Piotr Wandycz, *France and her Eastern Allies, 1919–1925* (Minneapolis, 1962), pp. 328–31, 338–40; Jon Jacobson, *Locarno Diplomacy: Germany and the West, 1925–1929* (Princeton, 1972), pp. 21–26.

68. Chamberlain told Sthamer that the German proposal offered "the possibility of creating a new concert of Europe" (Sthamer to Foreign Ministry, 19 Mar. 1925, PAB: 4509H/E125767–9). On British policy, see Northedge, pp. 252, 257–60, 312; Jacobson, pp. 12–26; Douglas Johnson, "Austen Chamberlain and the Locarno Agreements," *University of Birmingham Historical Journal* VIII (1961), pp. 62–81.

69. French Note, 16 June 1925, *Locarno-Konferenz*, no. 14.

70. *Schulthess 1925*, p. 49.

71. *Vermächtnis*, II, pp. 69, 74–81, 87–95, 99; Manfred Dörr, "Die

Deutschnationale Volkspartei 1925 bis 1928" (diss., Marburg, 1964), pp. 105–10, 135–38.

72. *Deutsche Zeitung; Kreuzzeitung*, both 21 June 1925. Dörr, pp. 138–45.

73. *Vermächtnis*, II, pp. 109–10.

74. Quoted in Hans Meier-Welcker, *Seeckt* (Frankfurt/Main, 1967), p. 470.

75. Cabinet, 24 June 1925, BAK: R 43 I/1403. Seeckt's objections in Meier-Welcker, pp. 448–50, and memorandum by Hasse, December 1924, PAB: L1837/L531927–64. Memorandum by Stresemann, 26 June 1925, PAB: 7129H/H147889–91.

76. Cabinet, 24 June 1925, BAK: R 43 I/1403.

77. Michael Stürmer, *Koalition und Opposition in der Weimarer Republik 1924–1928* (Düsseldorf, 1967), pp. 115–18. The Nationalists were interested in protective tariffs for agriculture, for which a bill was still in committee in the Reichstag, and their industrial backers wanted foreign credit, for which political détente was necessary.

78. Cabinet, 15 July 1925, BAK: R 43 I/1403. Stresemann's arguments are in *Vermächtnis*, II, pp. 111–26, 149–50, 156–61.

79. Memorandum by Schubert, 8 July, PAB: 4509H/E127066–70; German Note, 20 July 1925, *Locarno-Konferenz*, no. 16.

80. Stresemann told the Foreign Affairs Committee on 1 July 1925: "If we are in the League, then the whole framework put together for these arbitration treaties is of no account" (*Vermächtnis*, II, p. 117). Stresemann to Missions, 20 June 1925, PAB: 4509H/E126745–9.

81. *Vermächtnis*, II, p. 148.

82. Schubert's scathing criticism of a memorandum by Müller, who had reiterated the familiar case against membership, was a sign of the times. See Hoffmann (Berne) to Foreign Ministry, 10 Aug.; Bülow to Hoffmann, 22 Aug. 1925, PAB: L1837/L532310–47.

83. To Hoesch, Schubert confessed that the government could not surrender its position on article 16. A formula would have to be found "if only for reasons of saving face" (Schubert to Hoesch, 11 Aug. 1925, PAB: 4509H/E127001–5).

84. French Note, 24 Aug. 1925, *Locarno-Konferenz*, no. 17.

85. Ibid., nos. 3, 7, 9, 10, 11, 13, 15; Walsdorff, *Westorientierung*, pp. 59–138, recounts and analyzes the course of negotiation.

86. PAB: 7131H/H148305–8. See also, Stürmer, p. 122; Dörr, pp. 150–58; *Vermächtnis*, II, pp. 170–75.

87. Cabinet, 24 Aug. 1925, in Walther Hubatsch, *Hindenburg und der Staat* (Göttingen, 1966), pp. 192–97; *Vermächtnis*, II, pp. 179–82; *Locarno-Konferenz*, no. 24.

88. Spenz, pp. 88–89, 96.

89. *Locarno-Konferenz*, no. 26. The formula did not mention economic sanctions expressly, but the Allies did not challenge Stresemann's interpretation that Germany's participation in economic sanctions would be determined by her action on military sanctions (ibid., p. 176).

90. For the most recent work on the conference itself, see Walsdorff, pp. 140–45; Jacobson, pp. 60–63; Paul Wehn, "Germany and the Treaty of Locarno" (diss., Columbia, 1969).

91. The Allies further promised (at Locarno or immediately afterwards) to

settle the disarmament violations by negotiation, to reduce the IMCC, to withdraw some troops from the Coblenz and Mainz zones, and to alleviate the occupation regime (Cabinet, 19 Oct. 1925, in Hubatsch, pp. 197–204; Jacobson, p. 65; Salewski, p. 317).

92. Locarno also weakened Poland in another way: now that their eastern borders were secure, the French would need to rely less on their military alliance with Poland and, in consequence, reduce their commitment to Poland (Wandycz, pp. 367–68).

93. Walsdorff, pp. 145–51, considers Locarno a failure of German foreign policy, for it did not in fact result in binding pledges for the early evacuation of the entire Rhineland and for the abandonment of plans for permanent military inspection. This interpretation seems too narrow.

94. Turner, "Rede Stresemanns," p. 436; Stolberg-Wernigerode to Stresemann, 5 Sept.; Stresemann to Stolberg, 18 Sept. 1925, PAB: 7176H/H157041–5, 7177H/H157300–1.

95. Maxelon, pp. 168–70, 194–206, 218–19.

Chapter 4

1. *Akten zur deutschen auswärtigen Politik 1918–1945*, series B, I/1 (Göttingen, 1966), no. 3 (henceforth ADAP); Jacobson, *Locarno Diplomacy*, p. 64; Stürmer, *Koalition und Opposition*, pp. 143–44.

2. Turner, *Stresemann*, p. 216. For Stresemann's fears that Hindenburg would be susceptible to conservative influence, see *Vermächtnis*, II, p. 61; Stresemann to Stolberg-Wernigerode, 18 Sept. 1925, PAB: 7177H/H157300–1.

3. Andreas Dorpalen, *Hindenburg and the Weimar Republic* (Princeton, 1964), pp. 94–97. Hubatsch, *Hindenburg*, pp. 96–97, recounts these waverings without examining their motivation.

4. D'Abernon, *Ambassador of Peace*, III, p. 169; *Vermächtnis*, II, 60.

5. Among these friends were generals Cramon and Mackensen, Admiral Schröder, Count Cuno Westarp, and the landowners Elard von Oldenburg-Januschau and Martin Schiele (ADAP, B, I/1, p. 312 n; Dorpalen, pp. 96–97; *Vermächtnis*, II, p. 386).

6. ADAP, B, I/1, no. 6; *Verhandlungen*, 388:5151, 5161–66, 5206–9. Peter Haungs, *Reichspräsident und parlamentarische Kabinettsregierung* (Cologne, 1968), pp. 194–96, 200; Dörr, "Deutschnationale Volkspartei," pp. 203–6.

7. ADAP, B, I/1, no. 65; see unsigned memorandums, 3 Feb. 1926, PAB: 4584H/E178647–63.

8. ADAP, B, I/1, nos. 61, 76, 78, 88, 89, 252; *Verhandlungen*, 388:5228; unsigned memorandum, 6 Feb. 1926, BAK: R 43 I/486. Hindenburg's last attempt to commit the government to further conditions failed (*Locarno-Konferenz*, nos. 34, 37).

9. Other candidates were Belgium, China, Persia, Portugal, Siam, and Uruguay.

10. On the background and course of the crisis, see Georges Scelle, *Une crise de la Société des Nations* (Paris, 1927).

11. ADAP, B, I/1, no. 152. See also, David Carlton, "Great Britain and the League Council Crisis of 1926," *The Historical Journal* XI (1968), pp. 355–56, a careful study based on British documents.

12. ADAP, B, I/1, nos. 70, 83.

13. Ibid., no. 90. Dirksen pointed out that at the very moment the Foreign Ministry was speculating on the possibility of revising the borders in conjunction with the financial reorganization of Poland.

14. BAK: R 43 I/1409.

15. ADAP, B, I/1, no. 95.

16. Ibid., nos. 95, 101, 121; *Documents on British Foreign Policy,* ed. E. L. Woodward et al., ser. IA, I (London, 1966), no. 275 (henceforth DBFP); Carlton, p. 356. See also, ADAP, B, I/1, nos. 93, 99, 106, 109.

17. ADAP, B, I/1, no. 103, p. 258 n; Carlton, pp. 357–58.

18. *Vermächtnis,* II, p. 558; Cabinet, 24 Feb. 1926, BAK: R 43 I/1409. Müller urged the president and the chancellor to let the application be withdrawn in order to press the council powers (Hubatsch, pp. 228–29; Haungs, p. 198).

19. DBFP, ser. IA, I, no. 255; ADAP, B, I/1, nos. 113, 120, p. 200 n. Erik Lönnroth, "The Diplomacy of Östen Undén," in *The Diplomats, 1919–1939,* ed. Gordon A. Craig and Felix Gilbert (Princeton, 1953), pp. 92–99.

20. ADAP, B, I/1, nos. 113, 114, 118, 128.

21. Ibid., nos. 117, 128. Müller made a special trip to Berlin to speak to Hindenburg (Hubatsch, pp. 228–29).

22. ADAP, B, I/1, nos. 120, 128, 132; DBFP, ser. IA, I, nos. 287, 321. Stresemann left for Geneva "full of confidence and spirits," convinced that the obstacles could be overcome (D'Abernon, III, p. 227).

23. ADAP, B, I/1, no. 128; Carlton, p. 364.

24. Memorandum by Brazilian government, 5 Mar.; Köpke to German Delegation, 8 Mar. 1926, PAB: 4586H/E180652–8, E180627.

25. ADAP, B, I/1, no. 145; DBFP, ser. IA, I, nos. 327, 330.

26. Luther to Hindenburg, 7 Mar. 1926, PAB: 4586H/E180619–20; ADAP, B, I/1, nos. 127, 138.

27. ADAP, B, I/1, no. 147; DBFP, ser. IA, I, no. 331.

28. ADAP, B, I/1, nos. 153, 154, pp. 713–15; DBFP, ser. IA, I, nos. 336, 337.

29. DBFP, ser. IA, I, no. 341.

30. ADAP, B, I/1, no. 169, pp. 390 n., 712, 714, 716–17.

31. Ibid., no. 160; memorandum by Schubert, 14 Mar. 1926, PAB: 4586H/E180924–5.

32. Luther to Hindenburg, 14 Mar. 1926, PAB: 4586H/E180931–5; ADAP, B, I/1, no. 161.

33. ADAP, B, I/1, nos. 162, 163; memorandum by Schubert, 14 Mar. 1926, PAB: 4586H/E180915–6. Earlier the British had put great pressure on the French: if the French should block Germany's admission—and destroy the Locarno accord—the British would never again agree to guarantees of the kind given at Locarno (DBFP, ser. IA, I, no. 361).

34. ADAP, B, I/1, no. 166; DBFP, ser. IA, I, nos. 359, 360. The Germans suspected that certain European powers encouraged Brazil's intransigence—Italy perhaps, and France, where the government had little reason to be satisfied with the settlement (ADAP, B, I/1, no. 175. See also, Carlton, p. 361).

35. *Deutsche Tageszeitung,* 17 Mar.; *Der Tag,* 18 Mar.; *Kreuzzeitung,* 20 Mar. 1926; Dörr, pp. 207–8.

36. *Frankfurter Zeitung,* 18, 21 Mar.; memorandum by Pünder, 18 Mar. 1926, PAB: 4586H/E181128–31. D'Abernon (III, p. 238) remarked on the "paradoxi-

cal result" of the Geneva debacle—"the bargaining, the intrigues, and the compromises of the last fortnight have convinced the partisans of *Realpolitik* that they cannot afford not to be there. Hitherto, they had regarded Geneva as an assembly of ideologues—now they take the opposite view."

37. ADAP, B, I/1, no. 171; *Verhandlungen,* 390:6453–92, 6494–6512, 6528. The voting shows that Stresemann's policy commanded the support of nearly two-thirds of the Reichstag despite the fiasco at Geneva (*Verhandlungen,* 390:6570).

38. *Verhandlungen,* 390:6442–53; ADAP, B, I/1, nos. 175, 182, 184. Privately, Stresemann was not nearly as positive. In a dispatch to Hoesch, he voiced his doubts about Briand and his anxieties about public reaction (ibid., no. 182).

39. Memorandums by Poensgen, 25 Mar., by Bülow, 29 Mar. 1926, PAB: 4586H/E181323–34, E181346–8.

40. Cabinet, 31 Mar. 1926, BAK: R 43 I/1410; ADAP, B, I/1, p. 449 n.

41. ADAP, B, II/1, no. 69; memorandum by Gaus, 30 Mar. 1926, PAB: 4586H/E181349–54. The Germans informed the British and the French of these intentions several weeks before signing the treaty (ADAP, B, II/1, nos. 99, 100). The most recent account of the negotiations is in Walsdorff, *Westorientierung,* pp. 157–71.

42. ADAP, B, I/1, nos. 194, 210; Cabinet, 8 Mar. 1926, BAK: R 43 I/1412. Hindenburg argued that Germany should be represented only by an observer; his request came too late (ADAP, B, I/1, p. 463 n).

43. ADAP, B, I/1, nos. 222, 224; DBFP, ser. IA, I, no. 525. Committee on the Composition of the Council, League of Nations document C.299.M.139.1926.V.

44. The Nationalists wanted to return to the government once Germany had joined the League (Dörr, pp. 210–11, 215–16).

45. ADAP, B, I/1, no. 224; Spenz, *Diplomatische Vorgeschichte,* p. 161.

46. ADAP, B, I/2, no. 20; DBFP, ser. IA, II, no. 137.

47. ADAP, B, I/2, nos. 20, 30; DBFP, ser. IA, II, nos. 137, 149.

48. ADAP, B, I/2, nos. 23, 28, 33. The Germans did not respond to feelers from Poland that they compromise on the council seat in return for compensations elsewhere (ADAP, B, I/1, no. 295).

49. DBFP, ser. IA, II, no. 145; ADAP, B, I/2, no. 35.

50. Cabinet, 13 Aug. 1926, BAK: R 43 I/1414; ADAP, B, I/2, no. 22. Schubert explained the advantages of Germany's membership in terms designed to appeal to Field Marshal Hindenburg: "We must have the opportunity to appear on the battlefield of Geneva and go for the enemy's throat" (ADAP, B, I/2, no. 2).

51. Memorandum by Schubert, 19 Aug. 1926, PAB: 4586H/E182129–30; ADAP, B, I/2, no. 59. Spain resorted to an ultimatum, and her resignation reached Geneva on 11 September.

52. ADAP, B, I/2, no. 69; Committee on the Composition of the Council, League of Nations document C.597.M.234.1926.VII.

53. DBFP, ser. IA, II, no. 203; LNOJ, *Special Supplement 44,* pp. 50–55. In counterpoint to Stresemann's avowals in Geneva, the press in Germany listed the concrete rewards the Germans expected from membership: see, for example, *Kölnische Zeitung,* 5 Sept.; *Kreuzzeitung,* 8 Sept.; *Deutsche Allgemeine Zeitung, Germania,* both 9 Sept.; *Deutsche Zeitung,* 11 Sept. 1926.

Chapter 5

1. Bülow to Dufour (Geneva), 23 June 1927, PAB: L781/L229120–2; Kordt, *Nicht aus den Akten*, pp. 43–44.

2. Memorandum by Bülow, 12 Feb.; memorandum by Schubert, 15 Feb. 1926, PAB: 4585H/E179337–41, 4586H/E179806–7.

3. To fill this post, the Foreign Ministry selected the minister in the London embassy, Albert Dufour de Feronce. Sociable and well-informed, Dufour had established good connections in diplomatic circles in London, and these made him an obvious choice. With this appointment and that of Dufour's colleagues, the Germans broke with the League's practice of employing competent persons drawn from outside official ranks. The Germans all came from government service and were simply on leave of absence for the duration of their contracts in Geneva.

4. The Germans held ranking positions in the disarmament, financial-and-economic, health, information, intellectual cooperation, legal, political, and transit sections (ADAP, B, IV, no. 158; Unsigned memorandum, Oct. 1926, PAB: 3635/D804286–8).

5. The regular attendance of leading German politicians and diplomats helped set a pattern, and thereafter it became common practice for Europe's foreign ministers to participate in council meetings (Morley, *Society of Nations*, p. 377).

6. ADAP, B, V, no. 255, VII, no. 9; Bülow to Missions, 28 Dec. 1927, PAB: 3635/D804682–91.

7. Memorandum by Bülow, 28 Mar. 1927, PAB: 4585H/E179481–5. The Germans all retained close touch with the Foreign Ministry during their term with the secretariat. They reported to Berlin almost daily. In turn the Foreign Ministry kept them informed of its position on issues before the League and on occasion asked them to intervene informally with the secretary-general or other officials. In representing their government's interests and keeping it abreast of League affairs, the Germans differed little from representatives of other states in the secretariat. Unlike them, however, the Germans (and the Italians) were even less able to take their loyalties as international civil servants seriously (Morley, pp. 300–301; Arthur W. Rovine, *The First Fifty Years: The Secretary-General in World Politics 1920–1970* [Leyden, 1970], p. 38).

8. See, for example, *Vermächtnis*, III, p. 26; ADAP, B, I/2, no. 105, VII, no. 198.

9. Memorandum by Poensgen, 3 Nov. 1927, PAB: L1539/L466544–9. For further evidence of German satisfaction see Stresemann address to delegation, 10 Sept. 1927, PAB: 4675H/E222699–701; ADAP, B, VI, no. 221, VII, no. 9.

10. Bülow to Dufour, 23 June 1927, PAB: L781/L229120–2.

11. Dufour to Bülow, 5 Jan. 1926, PAB: K1764/K431912–7. The previous summer, Bülow had written an indignant memorandum on "anti-German tendencies" in the League, such as the League's refusal to accept German as one of its official languages and its revision of the procedures for dealing with minorities grievances. For Bülow, these tendencies were evidence that the League was girding itself to meet Germany's entry (memorandum, 2 July 1925, PAB: 3147H/D655331–5).

12. Paris *Gaulois*, quoted in *Literary Digest*, 25 Sept. 1926, as part of a survey of French press reactions.

13. Bülow recommended such a course, and Stresemann defended it (ADAP, B, I/2, nos. 76, 105; Stresemann in Foreign Affairs Committee, 7 Oct. 1926, PAB: L1539/L466501–12).

14. Renthe-Fink, a German official in the political section, charged that members of the secretariat failed to consult German colleagues on important issues (especially on sensitive political ones). Under-secretary Dufour complained that he was without influence on political and economic questions, and that Drummond's "autocratic regime" blocked all opportunities for change (Renthe-Fink to Schubert, 12 Dec.; Dufour to Stresemann, 4 Dec. 1928, PAB: 4585H/E179554–5, 7381H/H168675–82). Stresemann's successor did not ignore such complaints (Cabinet, 21 May 1930, BAK: R 43 I/1443).

15. See, for example, Köpke to Missions, 14 Sept. 1927; Schubert to Hoesch, 19 Jan. 1928, PAB: 3147H/D658912–3, 3154/D665980–7; ADAP, B, VII, nos. 84, 246.

16. Willy Ruppel, *Genfer Götterdämmerung: Werden, Wirken und Versagen des Völkerbunds* (Stuttgart, 1940), p. 43.

17. ADAP, B, V, no. 243, VII, nos. 68, 179; Stresemann interview, *New York Times*, 25 Feb. 1926.

18. Memorandum by Köpke, 9 Feb.; Weizsäcker to Missions, 24 Mar. 1928, PAB: 3241/D706760–6, 3635/D805065–73.

19. Weizsäcker to Missions, 24 Mar. 1928, PAB: 3635/D805065–73. In general, see Jacobson's description of this "Locarno diplomacy" (pp. 69–76), and, for a negative appraisal, Walters, *History of the League*, pp. 337–43.

20. Stolberg-Wernigerode to Stresemann, 5 Sept.; Stresemann to Stolberg, 18 Sept. 1925, PAB: 7176H/H157041–5, 7177H/H157300–1; *Vermächtnis*, II, pp. 503–4; "Das Werk von Locarno," *Deutsche Stimmen*, 23 Oct. 1925; *Deutsche Allgemeine Zeitung*, 2 Apr. 1926. See also, Weizsäcker to Dufour, 2 Oct. 1929, PAB: L1837/L532602–5.

21. *Vermächtnis*, III, pp. 34–35; Bülow to Missions, 28 Dec. 1927, PAB: 3635/D804682–91.

22. ADAP, B, IV, no. 219, V, no. 98, VI, no. 203; Stresemann in Foreign Affairs Committee, 7 Oct. 1926; memorandum by Schmidt, 9 Dec. 1928, PAB: L1539/L466501–12, 4587H/E184433–4.

23. DBFP, ser. IA, IV, p. 241 n, V, no. 188. "Expression of her defeat" comes from W. M. Jordan, *Great Britain, France, and the German Problem, 1918–1939* (London, 1943), p. 47.

24. ADAP, B, V, no. 39; Hoesch to Foreign Ministry, 3 Feb. 1928, PAB: 5138H/E297331–7; DBFP, ser. IA, III, no. 263.

25. DBFP, ser. IA, I, no. 1, V, no. 112. On Chamberlain and the League, see Walters, pp. 339–40; *Vermächtnis*, III, p. 195.

26. Walters, pp. 341, 343–46; Morley, pp. 343, 377–78; *Literary Digest*, 18 Sept. 1926; ADAP, B, I/2, no. 152.

27. ADAP, B, V, no. 255, VI, no. 71; Dufour to Bülow, 27 June 1927, PAB: K2342/K666781–5; Walters, pp. 337–42.

28. *Vermächtnis*, III, pp. 37–41, 212–13. See also, ADAP, B, I/2, no. 105, IV, no. 254.

29. ADAP, B, V, no. 255, VII, no. 9. Bülow added that Germany should seek

cooperation with the great powers without foreclosing the possibility of closing ranks with the smaller states and going into opposition (as Germany had done in March 1926 by collaborating with Sweden).

30. ADAP, B, VI, nos. 161, 163; Köpke to Missions, 14 Sept. 1927, PAB: 3147H/D658912–3.

31. ADAP, B, VI, nos. 167, 168, 175.

32. Ibid., nos. 35, 163, 173, 182.

33. Ibid., nos. 179, 184, 185, 221.

34. *Vermächtnis,* III, pp. 195–96, 214; Köpke to Missions, 14 Sept. 1927, PAB: 3147H/D658912–3.

35. Dufour to Stresemann, 4 Dec. 1928, PAB: 7381H/H168675–82.

36. Walters, pp. 346–47; Spenz, *Diplomatische Vorgeschichte,* pp. 173–75. For the characterization of the small states, see Bülow to Dufour, 23 June 1927, PAB: L781/L229120–2.

37. Ruppel, p. 44.

38. See DBFP, ser. IA, II, no. 241.

39. Turner, "Rede Stresemanns," pp. 421, 427; *Vermächtnis,* III, p. 58. See also, Heinrich Brüning, *Memoiren 1918–1934* (Stuttgart, 1970), p. 111.

40. On Stresemann's interest in exploiting a successful foreign policy to consolidate internal conditions see Turner, *Stresemann,* pp. 181, 233; Lothar Döhn, *Politik und Interesse: Die Interessenstruktur der Deutschen Volkspartei* (Meisenheim am Glan, 1970), pp. 378–95; Sigmund Neumann, *Die Parteien der Weimarer Republik* (Stuttgart, 1965), pp. 55–61.

41. Haungs, *Reichspräsident,* p. 251; Ernst von Weizsäcker, *Erinnerungen* (Munich, 1950), p. 80; Martin Vogt, ed., *Das Kabinett Müller II* (Boppard, 1970), pp. 125–28.

42. *Vermächtnis,* III, pp. 37–41, 73–75, 162–66, 187–94, 206–19; Weizsäcker, p. 80.

43. *Vermächtnis,* III, p. 195; ADAP, B, VII, no. 16. See also, DBFP, ser. IA, III, no. 83.

44. *Verhandlungen,* 392:9814–15.

45. Ibid., 392:9815, 394:12558; *Vermächtnis,* III, pp. 73–75, 162–66, 206–19; ADAP, B, IV, no. 253.

46. Ibid., I/2, pp. 665–69; *Verhandlungen,* 391:8141–42, 395:13898–99; *Vermächtnis,* III, pp. 61–62, 74, 76.

47. Stürmer, *Koalition und Opposition,* pp. 224, 226–27, 266; Becker, *Demokratie des sozialen Rechts,* p. 166. Ernst-Otto Czempiel, in a brief summary of party attitudes, points out that the SPD was the only party that even talked about the principles of international organization and that speculated on going beyond the League to a United States of Europe (*Macht und Kompromiss: Die Beziehungen der BRD zu den Vereinten Nationen, 1956–1970* [Düsseldorf, 1971], pp. 20–26).

48. *Verhandlungen,* 391:8136.

49. ADAP, B, IV, nos. 27, 64; Dörr, "Deutschnationale Volkspartei," pp. 256–60, 268–69, 314–20.

50. Memorandum by Hoetzsch, 11 Sept. 1927, PAB: 4587H/E183538–9; ADAP, B, IV, no. 201, VI, no. 156; Dörr, pp. 289–92, 314.

51. *Vermächtnis,* III, p. 250; *Verhandlungen,* 392:9815.

52. See, for example, ADAP, B, I/1, p. 746, I/2, pp. 666–68.

53. *Kreuzzeitung*, 12, 13 June; *Germania*, 13 June 1928; DBFP, ser. IA, II, nos. 392, 419, III, no. 201.

54. Memorandum by Poensgen, 3 Nov. 1927, PAB: L1539/L466544–9.

Chapter 6

1. The most recent work on Germany's efforts to cast off these restraints is Jacobson's *Locarno Diplomacy*, a careful and detailed study. See also, Maxelon, *Stresemann und Frankreich*, chap. 6.

2. DBFP, ser. IA, I, no. 432, III, nos. 1, 255, 279, V, no. 188; ADAP, B, I/1, pp. 3 n, 750–51. Contemporary studies on the occupation are heavily biased (see, for example, Karl Wachendorf, *Zehn Jahre Fremdherrschaft am Rhein* [Berlin, n.d.], with bibliography); no one seems yet to have exploited the pertinent archival material in Germany and England.

3. ADAP, B, I/1, nos. 35, 48, I/2, nos. 26, 41, 68; DBFP, ser. IA, I, no. 191, III, no. 36; Jacobson, pp. 76–83.

4. *Vermächtnis*, II, p. 555; Werner von Rheinbaben, *Kaiser, Kanzler, Präsidenten* (Mainz, 1968), pp. 231–32.

5. DBFP, ser. IA, III, no. 255. The occupation of the Rhineland would seem to have been a grievance greater even than the abominated eastern borders (save, perhaps, Danzig). Stresemann told the British ambassador in 1927, "for Germany as a whole the existence of the Armies of Occupation was distorting the whole political outlook and if it were not for them the German Nationals would lose half their seats in the Reichstag and the conduct of foreign policy would be greatly facilitated" (ibid., no. 93).

6. See ibid., I, no. 438, II, no. 93; *Vermächtnis*, II, pp. 261–62; Turner, "Rede Stresemanns," p. 428.

7. *Vermächtnis*, II, p. 553; ADAP, B, I/1, pp. 731–33. On the Dawes plan, see Rolf Lüke, *Von der Stabilisierung zur Krise* (Zurich, 1958), and Wolfram Fischer, *Deutsche Wirtschaftspolitik 1918–1945*, 3d ed. (Opladen, 1968).

8. Salewski, *Entwaffnung*, pp. 326–42; ADAP, B, I/2, nos. 27, 78.

9. Ibid., IV, no. 254; DBFP, ser. IA, II, no. 93.

10. ADAP, B, I/2, nos. 55, 95.

11. Ibid., I/1, no. 225. In December 1925 Berthelot had already suggested that the reparations debt might be commercialized to pay the Western powers to reduce the terms of occupation (ibid., no. 2).

12. Ibid., I/1, no. 264, I/2, nos. 11, 55, 73, p. 180 n. See also, Jacobson, pp. 85–87.

13. ADAP, B, I/2, nos. 88, 94; Georges Suarez, *Briand: sa vie–son oeuvre*, VI (Paris, 1952), pp. 218–27; DBFP, ser. IA, II, no. 238; *Documents diplomatiques belges 1920–40* (Brussels, 1964), II, nos. 128, 131 (henceforth DDB). See also, Heinz-Otto Sieburg, "Das Gespräch von Thoiry 1926," in *Gedenkschrift Martin Göhring*, ed. E. Schulin (Wiesbaden, 1968).

14. ADAP, B, I/2, pp. 665–69. On Stresemann's optimism, see Maxelon, p. 227.

15. Stresemann in Foreign Affairs Committee, 7 Oct. 1926, PAB: L1757/L512431–43; ADAP, B, I/2, nos. 95, 105. Stresemann told the Foreign Affairs

Committee of the Reichsrat that Thoiry would lead to evacuation in the "near future" and to the return of the Saar (12 Oct. 1926, PAB: L1757/L512447–51).

16. ADAP, B, I/2, nos. 98, 105; see also, nos. 114, 144, 175.

17. Ibid., nos. 153, 164; DBFP, ser. IA, II, nos. 226, 256; Cabinet, 13 Oct. 1926, BAK: R 43 I/1415. On pessimistic diplomats see D'Abernon, *Ambassador of Peace*, III, p. 266. On American reactions see Robert Gottwald, *Die deutsch-amerikanischen Beziehungen in der Ära Stresemann* (Berlin, 1965), pp. 75–87.

18. ADAP, B, I/2, nos. 136, 167, 173, 183; Émile Moreau, *Souvenirs d'un gouverneur de la Banque de France* (Paris, 1954), pp. 111–15.

19. ADAP, B, I/2, nos. 156, 159, 160, 167, 182, 188; Ernst Geigenmüller, "Botschafter Hoesch und die Räumungsfrage," in *Historische Zeitschrift* CC (1965), p. 611.

20. *Verhandlungen*, 391:8132–33, 8141–42, 8176, 8183–84.

21. See Foreign Affairs Committee, 7 Oct. 1926, PAB: L1757/L512431–43; ADAP, B, I/2, no. 144; *Vermächtnis*, III, p. 58.

22. Salewski, pp. 268–70, 342–57; ADAP, B, I/2, nos. 219, 225, 227, 231, 236; DBFP, ser. IA, I, no. 205, II, nos. 275, 300.

23. ADAP, B, I/2, nos. 233, 235, 237, 244; DBFP, ser. IA, II, nos. 326, 333.

24. See above, pp. 61–62.

25. ADAP, B, I/2, nos. 237, 242, 244.

26. Salewski, pp. 357–65; ADAP, B, I/2, nos. 261, 265; DBFP, ser. IA, II, nos. 333–55 passim.

27. *Vermächtnis*, III, pp. 73–76; ADAP, B, IV, pp. 602–4; memorandum, Dec. 1926, PAB: 3147H/D658363–5.

28. ADAP, B, I/2, nos. 262, 275, IV, no. 27.

29. Ibid., IV, nos. 26, 46, 157; DBFP, ser. IA, III, no. 7. For a close analysis of the French position, see Jacobson, pp. 104–13.

30. ADAP, B, IV, nos. 55, 201; see DBFP, ser. IA, II, no. 419. On the negotiations for the cabinet see Stürmer, *Koalition und Opposition*, pp. 182–90.

31. ADAP, B, IV, nos. 219, 240, V, no. 22. On Chamberlain's very positive assessment of Stresemann's chairmanship see DBFP, ser. IA, III, no. 46.

32. ADAP, B, IV, no. 220; DBFP, ser. IA, II, nos. 138, 392, 395, III, nos. 143, 201. See also, Jacobson, pp. 124–27.

33. At the June session, for example, the Germans at last realized a long-standing ambition—representation on the League's Mandates Commission (ADAP, B, V, no. 255).

34. On the June session see ADAP, B, V, nos. 227, 228, 237; DBFP, ser. IA, III, nos. 234, 241. On the September session see ADAP, B, VI, nos. 168, 203; DBFP, ser. IA, IV, no. 8.

35. ADAP, B, VI, nos. 167, 168; Jacobson, pp. 132–33.

36. ADAP, B, IV, nos. 15, 26, 46, 122, 215, V, nos. 143, 256; Maxelon, p. 252 n.

37. ADAP, B, IV, no. 254, V, no. 98; *Vermächtnis*, III, p. 197; Geigenmüller, pp. 615–16. "Secret conclaves" are in DBFP, ser. IA, IV, no. 8.

38. ADAP, B, IV, no. 253; Stresemann in Foreign Affairs Committee, 17 Mar. 1927, PAB: 3147H/D658503–30; *Verhandlungen*, 392:9882; Jacobson, p. 137. The German government was not nearly as convinced of the applicability of its legal rights under article 431 as it made out in public. It knew that the Western

powers believed that reparations would have to be paid in full before these rights obtained (ADAP, B, VII, no. 16; memorandum by Stresemann, 9 Dec. 1928, PAB: 4587H/E184477–86).

39. ADAP, B, VII, nos. 173, 219; Pünder to Chancellor, 12 Dec. 1927, PAB: 4587H/E183825–7. For Hoesch's rather skeptical reaction, see ADAP, B, VII, no. 240.

40. Foreign Affairs Committee, 17 Mar. 1928, PAB: 7348H/H165240–6; Jacobson, p. 145.

41. Stresemann (though neither Schubert nor Gaus) seems to have considered such surveillance a possible bargaining counter all along. On 15 Dec. 1926 he told the cabinet that such surveillance was worth discussing, though it was not to extend beyond 1935. In March 1927 he had told Chamberlain that Germany might agree to such surveillance in return for full evacuation (ADAP, B, I/2, no. 265, IV, no. 220).

42. *Verhandlungen,* 394:12490–95, 12556–60. On the reasons for new Reichstag elections see Stürmer, pp. 241–42; ADAP, B, VII, no. 219.

43. *Schulthess 1928,* pp. 278–81.

44. Hoesch to Foreign Ministry, 20 Jan., 3, 17 Feb. 1928, PAB: 7373H/H167120–6, 5138H/E297331–7, E297344–8.

45. Hoesch to Foreign Ministry, 1, 3 Feb.; memorandum by Schubert, 6 Mar. 1928, PAB: 5138H/E297327–37, 4587H/E183918–24. Berthelot's views were apparently shared by Poincaré but not by Briand (Jacobson, pp. 152–54, 158–64); Briand's position emerges clearly in DDB, II, no. 167.

46. *Verhandlungen,* 423:38–39.

47. Hoesch to Foreign Ministry, 22 June, 12 July 1928, PAB: 3241/D706862–5, D706873–81; Geigenmüller, pp. 616–17.

48. ADAP, B, VII, nos. 16, 219; Foreign Affairs Committee, 17 Mar. 1927, PAB: 3147H/D658503–30. See also, DBFP, ser. IA, V, no. 120.

49. Stresemann had alluded to the possibility of such a step in a meeting of the Foreign Affairs Committee on 17 Mar. 1928, PAB: 7348H/H165240–6. Schubert and Gaus both favored it, as did Chancellor Müller—see Schubert to Stresemann (Bühlerhöhe), 30 June; Gaus to Stresemann (Karlsbad), 1 Aug. 1928, PAB: 3241/D706854–7, 7378H/H168140–3; Jacobson, pp. 175, 177–78.

50. Schubert to Stresemann (Karlsbad), 24 July; unsigned memorandum, 20 Aug. 1928, PAB: 3058H/D607050–67, 5138H/E297436–48. The case against further occupation was made also in the press in Germany and abroad (DBFP, ser. IA, V, no. 188).

51. Stresemann (Karlsbad) to Schubert, 26 July; Schubert to Missions, 28 July 1928, PAB: 7150H/H151321–4, 4502H/E119214–22. On the cool reception in London and Brussels see DBFP, ser. IA, V, nos. 120, 123; DDB, II, no. 182.

52. Vogt, *Kabinett Müller II,* pp. 68–75; unsigned memorandum, 20 Aug. 1928, PAB: 5138H/E297436–48.

53. Pünder to Chancellery, 6, 8 Sept. 1928, PAB: 3147H/D659603–5, D659606–8; Vogt, *Kabinett Müller II,* pp. 77–84; DBFP, ser. IA, V, nos. 146, 149. Briand's position had been virtually the same in conversation with Hymans on 25 August (DDB, II, no. 183).

54. LNOJ, *Special Supplement 64,* pp. 58–59, 79–83.

55. Vogt, *Kabinett Müller II,* pp. 84–94, 97–106; Pünder to Chancellery, 13

Sept. 1928, PAB: 3147H/D659632–7. For the British and Belgian records of these conversations see DBFP, ser. IA, V, nos. 151, 156, 162; DDB, II, no. 187.

56. Chancellor Müller to Foreign Ministry, 14 Sept. 1928, PAB: 3147H/ D659638–43.

57. Vogt, *Kabinett Müller II*, pp. 107–12; Julius Curtius, *Der Young Plan* (Stuttgart, 1949), pp. 27, 31.

58. Vogt, *Kabinett Müller II*, pp. 113–22; DBFP, ser. IA, V, no. 161; DDB, II, no. 189.

59. DBFP, ser. IA, V, no. 161.

60. Vogt, *Kabinett Müller II*, pp. 128–31, 138–40, 177–80; Löbe to Stresemann, 5 Oct. 1928, PAB: 3147H/D659665; *Deutsche Allgemeine Zeitung*, 25 Sept. 1928; Jacobson, pp. 201–2.

61. *Frankfurter Zeitung*, 20 Sept.; Rieth (Paris) to Foreign Ministry, 1 Oct., Hoesch to Foreign Ministry, 3 Nov. 1928, PAB: 2406H/D506322–4, D506391–8. Similarly, the British "held that proposals for liquidating reparation liability should be made by Germany before we could promise evacuation" (DBFP, ser. IA, V, no. 159).

62. Arnold Toynbee, ed., *Survey of International Affairs 1929* (London, 1930), pp. 135–36 (henceforth *Survey*); John W. Wheeler-Bennett, *The Wreck of Reparations* (London, 1933), pp. 79–80; Link, *Amerikanische Stabilisierungspolitik*, pp. 438–45.

63. Erich Matthias and Rudolf Morsey, eds., *Das Ende der Parteien 1933* (Düsseldorf, 1960), pp. 283–88, 544–47. See also DBFP, ser. IA, V, nos. 175, 176. The impact and consequences of the election of 1928 deserve a monographic study.

64. *Verhandlungen*, 423:414–22, 426–35, 438–42, 464–70, 482.

65. Memorandum by Schubert, 5 Dec., PAB: 4587H/E184417–21; *Kreuzzeitung*, 5 Dec.; *Germania*, 6 Dec.; *Frankfurter Zeitung*, 6, 7 Dec.; *Deutsche Allgemeine Zeitung*, 7 Dec. 1928.

66. Memorandums by Schmidt, 9, 13 Dec.; memorandum by Stresemann, 9 Dec. 1928, PAB: 4587H/D184433–41, E184510–26, E184572–82, E184477–86; DBFP, ser. IA, V, nos. 287, 292.

67. Foreign Affairs Committee, 25 Jan. 1929, PAB: 3147H/D659781–90.

68. Hoesch to Foreign Ministry, 24 Jan.; Stresemann (Geneva) to Foreign Ministry, 7 Mar. 1929, PAB: 4502H/E120316–7, 4587H/E184870–2; Maxelon, pp. 266–67.

69. *Vermächtnis*, III, 393–95. On the margin of the copy of this letter that Stresemann sent to Adolf Müller in Berne is a penciled comment: "Confessions of someone duped despite all urgent warnings from Berne!" (30 Mar. 1929, PAB: L1815/L522486–91). See also, Vogt, *Kabinett Müller II*, pp. 652–55.

70. *Survey 1929*, pp. 141–42, 150–66; Wheeler-Bennett, pp. 87–88; Jacobson, pp. 250–58.

71. Vogt, *Kabinett Müller II*, introduction passim, pp. 1002–14; Fischer, *Deutsche Wirtschaftspolitik*, pp. 31–39; Turner, *Stresemann*, pp. 244–52.

72. Pünder (Madrid) to Chancellery, 11 June 1929, PAB: 4587H/E185111–9; Vogt, *Kabinett Müller II*, pp. 761–62.

73. Vogt, pp. 779–84. Hindenburg reminded the delegation that he would sign the Young plan only if (1) the Rhineland was evacuated at an early date, (2) France agreed to negotiate the return of the Saar, (3) there would be no control

commission of any kind (ibid., pp. 845–46).

74. *Verhandlungen*, 425:2802–15, 2860–62, 2868–72; Vogt, *Kabinett Müller II*, pp. 838–44.

75. *Survey 1929*, pp. 181–82; Wheeler-Bennett, pp. 108–10, 115–23; Jacobson, pp. 309–43.

76. *Vermächtnis*, III, pp. 556–57; Maxelon, pp. 270–71.

77. The committee of jurists, to which the proposal for a conciliation commission had been referred, had determined that the peace treaty did not justify such a commission (Jacobson, pp. 331–34).

78. *Vermächtnis*, III, pp. 560–63. Negotiations about the return of the Saar, which lasted from Nov. 1929 to July 1930, ended inconclusively.

Chapter 7

1. Gotthold Rhode, "Das Deutschtum in Posen und Pommerellen in der Zeit der Weimarer Republik," in *Die deutschen Ostgebiete zur Zeit der Weimarer Republik* (Cologne, 1966), pp. 88–132. In 1925 the Foreign Ministry put the number of German minorities at 1.5 million in Poland and 160,000 in the Baltic states, and it calculated that 400,000 Germans lived in Danzig and 90,000 in Memel (unsigned memorandum, 12 Sept. 1925, PAB: K1764/K431823–4). These figures are slightly higher than those in the official censuses (Wilhelm Winkler, *Statistisches Handbuch der europäischen Nationalitäten* [Vienna, 1931]).

2. On the drafting, character, and purpose of the minority treaties, see C. A. Macartney, *National States and National Minorities* (London, 1934), chaps. 7, 8; texts in *Protection of Linguistic, Racial or Religious Minorities by the League of Nations* (Geneva, 1927).

3. DBFP, ser. IA, V, no. 53. It may well have been difficult for the governments of the new states to prevent their people from settling old scores, and one should not forget that the authorities were simply not equipped to carry out their treaty obligations, especially in the first few years.

4. On the minorities and the treaties, see Macartney, pp. 381–95, and Herbert von Truhart, *Völkerbund und Minderheitspetitionen* (Vienna, 1931). An account of the real disadvantages and privations (and perhaps unadmitted advantages) of the minority experience remains to be written.

5. On the nature and politics of League procedures, see Macartney, chap. 9; Tennent H. Bagley, *General Principles and Problems in the International Protection of Minorities* (Geneva, 1950), pp. 42, 81–91; memorandum by Podewils, 29 Nov. 1926, PAB: K1764/K432287–92.

6. See, for example, *Vermächtnis*, I, pp. 581–82, 598–99, II, pp. 150–51, 172, 554; *Schulthess 1924*, pp. 83–84; Turner, "Rede Stresemanns," p. 435.

7. The loss of territory affected Prussia alone, but the sense of injury was felt by all the German states (Ian F. D. Morrow, *The Peace Settlement in the German-Polish Borderlands* [London, 1936], pp. 192–93).

8. There are two full-scale studies that reconstruct Germany's minority policy on the basis of documents from the Foreign Ministry archives: Carole Fink, "The Weimar Republic as the Defender of Minorities, 1919–33" (diss., Yale, 1969), and Helmut Pieper, *Die Minderheitenfrage und das Deutsche Reich 1919–1933/34* (Hamburg, 1974). Fink, whose main conclusions are incorporated in "Defender

of Minorities: Germany in the League of Nations, 1926–33," *Central European History* V (Dec. 1972), pp. 330–57, emphasizes Germany's contribution to the protection of minorities but largely ignores the false note injected by Germany's revisionist intentions. Pieper adds little more than detail to what we know. The books by Martin Broszat (*200 Jahre deutsche Polenpolitik,* rev. ed. [Frankfurt/Main, 1972]) and Harald von Riekhoff (*German-Polish Relations 1918–1933* [Baltimore, 1971]), also based on archival material, treat Germany's minority policy in a larger context.

9. *Verhandlungen,* 385:1931, 1946, 386:2229, 2236–37, 2240, 388:4545, 4590–91; Riekhoff, pp. 206–12.

10. Unsigned memorandum, Nov. 1923, Stresemann to Ministries, 13 Jan. 1925, PAB: 3241/D704692–4, 4555H/E147362–73; ADAP, B, I/1, no. 85, II/1, no. 64.

11. The economic and organizational aspects of government aid have been explored in detail by Norbert Krekeler, *Revisionsanspruch und geheime Ostpolitik der Weimarer Republik* (Stuttgart, 1973). See also, ADAP, B, I/1, nos. 178, 205, II/1, no. 205, V, no. 263; unsigned memorandums, 6 Feb., 10 Dec. 1929, PAB: 4555H/E147507–11, E148034–41.

12. Memorandum by Podewils, Jan. 1926, PAB: K1764/K431974–9; ADAP, B, I/1, pp. 751–52. To lend credibility to what it called its "moral offensive," the Foreign Ministry now urged a reluctant Prussian government to liberalize the treatment of national minorities within its territory—see Fink, diss., pp. 53–63; Martin Broszat, "Aussen- und innenpolitische Aspekte der preussisch-deutschen Minderheitenpolitik in der Aera Stresemann," in *Politische Ideologien und nationalstaatliche Ordnung,* ed. Kurt Kluxen and Wolfgang J. Mommsen (Munich, 1968), pp. 442–45.

13. Bülow to Missions, 22 Aug. 1925, PAB: K1764/K431779–86; Fink, diss., pp. 78–84, 94–95. German diplomats had been skeptical all along about the aid they could accord the minorities in the League (ADAP, B, I/1, no. 22).

14. Aschmann to Foreign Ministry, 18 June; memorandum by Soehring, 14 Oct. 1926, PAB: K1764/K432194–200, K432283–6.

15. Memorandums by Freytag, 25 Aug. 1927, 15 Aug. 1928, PAB: K1764/K432349–51, K432463–7.

16. Though the Foreign Ministry had originally asked for a position in the secretariat's minorities section, the diplomats dropped this request, for they believed that if Germans were employed there, representatives of minority states would also be employed, and this would "politicize" the section (DBFP, ser. IA, I, no. 276; ADAP, B, IV, no. 158).

17. ADAP, B, VII, no. 206; Schubert in press conference, 5 June 1929, PAB: 4587H/E184966–9; *Vermächtnis,* III, pp. 216–17. See also, memorandum by Drummond, 28 Nov. 1928, League of Nations Archives: Minorities Section Files, Box S. 353; Fink, diss., pp. 108–15.

18. Truhart, pp. 62–64.

19. Ibid., pp. 162–64; Weizsäcker to Missions, 23 June, 10 Oct.; memorandum by Dirksen, 14 Aug. 1928, PAB: 3635/D805096–109, D805202–15, 5462H/E369113–30.

20. Memorandum by Gaus, 19 Apr. 1930, PAB: 4570H/E169545–9.

21. Gaus to Schubert, 6 July 1926; memorandum by Dirksen, 16 Nov. 1925,

PAB: 5265H/E320523–30, 4569H/E168406–15.

22. *Vermächtnis*, II, pp. 69, 149, 173; Turner, "Rede Stresemanns," p. 429; LNOJ 1929, p. 520.

23. ADAP, B, VII, no. 206. See also Helmut Lippelt, " 'Politische Sanierung': Zur deutschen Politik gegenüber Polen 1925/26," *Vierteljahrshefte für Zeitgeschichte* XIX (1971), pp. 323–73.

24. ADAP, B, I/2, no. 225. Heinrich Sahm, *Erinnerungen aus meinen Danziger Jahren* (Marburg, 1958), pp. 124–25.

25. ADAP, B, I/1, nos. 22, 85, VII, no. 206.

26. ADAP, B, II/1, no. 74, VII, no. 22. After 1927, Stresemann worked for a more relaxed relationship with Poland, so as to demonstrate Germany's peaceful intentions—see Riekhoff, pp. 131–93; Maria Oertel, "Beiträge zur Geschichte der deutsch-polnischen Beziehungen 1925–30" (diss., Berlin, 1968), pp. 180–229, 240–307.

27. Memorandums by Poensgen, 7 Apr. 1928, by Freytag, 25 Apr. 1929, by Schneider, 26 Apr. 1930, PAB: K1764/K432401–2, K432631–2, L1675/L497537–9.

28. ADAP, B, VII, no. 79.

29. ADAP, B, IV, nos. 23, 95; Vogt, *Kabinett Müller II*, pp. 290–92; Oertel, pp. 129–32.

30. Foreign Affairs Committee, 17 Mar., 21 Oct. 1927, 17 Mar. 1929, PAB: 3147H/D658503–40, 7330H/H166464–88, 4587H/E184929–39. Memorandum by Weizsäcker, 31 Mar. 1930, PAB: K1764/K432628–30; Press Conference, 9 June 1928, PAB: 4587H/E184192–201. *Verhandlungen*, 395:13644, 13898, 423:61.

31. LNOJ 1928, pp. 875–76; *Protection . . . of Minorities* (1929), pp. 29–37.

32. DLV to Foreign Ministry, 4 Apr.; Völckers (Geneva) to Foreign Ministry, 1 Sept., Löbe to Stresemann, 5 Oct. 1928, PAB: K1764/K432405–8, K432473–80, 3147H/D659665.

33. Vogt, *Kabinett Müller II*, pp. 290–92.

34. Stresemann (Lugano) to Foreign Ministry, 16 Dec.; Weizsäcker to Missions, 28 Dec. 1928, PAB: 4587H/E184692–5, 3635/D805306–23; LNOJ 1929, pp. 68–70; DBFP, ser. IA, V, nos. 299, 303.

35. Foreign Ministry to Delegation, 15 Dec. 1928, PAB: 3147H/D659722–5; Jacobson, *Locarno Diplomacy*, pp. 234–35. On pressure, and on Foreign Ministry's efforts to evade it, see memorandum by Poensgen, 28 Apr.; unsigned memorandum, 1 Oct. 1928, PAB: K1764/K432410–1, K432486. Stresemann's tantrum earned him sheaves of congratulatory letters and telegrams (PAB: 7382H/H168769–813).

36. Dufour to Stresemann, 24 Jan. 1929, PAB: 3147H/D659761–71.

37. Memorandums by Reinebeck, 14 Jan., 9 Feb., by Freytag, 21 Jan. 1929, PAB: K1764/K432522–42, 3147H/D659848–68, K1772/K435877–85. The Prussian government criticized Reinebeck's strategy for not going "far enough." It would result in a "first-class funeral" of a promising initiative (unsigned memorandum, 16 Feb. 1929, PAB: 4555H/E147559–71).

38. Hoesch to Schubert, 8 Feb.; memorandum by Freytag, 13 Mar. 1929, PAB: 5544/E384707–10, K1772/K436037; Fink, diss., pp. 137–42.

39. Sthamer to Foreign Ministry, 16 Feb.; Hoesch to Foreign Ministry, 28

Feb.; Schubert in Foreign Affairs Committee, 19 Mar. 1929, PAB: 3147H/ D659892–3, D660014–6, 4555H/E147679–92. See also, Fink, diss., pp. 137–38, 152–54.

40. LNOJ 1929, pp. 515–22; Weizsäcker to Missions, 20 Mar. 1929, PAB: 3635/D805333–69.

41. LNOJ 1929, pp. 522–32; Weizsäcker to Missions, 20 Mar. 1929, PAB: 3635/D805333–69.

42. Memorandum by Schubert, 6 Mar.; unsigned memorandum, 7 Mar. 1929, PAB: 4587H/E184853–5, 4555H/E147652–3.

43. Stresemann in Press Conference, 6, 7 Mar.; unsigned memorandum, Mar. 1929, PAB: 4587H/E184850–2, E184873–9, 4555H/E147654–8. Stresemann's article, PAB: 4555H/E147669–74; press reaction, Fink, diss., pp. 154–55. Schubert was obliged to defend Germany's policy at Geneva at length in the Foreign Affairs Committee (19 Mar. 1929, PAB: 4555H/E147679–92).

44. LNOJ 1929, pp. 1133–55; memorandum by Reinebeck, 10 June 1929, PAB: 3147H/D660244–50; Fink, diss., pp. 158–59.

45. Memorandums by Schubert, 1, 12 June 1929, PAB: 4555H/E147246, 4587H/E185123–5.

46. Unsigned memorandum, 10 June 1929, PAB: 4587H/E185049–52.

47. Memorandum by Reinebeck, 10 June 1929, PAB: 3147H/D660244–50; *Protection . . . of Minorities* (1931), pp. 117–25.

48. Unsigned memorandum, 7 June 1929, PAB: 4587H/E184991.

49. Memorandum by Reinebeck, 10 June 1929, PAB: 3147H/D660244–50; *Protection . . . of Minorities* (1931), pp. 125–36.

50. Unsigned memorandum, 10 June 1929, PAB: 4587H/E185049–52; Vogt, *Kabinett Müller II,* pp. 731–33.

51. *Protection . . . of Minorities* (1931), pp. 136–45.

52. Pünder (Madrid) to Foreign Ministry, 11 June 1929, PAB: 4587H/ E185111–9.

53. Stresemann in Press Conference, 11, 13 June; Weizsäcker (Madrid) to Foreign Ministry, 11 June; Pünder (Madrid) to Chancellor, 13 June 1929, PAB: 4587H/E185098–106, E185107–9, E185138–46, E185111–19; *Protection . . . of Minorities* (1931), pp. 145–50.

54. *Verhandlungen,* 425:2826–28, 2837–38, 2852, 2857–59, 2869; *Germania,* 15 June 1929; Fink, diss., p. 174.

55. Walters, *History of the League,* pp. 427, 430–31; *Vermächtnis,* III, pp. 577–79. The Foreign Ministry interpreted Briand's plan as a scheme to secure the political and territorial status quo in Europe (J. W. Ewald, *Die deutsche Aussenpolitik und der Europaplan Briands* [Marburg, 1961]).

56. Curtius in Foreign Affairs Committee, 23 May; Weizsäcker to Missions, 18, 27 Oct. 1930, PAB: 3147H/D661194–218, 3635/D805696–716, D805716–45; Cabinet, 21 May 1930, 3 Oct. 1931, BAK: R 43 I/1443, 1453. On minority pressures see unsigned memorandum, July; memorandum by Weizsäcker, 1 Sept. 1930, PAB: K1773/K437432–5, K1764/K432665–6.

57. Krekelen, pp. 117–44. Curtius also continued Stresemann's practice of seeking reasonable relations with Poland, though he encountered considerable opposition in the Reichstag and the press (Riekhoff, pp. 146–57, 186, 270).

58. Kimmich, *Free City,* pp. 109–16.

59. DBFP, 2d ser., I, nos. 307, 308, 312, 318, 319; Karl-Dietrich Bracher, *Die Auflösung der Weimarer Republik*, 3d ed. (Stuttgart, 1960), pp. 290–91, 346–47; Wolfgang J. Helbich, *Die Reparationen in der Ära Brüning* (Berlin, 1962), pp. 12–16.

60. Rauscher (Warsaw) to Bülow, 5 June; unsigned memorandums, July, Aug. 1930, PAB: 4607H/E193737–9, K1773/K437432–5, K437463–6, K437491–3; Oertel, pp. 308–12.

61. Bülow to Curtius (Geneva), 15 Sept. 1930, PAB: 3147H/D661413–4; Julius Curtius, *Sechs Jahre Minister der deutschen Republik* (Heidelberg, 1948), pp. 171–72. At Geneva, Curtius turned down Briand's suggestion that they publish a communiqué stating their commitment to the policy of accommodation (memorandum by Curtius, 18 Sept. 1930, PAB: 4691H/H196945–52).

62. Wolfgang J. Helbich, "Between Stresemann and Hitler: The Foreign Policy of the Brüning Government," *World Politics*, XII (1959), pp. 32–39. On Brüning's fresh demands see DBFP, 2d ser., I, no. 308, *Schulthess 1930*, pp. 159–60; on eastern borders see memorandums by Gaus, 19 Apr., by Curtius, 15 May 1930, PAB: 4570H/E169545–9, 4587H/E185644–6; on new diplomatic style see memorandum by Curtius, 27 Oct. 1930, PAB: 4620H/E198557–60.

63. For more on Brüning's strategy, see below, pp. 155–57.

64. Bülow to Rauscher (Warsaw), 18 Nov. 1930, PAB: L683/L216380–3; Riekhoff, pp. 327–79.

65. "Anti-German Week" (19–26 Oct. 1930) was one of the more violent episodes in what was a rather violent election campaign thoughout Poland. That week, the Insurgents, a Polish paramilitary group, engaged in numerous acts of intimidation and maltreatment against the German community in Polish Upper Silesia. A detailed account can be found in the petition the Deutscher Volksbund, the local minority organization, filed with the League on 7 Jan. 1931 (LNOJ 1931, pp. 382–432). See also, Fink, diss., pp. 200–204.

66. Curtius to Missions, 28 Nov.; memorandum by Noebel, 1 Dec. 1930, PAB: 3147H/D661662–5, L683/L216396–9; LNOJ 1931, pp. 371–81, 432–52.

67. Trautmann to Missions, 19 Dec.; Hoesch to Foreign Ministry, 21 Dec. 1930, 13 Jan. 1931, PAB: L683/L216425–7, 3147H/D661691–5, D661726–8. See also, DBFP, 2d ser., I, no. 344.

68. LNOJ 1931, pp. 165–79; Walters, pp. 447–48. After the council session, Curtius felt obliged to explain to the diplomatic missions that all the agitation did not mean that Germany was about to demand the revision of the borders (Kimmich, pp. 103–4).

69. LNOJ 1931, pp. 237–38; Curtius in Foreign Affairs Committee, 2 Feb.; Weizsäcker to Missions, 12 Feb. 1931, PAB: 3147H/D661895–925, D661933–50; Cabinet, 28 Jan. 1931, BAK: R 43 I/1448. See also, Fink, diss., pp. 206–7.

70. LNOJ 1931, pp. 1145–50, 2442–47, 2262–63; Fink, diss., p. 209; Curtius (Geneva) to Foreign Ministry, 20 Sept. 1931, PAB: 3147H/D662627–8.

71. Ernst-Albrecht Plieg, *Das Memelland 1919–39* (Würzburg, 1962), pp. 68–85; Fink, diss., pp. 196–220.

72. Müller to Foreign Ministry, Jan. 1931, PAB: 3635/D805828–44.

73. Oertel, p. 174; Kimmich, p. 162; Müller to Foreign Ministry, Jan. 1931, PAB: 3635/D805828–44; Cabinet, 27 May 1931, BAK: R 43 I/1449.

Chapter 8

1. The various attempts between 1920 and 1925 to initiate general disarmament are recounted in John W. Wheeler-Bennett, *Information on the Reduction of Armaments* (London, 1925), and in Walters, *History of the League*, pp. 217–28, 361–63. See also, DBFP, ser. IA, III, no. 200, IV, no. 219.

2. Unsigned memorandum, 27 June 1927, PAB: 3147H/D658803–13. For a brief analysis of German policy in the 1920s, see Rolf Richter, "Der Abrüstungsgedanke in Theorie und Praxis und die deutsche Politik (1920–1929)," *Wehrwissenschaftliche Rundschau* XVIII (Aug. 1968), pp. 442–66.

3. The military's secret efforts to circumvent the restrictions—training men in excess of the legal limit, developing and testing proscribed weapons, stockpiling matériel imported from abroad—were of little practical value (Karl-Dietrich Bracher, et al., *Die nationalsozialistische Machtergreifung* [Cologne, 1960], pp. 766–84; Rainer Wohlfeil, "Heer und Republik," in *Handbuch zur deutschen Militärgeschichte 1648–1939* VI [Frankfurt/Main, 1970], pp. 204–40). For a contemporary assessment see DBFP, ser. IA, V, no. 268.

4. ADAP, B, I/1, no. 144; memorandum by Defense Ministry, 3 May 1926; memorandum by Weizsäcker, 2 Mar. 1931, PAB: 9126H/H243805–7, 9095H/H221374–83.

5. ADAP, B, I/1, nos. 45, 134, 144, 219; and see, ibid., V, no. 251. A careful reconstruction of the collaboration between the two ministries, done with much skill and subtlety, is in Gaines Post, Jr., *The Civil-Military Fabric of Weimar Foreign Policy* (Princeton, 1973). On disarmament policy, see especially pp. 303–16, 349–52.

6. Walters, p. 363; A. C. Temperley, *The Whispering Gallery of Europe* (London, 1938), pp. 57–58. Stresemann had first asked Adolf Müller, but Müller had declined (Müller to Foreign Ministry, 10 Jan. 1926, PAB: 4543H/E144480–1). Bülow then suggested Bernstorff, who as president of the Deutsche Liga für Völkerbund had impeccable credentials for representing pacifist principles (memorandum by Bülow, 14 Apr. 1926, PAB: 4543H/E144568–72; ADAP, B, I/2, no. 281).

7. The former Allies did not accept this argument, considering themselves at most under a moral obligation—see Salewski, *Entwaffnung*, pp. 34–35 (with references to contemporary literature); *Bulletin of International News*, 4 Dec. 1930.

8. League of Nations documents C.425.M.158.1926.IX; C.310.M.109.1927.IX; C.667.M.225.1927.IX; C.165.M.50.1928.IX. See also, ADAP, B, I/2, no. 219, IV, no. 246, V, no. 136. Bülow to Missions, 25 Mar., Bernstorff to Foreign Ministry, 2 Dec. 1927; memorandum by Bernstorff, 30 Mar. 1928, PAB: 3147H/D658551–82, D659432–40, 3635/D804851–2.

9. The British saw through these tactics (DBFP, ser. IA, V, nos. 377, 385). Any number of Foreign Ministry memorandums show that rearmament was never out of mind (ADAP, B, V, nos. 42, 251; memorandums by Weizsäcker, 4 Nov. 1927, by Köpke, 26 June, by Bülow, 25 Oct. 1929, PAB: 4543H/H145888–90, 9126H/H245729–31, H245734–6).

10. ADAP, B, V, no. 136, VII, no. 29.

11. League of Nations document C.310.M.109.1927.IX; ADAP, B, IV, no. 246, VII, no. 148; Directive, 8 Apr. 1929, PAB: 4543H/E145316–21.

12. Directive, 8 Apr.; Köpke to Missions, 17 May 1929, PAB: 4543H/E145316–21, 3147H/D660177–82; ADAP, B, V, no. 251.

13. ADAP, B, I/2, no. 219, V, no. 136; memorandum by Bülow, 16 Aug. 1928, PAB: 4543H/E145161–4. The Foreign Ministry urged the German press to assess the negotiations positively (Bülow to Zechlin, 3 May 1926, PAB: 9126H/H243803), and the government deliberately refrained from putting up a propaganda campaign.

14. On the work of the Preparatory Commission, see John W. Wheeler-Bennett, *Disarmament and Security since Locarno* (London, 1932); Walters, pp. 364–84, 440–42. For the British position see DBFP, ser. IA, II, no. 2, III, no. 202, IV, no. 219; for the French, Wolfers, *Britain and France*, chaps. 4, 22.

15. ADAP, B, IV, no. 246, V, nos. 81, 136; Köpke to Missions, 17 May 1929; memorandum by Weizsäcker, 29 Mar. 1928; Bülow to delegation, 18 Nov. 1930, PAB: 3147H/D659422–6, D660177–82, 3154H/D666209–10.

16. League of Nations document C.687.M.288.1930.IX.

17. League of Nations document C.195.M.74.1929.IX; Wheeler-Bennett, *Disarmament and Security*, pp. 73, 99–100.

18. Köpke to Missions, 12 Jan. 1931, PAB: 3154H/D666354–73. In a memorandum submitted to Curtius, Weizsäcker noted that the allusion to the peace treaty obliged the delegation to offer suggestions for improvement and to resort to blunt language; on its merits alone, the convention was entirely acceptable and probably the best that could be put together (memorandum, 2 Mar. 1931, PAB: 9095H/H221374–83).

19. LNOJ 1931, pp. 160–61, 223; *Schulthess 1931*, p. 41. Briand promptly protested against the threat implicit in Curtius's Reichstag remarks (Hoesch to Foreign Ministry, 11 Feb. 1931, PAB: L1837/L532695–6).

20. DBFP, 2d ser., I, no. 335; *Bulletin of International News*, 12 Feb. 1931. The British ambassador attributed Germany's "more forward foreign policy" to political pressures (DBFP, 2d ser., I, nos. 331, 334, 335, 337, 351).

21. Hugenberg to Brüning, 28 Nov., resolution, 28 Nov., Foreign Affairs Committee, Dec. 1930, PAB: 3635/D805775, 3154H/D666253, 3650H/D810952–5.

22. Directive, 24 Oct.; unsigned memorandum, 30 Oct. 1930; memorandum by Weizsäcker, 2 Mar. 1931, PAB: 3642H/D810811–14, D810816–20, 9095H/H221374–83.

23. On Brüning's foreign policy, see the sources cited above (p. 147 n); his own *Memoiren*, pp. 111, 193–95, 221–24, 274, 434–35, 492, 500; his foreign minister Curtius's *Sechs Jahre*, pp. 107–8, 162–63, 177–87; and Gottfried Reinhold Treviranus, *Das Ende von Weimar* (Düsseldorf, 1968), pp. 266–68. Brüning expounded his ideas to the American ambassador, see his memorandum dated 19 Dec. 1930, PAB: 3154H/D666302–6 (translated in part in Edward W. Bennett, *Germany and the Diplomacy of the Financial Crisis, 1931* [Cambridge, Mass., 1962] pp. 32–33). See also, Link, *Amerikanische Stabilisierungspolitik,* pp. 512–15.

24. Memorandum by Poensgen, 3 Nov. 1927; Bülow to Eisenlohr, 7 Aug.; Weizsäcker to Dufour, 2 Oct. 1929, PAB: L1539/L466544–9, L1712/L503247–51, L1837/L532602–5.

25. To an ambassador who had suggested that the Germans threaten to with-

draw from the League in order to gain a tactical advantage in a particular minorities case, Curtius wrote snappishly that only those states which had few interests in Europe and had their own sources of strength could forgo the League (Curtius to Embassy London, 3 Jan. 1931, PAB: L1837/L532689).

26. Memorandum by Weizsäcker, 16 Apr., PAB: L1837/L532623–41; see also draft of newspaper article by Weizsäcker, 3 Nov. 1930, PAB: L1837/L532679–84. Between 1930 and 1932, when the secretariat was being reorganized and restaffed, German diplomats worked hard to improve Germany's position there, for reasons both of expediency and of prestige (Weizsäcker to Dieckhoff [London], 20 Aug. 1930; Kamphoevener to Missions, 1 Nov. 1932, PAB: L779/L228223–34, 3147H/D663963–4011).

27. Memorandum by Drummond, 14 May 1930, PAB: 3147H/D661154–7.

28. Cabinet, 3 Oct. 1931, BAK: R 43 I/1453.

29. Hoesch to Foreign Ministry, 12 Feb., 11 Mar. 1931, PAB: L1837/L532697–9, 3154H/D666543–4. On Franco-German relations 1931, see also Bennett, passim.

30. Memorandums by Weizsäcker, 18 Feb., 13 Mar.; unsigned memorandums, 18 Mar., 11 July 1931, PAB: 9095H/H221345–8, 3154H/D666482–4, 3642H/D811005–9, 9126H/H245955–62; DBFP, 2d ser., III, no. 215.

31. Memorandums by Weizsäcker, 11 Feb., by Planck, 9 Apr., by Mackensen, 28 Mar. 1931, PAB: 3642H/H810988–93, D810998, D811022–31. Funds were also earmarked for domestic propaganda to rally support for Germany's position at the conference.

32. Unsigned memorandums, 18 Mar., 8 July 1931, PAB: 3642H/D811005–9, D811120–2. See also, DBFP, 2d ser., IV, nos. 110, 113.

33. Unsigned memorandums, 11 July, 7 May 1931, PAB: 9126H/H245955–62, H245912–7.

34. Memorandums by Weizsäcker, 2 Mar., by Frohwein, 10 July, Schleicher to Bülow, 18 May 1931, PAB: 9095H/H221374–83, H221384–86, 9126H/H245936–7. On German rearmament schemes, see Bracher, *Machtergreifung*, pp. 776–80; Walter Bernhardt, "Die Aufrüstung Hitlers von 1934 bis 1939 und ihre militärischen und politischen Konzeptionen" (diss., Kiel, 1968), pp. 28–30; Berenice Carroll, *Design for Total War* (The Hague, 1968), pp. 59–60. On the attitudes of the military, see Thilo Vogelsang, "Neue Dokumente zur Geschichte der Reichswehr 1930–33," *Vierteljahrshefte für Zeitgeschichte* II (1954), p. 410.

35. Memorandums by Frohwein, 25 July, 17 Nov. 1931, 6 Jan. 1932, by Feine, 29 Aug. 1931, PAB: 9095H/H221687–9, H221927–31, H222121–8, 9097H/H222421–30.

36. Cabinet, 15 Jan. 1932, BAK: R 43 I/1454; memorandums by Frohwein, 10 July; by Feine, 29 Aug. 1931, PAB: 9095H/H221374–86, 9097H/H222421–30. Thilo Vogelsang, *Reichswehr, Staat und NSDAP* (Stuttgart, 1962), pp. 430–31.

37. John W. Wheeler-Bennett, *The Pipedream of Peace* (London, 1934), p. 14; Walters, pp. 500–501; Norman Hillson, *Geneva Scene* (London, 1936), pp. 86–89; *Frankfurter Zeitung*, 3 Feb. 1932. The most detailed study of the disarmament conference, a vast repository of information, is Carl Loosli-Usteri, *Geschichte der Konferenz für die Herabsetzung und Begrenzung der Rüstungen 1932–34* (Zurich, 1940); Jordan, *Great Britain, France, and the German Problem*, chaps. 11–13, is still readable.

38. Walters, p. 501; Loosli-Usteri, p. 64; *Deutsche Allgemeine Zeitung*, 24 May 1931; *Deutsche Volkszeitung*, 1 Jan. 1932. On the Manchurian conflict the Germans tried to remain neutral before the League (Bülow to Bernstorff, 24 Sept. 1931, PAB: K2088/K555438).

39. Nadolny to Foreign Ministry, 18 Mar. 1932, PAB: 7360H/E535059–66; Temperley, pp. 179–89.

40. Conference for the Reduction and Limitation of Armaments, *Conference Documents*, I (Geneva, 1932), pp. 113–16; Walters, pp. 502–3.

41. *Records of the Conference for the Reduction and Limitation of Armaments*, ser. A, I (Geneva, 1932), pp. 67–70; Brüning, p. 525; Temperley, p. 188.

42. Brüning, p. 492; Treviranus, p. 265. Weizsäcker had been the Foreign Ministry's choice (memorandum by Frohwein, 10 Aug. 1931, PAB: 9095H/H221725–31). On Nadolny's unpopularity see Köpke to Bülow, 9 Apr. 1932, PAB: 4617/E195617–29. His own recollections of the conference are in *Mein Beitrag* (Wiesbaden, 1955), pp. 113–41.

43. *Conference Documents*, I, pp. 119–22. Nadolny's speech was well received by the German press (*Frankfurter Zeitung*, 19 Feb. 1932).

44. *Foreign Relations of the United States 1932*, I (Washington, 1948), pp. 59–62, 76–83 (henceforth FRUS); Temperley, pp. 190–91.

45. Nadolny to Foreign Ministry, 29 Feb. 1932, PAB: 3154H/D667119–20; DBFP, 2d ser., III, no. 239.

46. Nadolny to Foreign Ministry, 24, 29 Feb., 17 Mar.; Hoesch to Foreign Ministry, 27 Feb.; memorandum by Bülow, 25 Feb. 1932, PAB: 3154H/D667091–3, D667107–11, D667117–8, D667151–3, 3642H/D811614–20; Nadolny, pp. 115–16.

47. Nadolny to Bülow, 12 Mar. 1932, PAB: 7360H/E535052–3; Nadolny, p. 120.

48. Brüning, pp. 544–47, 552, 556–57; Vogelsang, *Reichswehr*, pp. 185–87; Link, p. 518.

49. Brüning, pp. 557–62; unsigned memorandum, April; memorandum by Bülow, 26 April; Bülow to Neurath (London), 4 May 1932, PAB: 3642H/D811917–9, 3154H/D667202–4, 4620/E200780–6; FRUS 1932, I, pp. 108–12. Stimson was to say that he and MacDonald found Brüning "more conciliatory towards making a reasonable compromise with the French on their fundamental issues than we had anticipated."

50. Walters, pp. 506–7; Wheeler-Bennett, *Pipedream*, pp. 33–34; *Frankfurter Zeitung*, 27 Apr. 1932. The Foreign Ministry assumed Tardieu's laryngitis to be a diplomatic illness (Bülow in Press Conference, 12 Dec. 1932, PAB: 3154H/D672219–36).

51. FRUS 1932, I, pp. 112–14.

52. *Frankfurter Zeitung*, 28 Apr. 1932; *Le Temps*, 29 Apr. 1932.

53. Bülow to Neurath, 4 May 1932, PAB: 4620/E200780–6; Cabinet, 2 May 1932, BAK: R 43 I/1456; Brüning, p. 563; *Verhandlungen*, 446:2594–95.

54. Nadolny to Foreign Ministry, 1 May; memorandum by Völckers, 4 May 1932, PAB: 7360H/E535208, E535214; FRUS 1932, I, pp. 112–13.

55. Hoesch to Foreign Ministry, 11 May 1932, PAB: 7360H/E535313–6.

56. Memorandum by Bülow, 2 June; memorandum by Planck, 4 June 1932, PAB: 3154H/D667304–12, 3642H/D811886–9.

57. Memorandum by Planck, 4 June 1932; Schleicher to Bülow, 9 June; memorandum by Defense Ministry, 15 June 1932, PAB: 3642H/D811886–9, 3154H/D667361, D671213–6. For indications that differences between the two ministries had been growing see memorandum by Bülow, 7 Jan.; Köpke to Bülow, 9 Apr. 1932, PAB: 9095H/H222106–7, 4617/E195617–29.

58. Memorandum, 7 June; Bülow to Schleicher, 16 June; Neurath to Nadolny, 20 June 1932, PAB: 3154H/D667355–9, D667391–8, 7360H/E535904–6.

59. Vogelsang, *Reichswehr,* pp. 230–34, 446; Wilhelm Deist, "Schleicher und die deutsche Abrüstungspolitik im Juni/Juli 1932," *Vierteljahrshefte für Zeitgeschichte* VII (1959), pp. 163, 165. On the military's political plans see Francis L. Carsten, *Reichswehr und Politik 1918–1933* (Cologne, 1964), pp. 339–421 passim; Wohlfeil, pp. 153–55, 297–98.

60. Nadolny, p. 121; DBFP, 2d ser., III, nos. 122, 129.

61. DBFP, 2d ser., III, nos. 144, 150, 151, 175, 179; memorandums by Neurath, 29 June; by Bülow, 12 July; Neurath to Missions, 15 July 1932, PAB: 3154H/D667445, 4619H/E197476–7, 7360H/E535526–62.

62. Walters, pp. 507–11; Loosli-Usteri, pp. 119–32; Vogelsang, *Reichswehr,* pp. 223–24.

63. Nadolny to Foreign Ministry, 10 July 1932, PAB: 7360H/E535513–4.

64. Neurath to Schleicher, 14 July; handwritten draft of Schleicher to Blomberg, July 1932, PAB: 7360H/E535933–4, E535935; Deist, pp. 173–74.

65. Memorandums by Bülow, 12 July 1932, PAB: 4619H/E197476–7, 7360H/E535902–3.

66. Nadolny to Foreign Ministry, Neurath to Schleicher, Neurath to Nadolny, all 20 July 1932, PAB: 3154H/D667487–90, D667493, D667496–8.

67. *Records of the Conference,* ser. B, I, pp. 186–87; Nadolny to Foreign Ministry, 23 July 1932, PAB: 3154H/D667508–10; Manfred Zahn, "Öffentliche Meinung und Presse während der Kanzlerschaft von Papens" (diss., Münster, 1953), pp. 106–7.

68. *Frankfurter Zeitung,* 27 July 1932; *New York Times,* 8 Aug. 1932; Cabinet, 15 Aug. 1932, BAK: R 43 I/1457. See also, Vogelsang, *Reichswehr,* pp. 294–95; Bracher, *Auflösung,* pp. 612–14. The liberal press decried Schleicher's interference in foreign affairs (Zahn, p. 109).

69. Neurath to Missions, 29 Aug. 1932, PAB: 3154H/D667555–8 (memorandum reproduced in Karl Schwendemann, *Abrüstung und Sicherheit,* 2d ed. [Berlin, 1933–5], I, pp. 408–13). Bülow defined Germany's wants much more concretely to the French and British ambassadors. He told them that Germany wanted sample weapons and a militia of 40–50,000 men. See DBFP, 2d ser., IV, no. 56; *Documents diplomatiques français,* 1st ser., I (Paris, 1964), no. 115 (henceforth DDF).

70. *Frankfurter Zeitung,* 2, 3 Sept.; *Le Temps,* 5 Sept. 1932. Schleicher took opportunity to make further pronouncements on equal rights and German aims, which Bülow criticized as going far beyond "Bessinge and the memorandum of 29 August" (Bülow to Neurath, 24 Sept. 1932, PAB: 3154H/D671863–9).

71. DBFP, 2d ser., IV, nos. 46, 54, 59; DDF, 1st ser., I, nos. 132, 169; Hoesch to Foreign Ministry, 27 Aug. 1932, PAB: 3154H/D667547–9.

72. Cabinet, 12 Sept., BAK: R 43 I/1457; Neurath to Missions, 12 Sept. 1932, PAB: 3154H/D667643–50.

73. Neurath to Henderson, 14 Sept. 1932, PAB: 3154H/D667664–6.

74. Bülow to Neurath, 4 Oct. 1932, PAB: 3154H/D667816–7; FRUS 1932, I, p. 448.

75. Memorandum by Bülow, 4 Oct.; Neurath to Missions, 15 Oct., PAB: 3154H/D671982–4, D672058–62; Cabinet, 7 Oct. 1932, BAK: R 43 I/1458.

76. DBFP, 2d ser., IV, nos. 152, 149; DDF, 1st ser., I, no. 250; Wilhelm Deist, "Die Haltung der Westmächte gegenüber Deutschland während der Abrüstungskonferenz 1932/33" (diss., Freiburg i.B., 1956), p. 176.

77. Memorandum in DDF, 1st ser., I, no. 331. Memorandum by Frohwein, 15 Nov. 1932; unsigned memorandum, 15 Nov. 1932, PAB: 3154H/D672144–52, D672401–5; Deutsche Allgemeine Zeitung, 15 Nov. 1932.

78. Memorandum in DBFP, 2d ser., IV, no. 170. Unsigned memorandum, 11 Nov. 1932, PAB: 3154H/D672381–3; Frankfurter Zeitung, 18 Nov. 1932.

79. Köpke to Embassy Paris, 12 Nov. 1932, PAB: 3154H/D672106–9; Cabinet, 17 Nov. 1932, BAK: R 43 I/1458. By November, the German press had become very censorious of Germany's diplomatic inactivity (Zahn, pp. 123–26).

80. Neurath to Foreign Ministry, 21, 22, 24 Nov. 1932, PAB: 3154H/D668262–3, D668265–7, D668278; DBFP, 2d ser., IV, nos. 187, 188, 190, 196.

81. Unsigned memorandum, 29 Nov. 1932, PAB: 3154H/D672669–79.

82. Neurath (Geneva) to Foreign Ministry, 6, 7 Dec. 1932, PAB: 3154H/D668333–6; DBFP, 2d ser., IV, nos. 210, 211.

83. Cabinet, 7 Dec. 1932, BAK: R 43 I/1458; Bülow to Neurath, 7 Dec. 1932, PAB: 3154H/D672519–20.

84. Neurath to Foreign Ministry, 8, 10 Dec. 1932, PAB: 3154H/D668340–1, D668350–4; DBFP, 2d ser., IV, nos. 215, 217.

85. Neurath to Foreign Ministry, 11 Dec. 1932, PAB: 3154H/D668357–60; Cabinet, 14 Dec. 1932, BAK: R 43 I/1458; DBFP, 2d ser., IV, no. 218; Schwendemann, I, pp. 480–81. The American record of these meetings is in FRUS 1932, I, pp. 489–528; the French record in DDF, 1st ser., II, nos. 71–93.

86. Cabinet, 14 Dec. 1932, BAK: R 43 I/1458; Bülow in Press Conference, 12 Dec. 1932, PAB: 3154H/D672219–36. Frankfurter Zeitung, 12, 13, 22 Dec. 1932; Schwendemann, I, pp. 481–83.

Chapter 9

1. Scholarly opinion on Hitler's foreign policy, especially its ideological content, remains divided. Some recent assessments include: Klaus Hildebrand, Deutsche Aussenpolitik 1933–45: Kalkül oder Dogma? (Stuttgart, 1970); Axel Kuhn, Hitlers aussenpolitisches Programm (Stuttgart, 1970); Gerhard Weinberg, The Foreign Policy of Hitler's Germany: Diplomatic Revolution in Europe 1933–36 (Chicago, 1970). Hitler's own exposition in Mein Kampf, 2 vols. (1925–27) and Hitlers Zweites Buch (1928; not published until 1961).

2. Hitler expounded his views on the League to Hermann Rauschning, Gespräche mit Hitler (Zurich, 1940), pp. 101–8. See also, Hitlers Zweites Buch, pp. 135, 144, 218.

3. Bracher, Machtergreifung, pp. 230–41.

4. From the very day that Hitler assumed power (and quite on their own), the diplomats tried hard to assure foreign governments that Germany's policy had

not changed, thus revealing (1) that they expected unfavorable reaction abroad and (2) that, mindful of 1918–19, they believed they could survive or contain another "revolution." See *Documents on German Foreign Policy 1918–1945,* ser. C, I (London, 1957), nos. 1, 10 (henceforth DGFP); DBFP, 2d ser., IV, no. 235.

5. Neurath's report (DGFP, C, I, no. 142) was based on a long, detailed memorandum drawn up by Bülow in March, after the results of the Reichstag elections seemed to confirm the new government's mandate. It is reproduced by Günter Wollstein in *Militärgeschichtliche Mitteilungen* XIII (1973), pp. 77–94. See also, Peter Krüger and Erich Hahn, "Der Loyalitätskonflikt des Staatssekretärs Bernhard Wilhelm von Bülow im Frühjahr 1933," *Vierteljahrshefte für Zeitgeschichte* XX (1972), pp. 376–410.

6. Kamphoevener to Missions, 1 June, 1 Nov. 1932; memorandum by Kamphoevener, 7 Sept. 1933, PAB: 3147H/D663547–67, D663963–4011. Referat Völkerbund, 76. Ratstagung. On Neurath's attitude toward the League see Walters, *History of the League,* p. 515; ADAP, B, III, no. 116.

7. German policy at Geneva in 1933 is treated in two studies, both unpublished: Christine Fraser, "Der Austritt Deutschlands aus dem Völkerbund" (diss., Bonn, 1969); Bernd Klinkhardt, "Die deutsche Politik auf der Abrüstungskonferenz und die Anfänge der deutschen Wiederaufrüstung" (thesis, Marburg, 1968).

8. DGFP, C, I, nos. 11, 16, 142; Directives, 11 Jan. 1933, PAB: 7616H/ H188329–37. See also, Klinkhardt, pp. 79–88; Gerhard Meinck, *Hitler und die deutsche Aufrüstung* (Wiesbaden, 1959), pp. 31, 86–89; Hans-Adolf Jacobsen, *Die nationalsozialistische Aussenpolitik 1933 bis 1938* (Frankfurt/Main, 1968), pp. 28–33, 398.

9. Though Blomberg adopted Schleicher's rearmament scheme virtually without change, he was much more radical in his policy toward the disarmament conference (memorandum by Nadolny, 13 Jan.; memorandum by Defense Ministry, Jan. 1933, PAB: 7616H/H188349–52, H188326–28). See also, Vogelsang, "Neue Dokumente," pp. 433–34; Post, *Civil-Military Fabric,* pp. 309–10.

10. *Records of the Conference,* Series B, II, pp. 220–21; Nadolny to Foreign Ministry, 6 Feb. 1933, PAB: 3154H/D668463–6; DGFP, C, I, no. 283; London *Times,* 6, 9, 10 Feb. 1933.

11. *Survey 1933,* p. 247.

12. Nadolny's position was strongly influenced by Blomberg, who at this time feared the rivalry of the Nazi stormtroopers and was therefore determined to preserve the integrity of the Reichswehr (DGFP, C, I, nos. 23, 26, 103; London *Times,* 11, 28 Feb. 1933).

13. DGFP, C, I, nos. 36, 37; telegrams and telephone messages, 20–27 Feb. 1933, PAB: 3154H/D668539–93.

14. London *Times,* 4 Mar.; Nadolny to Foreign Ministry, 1 Mar. 1933, PAB: 3154H/D668607–9. The discussions are chronicled in *Survey 1933,* pp. 238–45; Loosli-Usteri, pp. 314–20.

15. DGFP, C, I, nos. 46, 49; London *Times,* 4 Mar. 1933.

16. On Neurath's tactics see DGFP, C, I, nos. 20, 76; Schwendemann (Geneva) to Köpke, 7 Mar.; Frohwein (Geneva) to Köpke, 8 Mar.; Nadolny to Foreign Ministry, 10 Mar., PAB: 7360H/E536339–42, 7616H/H188369–71, 3154H/ D668680; London *Times,* 4 Mar. 1933. On reaction to MacDonald's initiative see

DGFP, C, I, no. 56; memorandum by Bülow, 4 Mar.; Köpke to Embassy Washington, 9 Mar. 1933, PAB: 7360H/E536255–7, E536311.

17. Neurath to Nadolny, 7 Mar. 1933, PAB: 3154H/D668645.

18. DGFP, C, I, no. 94; memorandum by Kreutzwald, 15 Mar. 1933, PAB: 3154H/D668746. In his memoirs, Rheinbaben recalls a fulminating and uncompromising Hitler (*Viermal Deutschland* [Berlin, 1954], pp. 272–76). On Hitler's preoccupation with domestic affairs at this time see Martin Broszat, *Der Staat Hitlers* (Munich, 1969), pp. 105–17, 130–50.

19. DGFP, C, I, nos. 97, 106; memorandums by Kreutzwald, 20, 22 Mar. 1933, PAB: 7360H/E536474–5, E536476; Klinkhardt, pp. 93–96.

20. *Conference Documents,* II, pp. 476–93; *Records of the Conference,* ser. B, II, pp. 352–57; DGFP, C, I, no. 103.

21. *Records of the Conference,* ser. B, II, pp. 421–24; London *Times,* 29 Apr. 1933; Walters, p. 544. Nadolny's demands here exceeded those of the military—see Schönheinz (Geneva) to Defense Ministry, 25 Apr. 1933, PAB: 3154H/D668891–2.

22. DGFP, C, I, nos. 209, 239; DBFP, 2d ser., V, nos. 110, 118; Nadolny to Foreign Ministry, 8 May 1933, PAB: 3154H/D669012–4; Weinberg, pp. 38–39. See also, Loosli-Usteri, pp. 390–411.

23. On the negotiations see DGFP, C, I, no. 239; DBFP, 2d ser., V, nos. 103–41 passim; FRUS 1933, I, pp. 129–32. As the pressure mounted, Neurath kept close telephone contact with the delegation (memorandums by Völckers and Feine, 8–12 May 1933, PAB: 3154H/D669011, D669028–9, D669075–6).

24. DBFP, 2d ser., V, nos. 123, 124; DDF, 1st ser., II, no. 260; FRUS 1933, I, pp. 133–34; Nadolny to Foreign Ministry, 9 May 1933, PAB: 3154H/D669021–3.

25. Schwendemann, II, pp. 386–91.

26. Nadolny to Foreign Ministry, 12 May, PAB: 3154H/D669072–3; London *Times,* 12 May 1933. When Nadolny finally became worried at Germany's isolation and suggested a possible compromise, Neurath was not interested (Nadolny to Foreign Ministry, 12 May, Neurath to Nadolny, 13 May 1933, PAB: 3154H/D669079–80, 7360H/E536688).

27. DGFP, C, I, no. 226.

28. On these internal developments see Broszat, pp. 117–26; London *Times,* 1 May 1933; DBFP, 2d ser., V, no. 130.

29. DGFP, C, I, nos. 243, 246; DBFP, 2d ser., V, no. 144; DDF, 1st ser., II, nos. 198, 251; FRUS 1933, I, pp. 143–45; Nadolny to Foreign Ministry, 12 May; Luther (Washington) to Foreign Ministry, 15 May, PAB: 3154H/D669079–80, D669109–10; London *Times,* 12, 13 May 1933.

30. Schwendemann, II, pp. 396–414. The speech was based in part on drafts prepared in the Foreign Ministry and in the Defense Ministry (DGFP, C, I, nos. 238, 241; unsigned memorandum, 17 May 1933, PAB: 3154H/D669322–5).

31. DBFP, 2d ser., V, no. 153.

32. DGFP, C, I, no. 251; Nadolny to Foreign Ministry, 20 May, PAB: 3154H/D669189–91; London *Times,* 19, 20 May, 28, 30 June 1933. See also, *Survey 1933,* pp. 272–91; Loosli-Usteri, pp. 422–67, 489–99.

33. *Survey 1933,* pp. 161–64, 182–83; Weinberg, pp. 52–55, 79–80, 87–107; Broszat, pp. 275–80.

34. Memorandum by Kamphoevener, 7 Sept. 1933, PAB: Referat Völker-

bund, 76. Ratstagung. Secretary-General Avenol apprised the Germans of these possibilities (memorandum by Gaus, 7 Aug. 1933, PAB: K2368/K670164–7).

35. Keller to Foreign Ministry, 23, 25, 26, 28 May; memorandum by Haas, 24 May; Kamphoevener to Missions, 24 June; Neurath to Delegation, 24 May 1933, PAB: 3147H/D665153–6, D665172, D665187–8, D665208–10, D665238–41, D665365–79, K2367/K670123–5. LNOJ 1933, pp. 838–40, 845–48, 929–33; London *Times*, 31 May, 7 June 1933.

36. London *Times*, 8 June 1933. In July, the Deutsche Liga für Völkerbund (now renamed Deutsche Gesellschaft für Völkerbundfragen) notified Neurath of its disagreement with the resolution at Montreux (DLV to Neurath, 15 July 1933, PAB: 8792H/E612553–6). See also memorandum by Haas, 13 May 1933, PAB: K2367/K670110–12.

37. DGFP, C, I, no. 426; memorandum by Kamphoevener, 9 Sept. 1933, PAB: Referat Völkerbund, 76. Ratstagung. In July, Bülow had implied in conversation that Germany might threaten to leave the League in an attempt to gain advantage in the disarmament talks or the Saar plebiscite (Weinberg, p. 94).

38. Unsigned memorandum, 24 Aug.; memorandum by Kamphoevener, 7 Sept. 1933, PAB: 8696H/E607864–7, Referat Völkerbund, 76. Ratstagung.

39. DGFP, C, I, nos. 449, 451, 452, 453; Keller to Foreign Ministry, 27 Sept., 2 Oct. 1933, PAB: 3147H/D665494–7, D665549–51; Paul Schmidt, *Statist auf diplomatischer Bühne* (Bonn, 1950), pp. 278–80; Max Beer, *Die auswärtige Politik des Dritten Reiches* (Zurich, 1934), pp. 80–81; London *Times*, 29 Sept. 1933.

40. DGFP, C, I, no. 456; memorandums by Bülow-Schwante; by Bülow, both 26 Sept.; Keller to Foreign Ministry, 2 Oct. 1933, PAB: 8792H/E612574–5, 3147H/D665481, D665549–51; LNOJ *Special Supplement 115*, p. 48, and *117*, pp. 26–29; London *Times*, 30 Sept., 3 Oct. 1933.

41. Keller to Foreign Ministry, 3, 4, 6 Oct. 1933, PAB: 3147H/D665553–60, D665561–7, D665593; LNOJ *Special Supplement 120*, pp. 20–55; London *Times*, 4, 5, 7 Oct. 1933.

42. DGFP, C, I, nos. 297, 367, 370; Koester (Paris) to Foreign Ministry, 12 July 1933, PAB: 3154H/D669449–50.

43. DGFP, C, I, nos. 370, 374; FRUS 1933, I, p. 205; memorandum by Neurath, 18 July 1933, PAB: 3154H/D669466; Nadolny, p. 138.

44. DGFP, C, I, nos. 447, 454, 466, 469; FRUS 1933, I, pp. 232–34; DDF, 1st ser., IV, no. 257. In the British records of these conversations Neurath appears much more conciliatory and open to agreement (DBFP, 2d ser., V, nos. 411, 419, 422).

45. DBFP, 2d ser., V, nos. 411, 422; memorandums by Frohwein, 27 Sept.; by Neurath, 29 Sept. 1933, PAB: 3154H/D669911–5, D669927–9.

46. DGFP, C, I, nos. 447, 454; DBFP, 2d ser., V, no. 419.

47. DGFP, C, I, no. 469; DBFP, 2d ser., V, no. 422; FRUS 1933, I, p. 236; London *Times*, 30 Sept. 1933.

48. DGFP, C, I, no. 475; DDF, 1st ser., IV, no. 276; DDB, III, nos. 61, 64; memorandums by Neurath, 30 Sept.; by Bülow, 5 Oct. 1933, PAB: 3154H/ D669947, D669983–5.

49. DGFP, C, I, no. 480; memorandums by Schwendemann, by Neurath, both 30 Sept. 1933; Directives, 4 Oct. 1933, PAB: 7668H/E547514–5, 3154H/ D669947, 7360H/E537586–9.

50. DGFP, C, I, no. 478; memorandum by Bülow, 4 Oct. 1933, PAB: 3154H/D669974. Simon's draft is in DBFP, 2d ser., V, p. 669 n.

51. For the telling allusion in Hitler's broadcast speech on 14 Oct. 1933 see Schwendemann, II, p. 473.

52. DBFP, 2d ser., V, nos. 415, 492, 511; FRUS 1933, I, pp. 285–86, 291, II, pp. 263–67, 301–2, 304; DDF, 1st ser., IV, nos. 314, 328; DDB, III, no. 61; London *Times*, 6, 16 Oct. 1933; Broszat, pp. 256–65, 175–79.

53. London *Times*, 16 Oct. 1933; Broszat, pp. 151–61.

54. DGFP, C, I, no. 499. The powers had confined themselves to paper protests (*Survey 1934*, pp. 442–48).

55. DBFP, 2d ser., V, no. 471; DDB, III, no. 61; correspondence between Bülow and Blomberg, 25–30 Sept. 1933, PAB: 7360H/E537467, E537476–8, E537500–1, D537558–9; Meinck, p. 31. Neurath later claimed to have encouraged Hitler in his decision (Fraser, p. 228).

56. DGFP, C, I, no. 479. Bülow promptly had Neurath's office inform the foreign minister that Hitler and Blomberg were considering "the necessity of a complete break with Geneva" (memorandum by Bülow, 4 Oct. 1933, PAB: 3154H/D669974). Neurath returned "abruptly"—probably on 6 October (DDF, 1st ser., IV, no. 301).

57. DGFP, C, I, no. 484. On 5 Oct., Bülow told the British ambassador that if the powers treated Germany unfairly, "she would leave Geneva" (DBFP, 2d ser., V, no. 427; memorandum by Bülow, 5 Oct. 1933, PAB: 3154H/D669983–5).

58. DBFP, 2d ser., V, nos. 434, 435, 443; Hassell to Foreign Ministry, 5 Oct.; Bismarck to Foreign Ministry, 6 Oct. 1933, PAB: 3154H/D669988, D670001–3; London *Times*, 7 Oct. 1933.

59. DGFP, C, I, no. 493; DBFP, 2d ser., V, no. 438; Nadolny to Foreign Ministry, 8, 10 Oct. 1933, PAB: 3154H/D670016–8, D670038–42.

60. DGFP, C, I, nos. 489, 495; Nadolny to Foreign Ministry, 12 Oct. 1933, PAB: 7360H/E537789; Nadolny, p. 139.

61. DGFP, C, I, no. 494. Mussolini was worried about German rearmament and had repeatedly offered to mediate, but Germany had not responded (Ibid., nos. 431, 441, 442, 445, 474; DBFP, 2d ser., V, nos. 444, 448; FRUS 1933, I, pp. 258, 304; Weinberg, p. 48).

62. Nadolny, pp. 139–40. See also, DBFP, 2d ser., V, no. 447; FRUS 1933, I, pp. 257–58.

63. DBFP, 2d ser., V, nos. 449, 469; FRUS 1933, I, p. 288; memorandum by Schwendemann, 13 Oct., PAB: 3154H/D670070–1; London *Times*, 14 Oct. 1933.

64. DGFP, C, I, no. 499; DBFP, 2d ser., V, no. 469. Broszat (pp. 127–28) concludes that the plebiscite served the same purpose as the popular *Friedensrede* in May: in both cases the world was presented with a national protest which was also a vote of confidence in the new regime.

65. DGFP, C, I, no. 498.

66. DBFP, 2d ser., V, no. 451.

67. Memorandum by Völckers; Frohwein to Foreign Ministry, both 14 Oct. 1933, PAB: 3154H/D670081, D670082–8; Rheinbaben, *Viermal*, pp. 277–78.

68. Memorandum by Bülow, 14 Oct. 1933, PAB: 3147H/D665645.

69. DGFP, C, I, no. 499. The cabinet minutes suggest that Hitler had no direct knowledge of Simon's speech.

70. DBFP, 2d ser., V, no. 452; DDF, 1st ser., IV, no. 307; DDB, III, no. 61; FRUS 1933, I, pp. 281–82; memorandum by Kamphoevener (Geneva), 14 Oct. 1933, PAB: 8692H/E607639–40. Schwendemann, II, pp. 461–65.

71. Reproduced in *Survey 1933*, p. 306.

72. Schwendemann, II, pp. 467–80. Neurath promptly informed the Missions of the official line (14 Oct. 1933, PAB: 3154H/D670099–101). On support in the press see *Deutsche Allgemeine Zeitung, Berliner Tageblatt*, both 15 Oct. 1933.

73. Bülow to Trendelenburg, 19 Oct.; Kamphoevener to Trendelenburg, 8 Nov.; Kamphoevener to Missions, 11 Nov. 1933, PAB: 8692H/E607649–50, E607226–9, 3642H/D808791–826.

74. League of Nations document C.605.M.282.1933.V; Krauel (Geneva) to Foreign Ministry, 21 Oct. 1933, PAB: 3147H/D665667. Germany withdrew officially from the ILO shortly thereafter (memorandum by Völckers, 23 Oct. 1933, PAB: 3147H/D665668).

75. Schwendemann, II, pp. 494–506.

76. DDF, 1st ser., IV, no. 307.

77. DGFP, C, II, nos. 13, 18; DBFP, 2d ser., V, nos. 457, 476; FRUS 1933, I, pp. 267–70, 288, 296; DDF, 1st ser., IV, no. 307; DDB, III, no. 60; London *Times*, 16, 17, 18 Oct. 1933; Fraser, pp. 248–53.

78. FRUS 1933, I, pp. 271, 280–81.

79. DBFP, 2d ser., V, nos. 457, 482; FRUS 1933, I, pp. 268–70, 277; *Survey 1933*, pp. 310–11.

80. DGFP, C, II, no. 9; Rauschning, p. 101.

81. Germans of all political persuasions, the British ambassador in Berlin commented, "felt that on this occasion they were avenging themselves on the League for its manifold delinquencies of the past" (DBFP, 2d ser., VI, no. 39).

82. DGFP, C, II, nos. 23, 117; DBFP, 2d ser., V, no. 489, VI, no. 80; Trendelenburg to Bülow, 2 Nov., PAB: 8692H/E607739–43; London *Times*, 16 Oct. 1933; Meinck, pp. 54–55.

83. DGFP, C, II, no. 159; DBFP, 2d ser., VI, nos. 143, 160, 193; FRUS 1933, I, pp. 311–12; Meinck, pp. 59–63; Weinberg, pp. 170–72.

84. DGFP, C, II, nos. 120, 164, 172, 178, 208, 250; DBFP, 2d ser., VI, nos. 161, 164; Fraser, pp. 261–72.

85. DGFP, C, II, nos. 117, 245; DBFP, 2d ser., VI, nos. 77, 140, 206, pp. 947–51; FRUS 1933, I, pp. 346–47; London *Times*, 8, 25, 28 Nov. 1933.

86. DGFP, C, II, no. 164; DBFP, 2d ser., VI, nos. 161, 235, 245; FRUS 1934, I, p. 2; DDF, 1st ser., V, nos. 118, 449; London *Times*, 19, 22 Dec. 1933.

87. DGFP, C, II, nos. 120, 208, 271; DBFP, 2d ser., VI, no. 304; Bülow to Trautmann, 30 Nov. 1933; memorandum by Neurath, 16 Dec. 1933; Köpke to Missions, 18 Dec. 1933; PAB: 4620/E201029–32, 4691H/E197855, 8691H/E607551–2.

88. See, DGFP, C, III, nos. 434, 446.

89. DGFP, C, II, no. 506, III, nos. 446, 555, IV, nos. 37, 102, pp. 171–78; Fraser, pp. 283, 285–87. In 1936, Hitler tried the same tactics after Germany had broken the Locarno pact and reoccupied the Rhineland (Jacobsen, pp. 416–19; Weinberg, pp. 253–63).

90. The German government quietly paid its dues to the League, on which it was in arrears, and dissolved the Liga für Völkerbund (League of Nations

Treasury to German Consul General, 14 Oct., League of Nations Archives: 1933–46, 17/20/1; memorandum by Neurath, 5 Nov. 1935, PAB: 3147H/ D665767).

Chapter 10

1. The phrase is in René Albrecht-Carrié, *A Diplomatic History of Europe,* rev. ed. (New York, 1973), p. 421.

2. Quoted in Meier-Welcker, *Seeckt,* p. 474 n; Jacobson, *Locarno Diplomacy,* p. 384.

3. DBFP, ser. IA, III, no. 263.

4. Ibid., I, no. 141, II, no. 392; 2d ser., I, no. 308.

5. See Jacobson, pp. 356–57, 372–73, 378–79; ADAP, B, IV, nos. 15, 26; DBFP, ser. IA, V, nos. 123, 188.

6. Schubert address in council, 13 Jan. 1930, PAB: 4587H/E185475–8.

7. Thus, in 1927 the Germans distorted a Polish proposal for a general non-aggression pact (see above, pp. 98–100), sabotaged the work of the Security and Arbitration Committee, which was to have cleared away obstacles to progress in the disarmament talks (ADAP, B, VII, no. 246), and, in 1928, resisted a full-scale investigation under article 213 into a suspicious arms shipment discovered at Szent-Gotthard (see above, p. 95). This last episode provoked angry criticism in France (Hoesch to Foreign Ministry, 14 Mar. 1928, PAB: 3147H/ D659412–4; DBFP, ser. IA, IV, p. 241 n). In general, see Bülow to Missions, 5 Oct. 1929, PAB: 3147H/D659059–96.

8. Kimmich, *Free City,* p. 160.

9. Walters, *History of the League,* p. 440. For their part, German diplomats characterized the experiences of the German delegates in the council as a "bath in a crocodile pond" (Curtius, *Sechs Jahre,* p. 153).

10. See, for example, Bülow in Dec. 1925 (ADAP, B, I/1, no. 22) and Weizsäcker in Apr. 1930 (see above, p. 157), n. 26).

11. A good example of this "functional" approach is the anonymous work *Der Kampf um die deutsche Aussenpolitik* (Leipzig, 1931), especially pp. 17–23, 47–55, 74–99. Only a few left-wing liberals did not share this general attitude (Czempiel, *Macht und Kompromiss,* p. 26).

12. This flight from responsibility is well illustrated by the interpretation placed on article 16 of the covenant at Locarno. See above, p. 74; DBFP, ser. IA, I, pp. 847–48.

13. See above, pp. 35–37, 98, and the references given there. An excellent analysis of the League's intrinsic weakness is in Hinsley, *Power and the Pursuit of Peace,* pp. 309–22.

14. Bülow speculated along these lines in 1925–26 (ADAP, B, I/1, nos. 22, 65).

15. Rheinbaben, *Viermal,* p. 256; similarly, Weizsäcker, *Erinnerungen,* p. 94.

16. Czempiel considers the Germans' opposition to cooperation and compromise abroad and their opposition to democratic government at home as two sides of the same coin (pp. 11–29).

17. ADAP, B, I/1, no. 22. On the differences between Stresemann and Brüning see *Verhandlungen,* 395:13898; Brüning, *Memoiren,* pp. 355–56.

18. On the growing skepticism within the League see Weizsäcker to Missions,

12 Oct. 1928; Kamphoevener to Missions, 22 Oct. 1931; Köpke to Missions, 31 Mar. 1932, PAB: 3635/D805216–58, D805994–6029, D806064–84.

19. Andreas Hillgruber, *Deutschlands Rolle in der Vorgeschichte der beiden Weltkriege* (Göttingen, 1967), and *Kontinuität und Diskontinuität in der deutschen Aussenpolitik von Bismarck bis Hitler* (Düsseldorf, 1969); Klaus Hildebrand, *Deutsche Aussenpolitik 1933–45: Kalkül oder Dogma?* (Stuttgart, 1970); John C. G. Röhl, ed., *From Bismarck to Hitler* (New York, 1970). For an earlier interpretation see Ludwig Dehio, *Deutschland und die Weltpolitik im 20. Jahrhundert* (Munich, 1955).

20. See Neumann, *Parteien der Weimarer Republik,* pp. 54–61. For a different perspective see Hans-Ulrich Wehler, *Das deutsche Kaiserreich 1871–1918* (Göttingen, 1973).

21. *Vermächtnis,* II, p. 172; ADAP, B, I/1, pp. 729–30, 735, IV, pp. 593–96.

22. See Stresemann to Ministries, 13 Jan. 1925; Weizsäcker to Missions, 28 Dec. 1928, PAB: 4555H/E147362–73, 3635/D805306–23.

23. ADAP, B, I/2, pp. 667–68, IV, p. 593.

24. Waldemar Besson, *Die Aussenpolitik der Bundesrepublik* (Munich, 1970), p. 49. In a different context is Fritz Fischer's "Kontinuität des Irrtums: Zum Problem der deutschen Kriegszielpolitik im ersten Weltkrieg," *Historische Zeitschrift* CXCI (1960), pp. 83–100. The phrase "world hegemony" is in Fischer, *Griff nach der Weltmacht,* p. 108.

25. Troeltsch, *Spektator-Briefe,* pp. 69, 91, 109; *Kreuzzeitung,* 10 Jan. 1923.

26. ADAP, B, I/1, no. 144 (excerpts translated in Röhl, *From Bismarck to Hitler,* p. 111).

27. ADAP, B, I/, no. 22, I/2, no. 76.

Bibliography

This bibliography contains the primary and secondary sources I found particularly useful. It also contains very recent publications based on the documents. Filmed documents are identified by their serial numbers. The films are available in the National Archives, Washington, and in the Foreign and Commonwealth Library, London.

Archival Sources

1. Politisches Archiv, Bonn

Büro Reichsminister
Völkerbund, 1920–35: 3147H; Abrüstung, 1927–35: 3154H; Stresemann Nachlass, 1924–29: 3241H

Büro Staatssekretär
Sicherheitsfrage, 1924–29: 4509H; Abrüstung, 1926–32: 4543H, 4604; Minderheiten, 1925–29: 4555H; Völkerbund, 1923–30: 4584H–4587H; Schriftwechsel, 1930–36: 4606, 4620

Abteilung II F—Abrüstung
Deutsche Delegation zur Abrüstungskonferenz, 1932: 7616H; Vorbereitende Kommission für die Abrüstungskonferenz, 1925–36: 9126H; Vorbereitung der allg. Abrüstungskonferenz, 1930–32: 9095H; Allg. Abrüstungskonferenz, 1932–36: 7360H; Abrüstungskonferenz, Allg., 1931–35: 7668H

Referat Völkerbund
Deutsche Liga für Völkerbund, 1920–36: K2317, 6429H; Minderheitsfragen, 1920–36: K1764; Kritik am Völkerbund, 1933–36: 8691H, 6403H; Ratssitz, Allg., 1921–36: K2342, L1538; 76.—79. Ratstagung, 1933–34; Deutschland, 1919–36: L1511, L1539, L1837; Deutschland und das Judentum, 1933–36: K2367; Deutschland—Austritt aus dem Völkerbund, 1933–36: 8692H; Deutschland—Wiedereintritt in den Völkerbund, 1934–36: 8697H

Referat Deutschland
Allg. auswärtige Politik, 1920–35: L756, L1757; Judenfrage vor
dem Völkerbund, 1933–34: 8792H
Stresemann Nachlass
Allg. und Politische Akten, 1923–30: 7112–25, 7142–80,
7336–50, 7355, 7369–92, 7414–15
Handakten
Dirksen, 1925–29: 5462H; von Simson, 1919; Simons, 1919

2. Bundesarchiv, Koblenz

Reichsministerial- und Kabinettssitzungen, 1919–32:
R 43 I/1348–1458; Völkerbund, 1919–33: R 43 I/483–96, 509;
Abrüstung, 1921–34: R 43 I/516–20, 533–36; Nachlass Schück-
ing; Nachlass Wehberg

3. League of Nations Archives, Geneva

General Files; Minorities Section; Council Documents

Published Sources

1. Documents

Akten zur deutschen Auswärtigen Politik 1918–1945. Ser. B, 7 vols.
   Göttingen, 1966–74.
Akten der Reichskanzlei 1919–1938. Ed. Karl-Dietrich Erdmann
   and Wolfgang Mommsen. Boppard, 1968–73:
   Das Kabinett Scheidemann. Ed. Hagen Schulze. 1970.
   Das Kabinett Müller I. Ed. Martin Vogt. 1971.
   Das Kabinett Cuno. Ed. Karl-Heinz Harbeck. 1968.
   Die Kabinette Marx I und II. Ed. Günter Abramowski. 1973.
   Das Kabinett Müller II. Ed. Martin Vogt. 1970.
Czernin, Ferdinand, ed. *Versailles 1919.* New York, 1965.
Deutsche Liga für ·Völkerbund. *Memorandum zur Vertrauenskrise
   des Völkerbunds.* Berlin, 1932.
Deutscher Geschichtskalender, 1918–26. Ed. Friedrich Purlitz. 9
   vols. Leipzig, n.d.
Documents on British Foreign Policy 1919–1939. Ed. E. L. Wood-
   ward et al. 1st ser., ser. IA, 2d ser. London, 1948–73.
Documents diplomatiques belges 1920–40. Ed. C. de Visscher and F.
   Vanlangenhove. Vols. 1–3. Brussels, 1964.
Documents diplomatiques français 1932–39. 1st ser. 5 vols. Paris,
   1964–70.
Documents on German Foreign Policy 1918–1945. Ser. C. 5 vols.
   London, 1957–66.

Foreign Relations of the United States, 1919, 1931–34. Washington, 1943–51.

League of Nations, Conference for the Reduction and Limitation of Armaments. *Conference Documents.* 2 vols. Geneva, 1932–35.

————. *Records of the Conference for the Reduction and Limitation of Armaments.* Ser. A, B. Geneva, 1932–33.

————. *Official Journal.* Geneva, 1920–33.

————. *Protection of Linguistic, Racial or Religious Minorities by the League of Nations.* Geneva, 1927, 1929, 1931.

Locarno-Konferenz 1925: Eine Dokumentensammlung. Ed. Ministerium für Auswärtige Angelegenheiten der DDR. Berlin, 1962.

Luckau, Alma. *The German Delegation at the Paris Peace Conference.* New York, 1941.

Material zur Behandlung der Minderheitenfrage im Völkerbund 1932. Berlin, 1933.

Matthias, Erich, and Morsey, Rudolf, eds. *Der Interfraktionelle Ausschuss 1917/18.* 2 vols. Düsseldorf, 1959.

————. *Die Regierung des Prinzen Max von Baden.* Düsseldorf, 1962.

Matthias, Erich, and Miller, Susanne, eds. *Die Regierung der Volksbeauftragten.* 2 vols. Düsseldorf, 1969.

Schücking, Walter, and Wehberg, Hans. *Die Satzung des Völkerbunds.* 2d ed. Berlin, 1924.

Schulthess' Europäischer Geschichtskalender, 1918–30. Ed. Wilhelm Stahl and Ulrich Thürauf. Munich, 1922–31.

Schwendemann, Karl. *Abrüstung und Sicherheit.* 2 vols. 2d ed. Berlin, 1933–35.

Stresemann, Gustav. *Vermächtnis: Der Nachlass in drei Bänden.* Ed. Henry Bernhard et al. Berlin, 1932–33.

Turner, Henry A., Jr. "Eine Rede Stresemanns über seine Locarnopolitik." In *Vierteljahrshefte für Zeitgeschichte* XV (1967), pp. 412–36.

Verhandlungen des Deutschen Reichstags, Stenographische Berichte. Vols. 326–456. Berlin, 1919–32.

Vogelsang, Thilo. "Neue Dokumente zur Geschichte der Reichswehr 1930–33." In *Vierteljahrshefte für Zeitgeschichte* II (1954), pp. 397–436.

2. Memoirs

Beer, Max. *Die Reise nach Genf.* Berlin, 1932.

Bernstorff, Johann. *Erinnerungen und Briefe.* Zurich, 1936.

Brüning, Heinrich. *Memoiren 1918–1934.* Stuttgart, 1970.

Cecil, Robert. *A Great Experiment.* London, 1941.
Curtius, Julius. *Sechs Jahre Minister der deutschen Republik.* Heidelberg, 1948.
D'Abernon, Edgar Vincent. *An Ambassador of Peace.* 3 vols. London, 1929–30.
Dell, Robert. *The Geneva Racket, 1920–39.* London, 1941.
Dirksen, Herbert von. *Moskau, Tokio, London.* Stuttgart, 1949.
Eden, Anthony. *Facing the Dictators.* London, 1962.
François-Poncet, André. *Souvenirs d'une ambassade à Berlin.* Paris, 1946.
Hillson, Norman. *Geneva Scene.* London, 1936.
Jäckh, Ernst. *Der Goldene Pflug.* Stuttgart, 1954.
Kessler, Harry. *Tagebücher 1918–1937.* Frankfurt/Main, 1961.
Kordt, Erich. *Nicht aus den Akten.* Stuttgart, 1950.
Nadolny, Rudolf. *Mein Beitrag.* Wiesbaden, 1955.
Rheinbaben, Werner von. *Kaiser, Kanzler, Präsidenten.* Mainz, 1968.
———. *Viermal Deutschland.* Berlin, 1954.
Ruppel, Willy. *Genfer Götterdämmerung: Werden, Wirken und Versagen des Völkerbunds.* Stuttgart, 1940.
Schmidt, Paul. *Statist auf diplomatischer Bühne 1923–45.* Bonn, 1950.
Slocombe, George. *A Mirror to Geneva.* New York, 1938.
Temperley, A. C. *The Whispering Gallery of Europe.* London, 1938.
Treviranus, Gottfried. *Das Ende von Weimar: Heinrich Brüning und seine Zeit.* Düsseldorf, 1968.
Weizsäcker, Ernst von. *Erinnerungen.* Munich, 1950.

Secondary Sources

Albrecht-Carrié, René. *Britain and France: Adaptations to a Changing Context of Power.* New York, 1970.
Bagley, Tennent H. *General Principles and Problems in the International Protection of Minorities.* Geneva, 1950.
Barros, James. *Betrayal from Within.* New Haven, 1969.
Becker, Werner. *Demokratie des sozialen Rechts.* Göttingen, 1971.
Beloff, Max. *Imperial Sunset,* vol. I. New York, 1970.
Bernhardt, Walter. "Die Aufrüstung Hitlers von 1934 bis 1938 und ihre militärischen und politischen Konzeptionen." Diss., Kiel, 1968.
Bracher, Karl-Dietrich. *Die Auflösung der Weimarer Republik.* 3d ed. Stuttgart, 1960.
Bracher, Karl-Dietrich; Sauer, Wolfgang; and Schulz, Gerhard.

Die nationalsozialistische Machtergreifung. Cologne, 1960.

Brink, Marianne. "Deutschlands Stellung zum Völkerbund in den Jahren 1918/19 bis 1922 unter besonderer Berücksichtigung der politischen Parteien und der pazifistischen Vereinigungen." Diss., Berlin, 1968.

Broszat, Martin. *Der Staat Hitlers.* Munich, 1969.

Bülow, Bernhard W. von. *Der Versailler Völkerbund: Eine vorläufige Bilanz.* Stuttgart, 1923.

Carlton, David. "Great Britain and the League Council Crisis of 1926." *The Historical Journal* XI (1968), 354–64.

Craig, Gordon A., and Gilbert, Felix, eds. *The Diplomats, 1919–1939.* Princeton, 1953.

Czempiel, Ernst-Otto. *Macht und Kompromiss: Die Beziehungen der BRD zu den Vereinten Nationen 1956–1970.* Düsseldorf, 1971.

Deist, Wilhelm. "Die Haltung der Westmächte gegenüber Deutschland während der Abrüstungskonferenz 1932/33." Diss., Freiburg i.B., 1956.

———. "Schleicher und die deutsche Abrüstungspolitik im Juni/Juli 1932." *Vierteljahrshefte für Zeitgeschichte* VII (1959), pp. 163–76.

Döhn, Lothar. *Politik und Interesse: Die Interessenstruktur der Deutschen Volkspartei.* Meisenheim/Glan, 1970.

Dörr, Manfred. "Die Deutschnationale Volkspartei 1925 bis 1928." Diss., Marburg, 1964.

Fink, Carole. "Defender of Minorities: Germany in the League of Nations, 1926–1933." *Central European History* V (1972), pp. 330–57.

———. "The Weimar Republic as the Defender of Minorities 1919–1933." Diss., Yale, 1969.

Fischer, Fritz. *Griff nach der Weltmacht.* Düsseldorf, 1964.

———. "Kontinuität des Irrtums: Zum Problem der deutschen Kriegszielpolitik im ersten Weltkrieg." *Historische Zeitschrift* CXCI (1960), pp. 83–100.

Fischer, Wolfram. *Deutsche Wirtschaftspolitik 1918–1945.* 3d ed. Opladen, 1968.

Fox, John P. "Britain and the Inter-Allied Military Commission of Control 1925–26." *Journal of Contemporary History* IV (1969), pp. 143–64.

Fraenkel, Ernst. "Das deutsche Wilsonbild." *Jahrbuch für Amerikastudien* (1960), pp. 66–120.

———. "Idee und Realität des Völkerbundes im deutschen politischen Denken." *Vierteljahrshefte für Zeitgeschichte* XVI (1968), pp. 1–14.

Fraser, Christine. "Der Austritt Deutschlands aus dem Völker-

bund: Seine Vorgeschichte und seine Nachwirkungen." Diss.,
Bonn, 1969.

Geigenmüller, Ernst. "Botschafter Hoesch und die Räumungsfrage." *Historische Zeitschrift* CC (1965), pp. 606–20.

Gnichwitz, Siegfried. "Die Presse der bürgerlichen Rechten in
der Aera Brüning." Diss., Münster, 1956.

Göppert, Otto. *Organisation und Tätigkeit des Völkerbundes.*
Stuttgart, 1938.

Graml, Hermann. "Die Rapallo-Politik im Urteil der
westdeutschen Forschung." *Vierteljahrshefte für Zeitgeschichte*
XVIII (1970), pp. 366–91.

Guggenheim, Paul. *Der Völkerbund: Eine systematische Darstellung
seiner Gestaltung in der politischen und rechtlichen Wirklichkeit.*
Leipzig, 1932.

Haungs, Peter. *Reichspräsident und parlamentarische Kabinettsregierung: Eine Studie zum Regierungssystem der Weimarer Republik in den Jahren 1924–29.* Cologne, 1968.

Helbich, Wolfgang J. "Between Stresemann and Hitler: The
Foreign Policy of the Brüning Government." *World Politics*
XII (1959), pp. 32–39.

———. *Die Reparationen in der Ära Brüning.* Berlin, 1962.

Hildebrand, Klaus. *Deutsche Aussenpolitik 1933–45: Kalkül oder
Dogma?* Stuttgart, 1970.

Hillgruber, Andreas. *Deutschlands Rolle in der Vorgeschichte der
beiden Weltkriege.* Göttingen, 1967.

———. *Kontinuität und Diskontinuität in der deutschen Aussenpolitik
von Bismarck bis Hitler.* Düsseldorf, 1969.

Hinsley, F. H. *Power and the Pursuit of Peace.* Cambridge, 1963.

Hubatsch, Walther. *Hindenburg und der Staat.* Göttingen, 1966.

Jacobsen, Hans-Adolf. *Die nationalsozialistische Aussenpolitik 1933
bis 1938.* Frankfurt/Main, 1968.

Jacobson, Jon. *Locarno Diplomacy: Germany and the West, 1925–
1929.* Princeton, 1972.

Jordan, William M. *Great Britain, France, and the German Problem
1918–1939.* London, 1943.

Kimmich, Christoph M. *The Free City: Danzig and German Foreign
Policy, 1919–1934.* New Haven, 1968.

Klinkhardt, Bernd. "Die deutsche Politik auf der Abrüstungskonferenz und die Anfänge der deutschen Wiederaufrüstung 1932/33." Thesis, Marburg, 1968.

Krekeler, Norbert. *Revisionsanspruch und geheime Ostpolitik der
Weimarer Republik.* Stuttgart, 1973.

Krüger, Peter, and Hahn, Erich. "Der Loyalitätskonflikt des
Staatssekretärs Bernhard Wilhelm von Bülow im Frühjahr

1933." *Vierteljahrshefte für Zeitgeschichte* XX (1972), pp. 376–410.

Kuhn, Axel. *Hitlers aussenpolitisches Programm.* Stuttgart, 1970.

Link, Werner. *Die amerikanische Stabilisierungspolitik in Deutschland 1921–32.* Düsseldorf, 1970.

Lipgens, Walter. "Europäische Einigungsidee 1923–30 und Briands Europaplan im Urteil der deutschen Akten." *Historische Zeitschrift* CCIII (1966), pp. 46–89, 316–63.

Lippelt, Helmut. "'Politische Sanierung': Zur deutschen Politik gegenüber Polen 1925/26." *Vierteljahrshefte für Zeitgeschichte* XIX (1971), pp. 323–73.

Loosli-Usteri, Carl. *Geschichte der Konferenz für die Herabsetzung und Begrenzung der Rüstungen 1932–34.* Zurich, 1940.

Lüke, Rolf. *Von der Stabilisierung zur Krise.* Zurich, 1958.

Matthias, Erich, and Morsey, Rudolf, eds. *Das Ende der Parteien 1933.* Düsseldorf, 1960.

Maxelon, Michael-Olaf. *Stresemann und Frankreich: Deutsche Politik der Ost-West-Balance.* Düsseldorf, 1972.

Mayer, Arno J. *Politics and Diplomacy of Peacemaking.* New York, 1967.

Meinck, Gerhard. *Hitler und die deutsche Aufrüstung 1933–37.* Wiesbaden, 1959.

Morley, Felix. *The Society of Nations.* Washington, 1932.

Munch, Peter, ed. *Les origines et l'oeuvre de la Société des Nations.* 2 vols. Copenhagen, 1923–24.

Neumann, Sigmund. *Die Parteien der Weimarer Republik.* Stuttgart, 1965.

Northedge, F. S. *The Troubled Giant: Britain among the Great Powers 1916–39.* New York, 1966.

Oertel, Maria. "Beiträge zur Geschichte der deutsch-polnischen Beziehungen 1925–30." Diss., Berlin, 1968.

Pieper, Helmut. *Die Minderheitenfrage und das Deutsche Reich 1919–1933/34.* Hamburg, 1974.

Plieg, Ernst-Albrecht. *Das Memelland 1919–39.* Würzburg, 1962.

Post, Gaines, Jr. *The Civil-Military Fabric of Weimar Foreign Policy.* Princeton, 1973.

Rhode, Gotthold. "Das Deutschtum in Posen und Pommerellen in der Zeit der Weimarer Republik." In *Die Deutschen Ostgebiete zur Zeit der Weimarer Republik.* Cologne, 1966.

Riekhoff, Harald von. *German-Polish Relations 1918–1933.* Baltimore, 1971.

Rürup, Reinhard. "Problems of the German Revolution 1918–19." *Journal of Contemporary History* III (1968), 109–35.

Salewski, Michael. *Entwaffnung und Militärkontrolle in Deutschland*

1919–1927. Munich, 1966.

Schwabe, Klaus. *Deutsche Revolution und Wilson-Frieden: Die amerikanische und deutsche Friedensstrategie zwischen Ideologie und Machtpolitik 1918/19.* Düsseldorf, 1971.

Schwarz, Gotthard. *Theodor Wolff und das "Berliner Tageblatt".* Tübingen, 1968.

Scott, George. *The Rise and Fall of the League of Nations.* London, 1973.

Spenz, Jürgen. *Die diplomatische Vorgeschichte des Beitritts Deutschlands zum Völkerbund 1924–1926.* Göttingen, 1966.

Stambrook, F. G. "'Das Kind'—Lord D'Abernon and the Origins of the Locarno Pact." *Central European History* I (1968), pp. 233–63.

Stürmer, Michael. *Koalition und Opposition in der Weimarer Republik 1924–1928.* Düsseldorf, 1967.

Survey of International Affairs, 1926, 1927, 1929, 1932, 1933. Ed. Arnold Toynbee. London, 1928–34.

Thimme, Annelise. *Flucht in den Mythos.* Göttingen, 1969.

———. *Gustav Stresemann: Eine politische Biographie zur Geschichte der Weimarer Republik.* Frankfurt/Main, 1957.

Troeltsch, Ernst. *Spektator-Briefe.* Tübingen, 1924.

Truckenbrodt, W. *Deutschland und der Völkerbund: Die Behandlung reichsdeutscher Angelegenheiten im Völkerbundsrat 1920–39.* Essen, 1941.

Truhart, Herbert von. *Völkerbund und Minderheitspetitionen.* Vienna, 1931.

Turner, Henry A., Jr. *Stresemann and the Politics of the Weimar Republic.* Princeton, 1963.

Vogelsang, Thilo. "Papen und das aussenpolitische Erbe Brünings: die Lausanner Konferenz 1932." In C. P. Claussen, ed., *Neue Perspektiven aus Wirtschaft und Recht.* Berlin, 1966.

———. *Reichswehr, Staat und NSDAP.* Stuttgart, 1962.

Walsdorff, Martin. *Westorientierung und Ostpolitik: Stresemanns Russlandpolitik in der Locarno-Ära.* Bremen, 1971.

Walters, Francis P. *A History of the League of Nations.* London, 1960.

Wandycz, Piotr S. *France and her Eastern Allies, 1919–1925.* Minneapolis, 1962.

Wehn, Paul. "Germany and the Treaty of Locarno." Diss., Columbia, 1969.

Weidenfeld, Werner. *Die Englandpolitik Gustav Stresemanns: Theoretische und praktische Aspekte der Aussenpolitik.* Mainz, 1972.

Weinberg, Gerhard L. "The Defeat of Germany in 1918 and the

European Balance of Power." *Central European History* II (Sept. 1969), pp. 248–60.

———. *The Foreign Policy of Hitler's Germany: Diplomatic Revolution in Europe, 1933–36.* Chicago, 1970.

Wheeler-Bennett, John W. *Disarmament and Security since Locarcarno, 1925–31.* London, 1932.

———. *The Pipedream of Peace.* London, 1934.

———. *The Wreck of Reparations.* London, 1933.

Wohlfeil, Rainer. "Heer und Republik." In *Handbuch zur deutschen Militärgeschichte 1648–1939,* vol. VI. Frankfurt/Main, 1970.

Wolfers, Arnold. *Britain and France between Two Wars.* New York, 1940.

Zahn, Manfred. "Öffentiliche Meinung und Presse während der Kanzlerschaft von Papens." Diss., Münster, 1953.

Zimmern, Alfred E. *The League of Nations and the Rule of Law, 1918–35.* 2d ed. London, 1939.

Zwoch, Gerhard. "Die Erfüllungs- und Verständigungspolitik der Weimarer Republik und die deutsche öffentliche Meinung." Diss., Kiel, 1950.

Index